A History of
MILTON KEYNES
AND DISTRICT

Volume II – from 1800 to about 1950

It needs great courage to be a historian,
for one can never discover the whole truth
about anything, let alone what happened
when our grandfathers were young.

We wish to thank Mr P. S. Billings, also Legal & General
Assurance Society for their support in enabling this
reprint to take place.

A History of
MILTON KEYNES
AND DISTRICT

Volume II – from 1800 to about 1950

by

SIR FRANK MARKHAM

DL, MA, BLitt
former President of the Museums Association
and MP for the Buckingham Division 1951–64

Isometric plan of the Guildhall and Chantry at Fenny Stratford and Appendix
by Paul Woodfield, MKDC

Plans of Buckinghamshire Railways and Wolverton Works 1841 drawn by
Susan Oxley
Plan of New Bradwell 1860 drawn by Moira Courtman
And fifty illustrations from various sources

WHITE CRESCENT PRESS LIMITED
LUTON

ISBN 0 900804 30 0

Printed in England by White Crescent Press Limited, Luton, Bedfordshire

CONTENTS

ILLUSTRATIONS

Preface

The last part of a book to be written, and probably the hardest, is the Preface, for in it one faces the impossible task of thanking adequately all those who have helped. There are scores of such friends, some from the villages in the area – others from as far afield as Australia or California. Their contributions vary from substantial additions to the text, or the loan of basic material, to the reading of typescripts and printed proofs, or to the loan of historic postcards or sketches to serve as illustrations. Some such contributors are mentioned in footnotes or captions. I am proud to say that their help has made this book possible and I pay the warmest tribute I can to them all.

The selected list is as follows:

Robert J. Ayers, Stony Stratford
Ian Beckett, Whitchurch
Walter Beesley, OBE, Hanslope
A. H. Bennett, Beaconsfield
Ray Bellchambers, Old Bradwell
G. A. Boddington, Wolverton
J. P. Bristow, London Brick Co, Stewartby
Dr O. F. Brown, Stony Stratford
F. G. Cockman, Bedford
Moira Courtman, London
Brigadier Hamilton Cox, Claydon House
Aidan Crawley, London
J. L. Day, Mursley
Miss Dickens, Newton Longville
Mrs Dimmock, Newton Longville
Sir Philip Duncombe, Bt, Great Brickhill
Rev John Elkerton, Milford-on-Sea
John Franklin, Church Farm, Great Brickhill
Walter J. Franklin, Stony Stratford
Arthur Grigg, Bletchley
Mrs Harrowell, Newton Longville

Harold Hepworth, Bletchley
Huntingdon Library, California
Dr Peter Jarvis, Bletchley
Baroness Kinloss, House of Lords
Rev W. H. Kimberley, Buckingham
Col M. H. S. Last, Beachampton
Edward Legg, Fenny Stratford
Mrs Lickorish, Bletchley
Dennis Lovett, Fenny Stratford
James Martin, Leighton Buzzard
Capt W. G. Mells, Great Missenden
Milton Keynes Development Corporation
A. I. O'Dell, Simpson Road, Bletchley
Mrs Pacey, Woburn Sands
John Platt, Milton Keynes DC
Harold Price, OBE, Bletchley
Miss Margaret Salmons, Newport Pagnell
The Selby-Lowndes family, Bow Brickhill
K. W. B. Sharp, BSC, Wolverton
John Smithie, OBE, Bletchley
Ron Staniford, Bletchley
The Spalding family, Como, Western Australia
Mrs J. Smith, Leighton Buzzard
David Stimson, Wolverton
Geoffrey Tew, MA etc, British Rail, Wolverton
Murray Tompkins, Bletchley
Keith Tull, Haversham
Sir Ralph Verney, KBE, Middle Claydon
Valentin, Ord & Nagle Ltd, Fenny Stratford
The Wells family, Bletchley
Paul Woodfield, Milton Keynes DC

Added to all these, the officers of every local authority have loaned documents and maps to an almost bewildering degree, and the great national institutions, such as the British Museum, Science Museum and the County Record Office at Aylesbury (E. J. Davis) have helped considerably.

This second volume, like the first, is incomplete. It has ragged ends, because history is still in the making, and indeed much vital information will not be available until the files of the various Ministries are opened to the public in a few years' time.

Prices

Once again one comes up against the tremendous difficulty of trying to give the younger generation an idea of what pounds, shillings and pence were really worth. If we keep our thinking in terms of pounds sterling it is possible to say that a pound's worth of goods in 1800 would have cost £5 by 1900, and the £5 worth in 1900 would cost about £45 in 1974. A week's work of a farm labourer in 1800 would have earnt about 9s or 45p. Today the equivalent work earns about £25, so that there seems to be almost a grim equality with a slight edge in favour of wages over prices. But if we take other factors such as the income of the clergy in 1800 and today we see that the clergy have really lost out in the process, and that charities and trusts which were really wealthy in 1800 have not only had their purchasing power reduced to one-fortieth at least, but owing to government pressure for them to invest in Consols and other government stocks a century ago, the income has diminished still more. An endowment of £100 in 1816 would produce £3 a year in interest. It still does, but whereas then it equalled six weeks' wages, now it only equals a few hours.

Shillings and pence, halfpennies and farthings, were the coins our grandfathers thought and reckoned with and it would be as absurd to decimalise these as to try to decimalise the Biblical shekel or the widow's mite.

As I indicated in volume I, the amount of material available for a history since 1800 is absolutely torrential. Most of the records of parishes, manors, district and parish councils are all intact: the local press for a hundred years has been pouring out the raw material for any history. I am not exaggerating when I say that for the area now known as Milton Keynes and the adjacent parishes there are millions of documents available to the research worker.

Choice has been difficult. It has been impossible to write anything like a clear history of each town or parish, of each church, chapel or mansion, or of the Newport Pagnell RDC and UDC. Had all these been even partially included it would need ten or a dozen volumes more from my successors for the next generation – by which time there would be thirty years more of historic records. Impossible to cope!

This volume finishes unevenly about 1951, leaving untold the story of the last quarter of a century which is not only within the minds of most of us but still a subject of political discussion and present debate. The volume covers in a way such great subjects as the triple transport revolution – canals – railways – motor transport; the great revolution in government from the peers and squires of the Napoleonic era to the democracies from 1867 on, and the rise of the trade unions and local bureaucracies since about 1894.

So this volume gives only the main streams affecting the area – the broadest of which is the passing of power from the aristocracy and the squires to the trade unions and the local officials. How did it happen? Who got hurt in the process? Who gained? This is the main theme, and I can but apologise again for disappointing so many who hoped for a more precise, a more detailed history of each parish. The second main theme is how the area passed from a serene rural region to one of the fastest growing industrial areas in England.

The story is unfinished – and it never will be finished, for next week's local newspapers will add still more material for the dedicated historian to consider in years to come.

Once again, my warmest thanks to all those who have helped; most of all to my wife, whose assistance and advice since the book was first thought of several years ago, have been absolutely invaluable.

Frank Markham

1 The Powerhouse of Stowe

Saturday 31 May 1800 was one of the greatest days in the 1,000 year old history of Fenny Stratford and Water Eaton for on that day the Marquess of Buckingham opened that portion of the Grand Junction Canal from Tring to Fenny which had been two years digging and building. At last it was completed, and a procession of horse-drawn barges started from Tring in the morning; reached Leighton Buzzard at 1 pm, and on arrival at Fenny Stratford was joined by the Marquess of Buckingham with his friends and principal shareholders. They were met by the band and a detachment of the Bucks Militia, and then went in a grand procession to Fenny Stratford crossroads where they were received with the booming of cannon (the Fenny Poppers possibly), the ringing of bells and other demonstrations of joy.

For centuries Fenny Stratford's contacts with the outer world had been by road, and the famous Watling Street did indeed give it access at some peril to London and to the Midlands, but now it had water access too. The Ouzel alongside which the canal ran was a relatively small river, excellent for mills, but hardly capable of taking a water craft larger than a punt, and that only between one mill and another. Now there was a waterway on which barges 72ft long and 12ft wide could bring so much that the area wanted, from bricks and slates and coal, to manure and lime, and merchandise of all kinds provided it was not perishable. It was a great occasion. The newly created wharves at Fenny and Water Eaton naturally looked forward to a prosperous time.

In our first volume (pp311–24) we described the economic effect of the canal on the locality. Our concern now is why the Marquess of Buckingham should receive all the honours the market town of Fenny Stratford could confer on him?

We have seen that in June 1792 he called a meeting of local worthies at an inn in Stony Stratford, and with the engineer James Barnes, launched the idea of a canal from London to Braunston, in Northants, where it would link up with the Oxford

1

Canal and save several days in transporting goods across England. The cost would be £500,000. The meeting not only approved the plan: it guaranteed the money, and the principal guarantor was George Nugent-Temple, Marquess of Buckingham, then in his fortieth year. How did he get his title, and where did his money come from?

He was the grandson of one Hester Temple, who deserves a page or two, and nephew of another Hester Temple who deserves a paragraph or two.

The Two Hester Temples

The first Hester Temple was born in 1690. She grew up to be vivacious, beautiful and extremely intelligent. By the time she reached her late teens she knew that her elder brother, Sir Richard Temple (1669–1749) who was the owner of the great palace of Stowe, near Buckingham, would probably never produce a legitimate heir, although married to an heiress, and that she would possibly inherit the great Temple estates. She was not only a girl in a million, but looked like being a girl with a million.

It was important as to whom she would marry, and according to the custom of the time her brother should find her a suitable husband. But Hester made her own choice.

Her brother, who had been a local MP since 1697, was now (1714) made a baron, and in 1718 created Viscount Cobham, mainly for his services as a lieutenant-general and as a diplomat. Poets and writers of the day talked of his gracefulness, his winning address and charm. Hester had the same qualities. Her romantic choice fell on the young and handsome Richard Grenville, 'Esquire', of Wotton Underwood, Bucks, who already owned many manors in mid-Bucks.

As Mr and Mrs Grenville, she and her husband now settled down at Stowe in wealthy but untitled state. Children were born, and all seemed serene and happy for seventeen years. Then Richard died. Many women have suffered a similar loss, and remarried, but Hester Temple-Grenville had other ideas. She became a great political hostess. Such still was her influence and charm that when her brother, by now a field-marshal, but still childless, died in 1749, she succeeded him as Viscountess Cobham, but the King was persuaded to make her Countess Temple –

an unusual promotion! It meant that her son would, after her death, become Earl Temple.

Among her children Richard, the eldest, became our gawky local member of parliament for twenty years and a cabinet minister, whilst her daughter, also called Hester, married in 1754 a young politician by the name of William Pitt, (later Earl of Chatham). Stowe now became a great political centre.

How the Grenvilles electioneered is interesting, for fortunately we have a direct account from the gentle poet, William Cowper, who was then living at Olney. Norman Wilkinson, in his biography of the poet, writes:

> 'In 1783 life at Olney was full of small adventures. Apart from his occasional melancholy, Cowper never seems to have been bored, and he reacts with such spontaneity to every happening and every change. The clash and clatter of our elections seem dull beside the lasting amusement gained from the visit of the candidate, Mr. Grenville, who came in by the back-door, shook Cowper by the hand, refused to believe that he had no influence, kissed the ladies and even the maid in the kitchen, "and seemed a most loving, kissing, kind-hearted gentleman".'

In the pursuit of power the Grenvilles knew that kissing was a definite aid to progress. But from then on the Grenvilles 'arranged' the elections and there was no contest for forty-seven years!

Cowper was not the only one to be bewitched by the Grenville charm, and few were surprised when George Temple-Grenville (1753–1813) who had been a Bucks MP for several years and succeeded his uncle as Earl Temple in 1779, was created Marquess of Buckingham in 1784 and made a Knight of the Garter two years later. He had married in 1775 Lady Mary Nugent, the heiress of Robert, Earl Nugent, and so lengthened the surname to Temple-Nugent-Grenville. Like most of the new generation of Temple-Grenvilles the first Marquess was a hard worker and a greedy placeman, excessively proud and touchy. He had been made a Secretary of State in 1784 but resigned after three days in office because he was made a marquess and not a duke.[1]

He had a great capacity for the making and management of

1 *Records of Bucks,* 1973 130.

money. The Marquess was interested in everything from stocks and shares, merchant adventures, and most important to this area, in canals. This was the man who brought the canal to Water Eaton, Fenny Stratford, Linford, Wolverton and Cosgrove. He was the son of one prime minister, had called another uncle, and a cousin was at this moment of time the third of his immediate relatives to be called to the office. It was the latter, William Pitt, the younger, who had made him a marquess in 1784.

THE CANALS

When the Marquess started up the canal idea in 1792 it was as a commercial venture with certain risks, but he and everybody else knew that whatever was wanted in terms of Acts of Parliament would be obtainable, which was an asset of great value.

We have already seen that when the Grand Junction Canal was opened as far as Fenny Stratford in 1800 he was there leading the rejoicings and receiving the honours. And now he was determined that when the canal reached Cosgrove, the branch from there through Old Stratford to Buckingham should be cut and finished at all speed. It was accomplished in eight months.[2] Let us quote from the *Gentleman's Magazine* for 1801:

'The branch of the canal from Buckingham to the Grand Junction canal (at Cosgrove) was opened this day with great rejoicing. A barge with the Marquess of Buckingham Mr. Praed and Mr. Selby (Gentlemen of the Committee) and Mr. Box, the Treasurer, accompanied by a large party of ladies and gentlemen and a band of music led the way to a procession of 12 barges laden with coal, slate and a variety of merchandise.

'Upon their entrance into the bason at Buckingham they were welcomed by the firing of several pieces of cannon. A numerous party were handsomely entertained by the Marquis of Buckingham at the *Cobham Arms* Inn on this occasion, and a liberal supply of beer was given to the population.'

Then, as now, there was a rapturous, wild and ineffable pleasure of drinking at somebody else's expense.

Before very long the canal was carrying out unexpected business. The long Blisworth tunnel was opened in 1805 and in May

2 See *History of Milton Keynes and District* 312–13 and 321.

1806 'A barge went from Northampton with a cargo of 100 live fat sheep for the London market. Being the first attempt of its kind it created considerable excitement; the boat was 53 hours making the journey of 95 miles; it was a success, and a boat is to be sent up once a week.'[3]

In 1822 there was another and more striking development. The War Office decided that troops going to and from Ireland should travel by canal, and in June 600 Foot Guards travelled from London to Liverpool at about 2mph, and two months later the relieved Grenadier Guards, 750 men all told, travelled from Liverpool to London in thirty boats. At that time there were few public houses on the canal side, but those that were, like the *Black Horse* at Linford and the *Navigation Inn* (now *The Bridge*) at Fenny Stratford must have done a roaring trade.

In September 1826 the first steamboat made the journey from London to Birmingham.

The canals prospered and added still more to the Temple-Nugent-Grenville fortunes. Before long the £100 Grand Junction Canal shares had risen to £240. Stowe was beautified more and more, and again and again the Pitts, the Grenvilles, the Temples, the Lyttletons and the Graftons (Fitzroys) met there to discuss, to argue and sometimes even to agree. Stowe was a power in the land. It was the hub of British politics: it was the dynamo that set all sorts of things in motion.

Within the space of forty years the Stowe group provided four prime ministers – a record unequalled by any other part of the country. The attached short genealogical tree may help.[4]

Meanwhile the Marquess was adding to his political power. More 'rotten boroughs' were acquired. More friends or relatives were nominated as MPs or to other positions of influence. In Parliament there were no organised political parties, only organised personal factions, and of all these that headed by the Grenvilles was one of the strongest.

THE SECOND MARQUESS OF BUCKINGHAM

When the first marquess died in 1813 he was succeeded by the

---

3 Gibbs, *Buckinghamshire Local Records* III.
4 *Records of Bucks* XI 435 *seq* in reviewing the *Temple Memoirs* (London 1925–26) gives many pedigrees, and all the members of the family are treated with engaging candour. See also *VCH* III 484, Sheahan p251, Lipscomb p599, *Burke's Peerage* 1837, and the *Grenville Memoirs* p18.

THE TEMPLES AND GRENVILLES OF STOWE

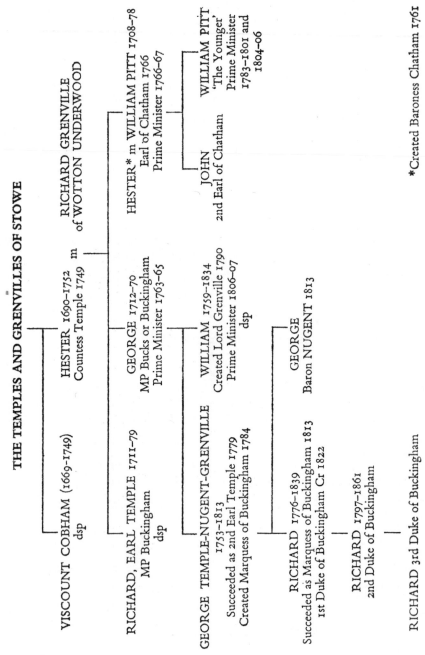

VISCOUNT COBHAM (1669–1749)
dsp

HESTER 1690–1752 m RICHARD GRENVILLE
Countess Temple 1749   of WOTTON UNDERWOOD

RICHARD, EARL TEMPLE 1711–79
MP Buckingham
dsp

GEORGE 1712–70
MP Bucks or Buckingham
Prime Minister 1763–65

HESTER* m WILLIAM PITT 1708–78
Earl of Chatham 1766
Prime Minister 1766–67

GEORGE TEMPLE-NUGENT-GRENVILLE
1753–1813
Succeeded as 2nd Earl Temple 1779
Created Marquess of Buckingham 1784

WILLIAM 1759–1834
Created Lord Grenville 1790
Prime Minister 1806–07
dsp

GEORGE
Baron NUGENT 1813

JOHN
2nd Earl of Chatham

WILLIAM PITT 1708–78
'The Younger'
Prime Minister
1783–1801 and
1804–06

RICHARD 1776–1839
Succeeded as Marquess of Buckingham 1813
1st Duke of Buckingham Cr 1822

RICHARD 1797–1861
2nd Duke of Buckingham

RICHARD 3rd Duke of Buckingham

*Created Baroness Chatham 1761

6

most colourful character Stowe had ever produced. The new marquess, who also succeeded to the earldoms of Temple and Nugent and to the viscounty of Cobham, had long been aware that he deserved much. When in 1796 at the age of 19 he married Anne-Elizabeth, the only daughter and heiress of James Brydges, the third and last Duke of Chandos, both he and she felt that he had a right to the extinct dukedom, but more than this they knew that she was the sole representative of a former Duke of Suffolk who had married Mary, Queen Dowager of France, sister of Henry VIII, and that if that much-married monarch's will had been properly carried out he and she would now be King and Queen of England.[5] Few were surprised when he lengthened his name to

A clever caricature of the Marquess of Buckingham in 1811 entitled 'View of a Temple near Buckingham' published by Dighton. The original, which is at Claydon House, is in colour with a scarlet tunic, golden epaulettes etc. The second Marquess became Duke of Buckingham in 1822.

5 Sheahan pp226–27 and 302, says bluntly that if the will of Henry VIII had been carried into effect the Duke of Buckingham would have been King of England.

Richard Temple-Nugent-Brydges-Chandos-Grenville. It was the fashion at that time that if a man married an heiress of some worth he added her name to his own. When his father died in 1813 he became the largest landowner in Bucks and one of the richest men in England, and spent accordingly.

Even for those days he had a belly of magnificent proportions, whether belted or bare, and a heavy, dull, sunless face. As a young man he had a magnificent build before his stomach went in for a career of its own.

THE FIRST DUKE OF BUCKINGHAM AND CHANDOS

All Buckingham knew that the Marquess of Buckingham was highly delighted when King George IV in February 1822, on the recommendation of the Duke of Wellington, made him Duke of Buckingham and Chandos, and Marquess of Chandos. It was a delicate question as to why he had been made a duke for he had not been a great commander during the Napoleonic wars, nor had he been a prime minister, which usually rated an earldom, nor had he married a regular royal princess.

The 62 year old Duke of Wellington, the victor of Waterloo, had never recommended anybody for a dukedom before. Even after Waterloo the highest honour he sought for any of his great captains was a marquisate for the Earl of Uxbridge – one of the illiterate Pagets – who commanded the cavalry and artillery at Waterloo, and lost a leg there. There is a story that at the battle when Wellington and Uxbridge were riding side by side during a great cannonade, Uxbridge suddenly said, 'Gad Sir, I've lost a leg'. The Duke looked down and said 'Gad Sir, so you have'.

Buckingham's elevation to a dukedom was one of the most peculiar transactions in English political history, and the story of how our particular Grenville managed to secure a dukedom was told by another Prime Minister, the Earl of Rosebery, at a meeting of the Bucks Archaeological Society at Aylesbury in 1904.[6] Part of his speech is well worth quoting:

'Politics have been the pride of Bucks. Her political position was achieved in the 18th century, and lasted till politics passed out of the hands of the grandees and became popular and democratic. I claim for Bucks that she is the most famous

6 *Records of Bucks* IX 94 *seq.*

of English counties in the field of politics during that period . . .

'. . . Why was this? The reason seems to lie in the Palace of Stowe and its inhabitants . . .

'The political power began under the fostering influence of Lord Cobham, who was not only a politician but a Field-Marshal: and at Stowe there was gathered that remarkable group which was known as the Cobham Cousins – Grenvilles – Lyttletons and Pitts. This powerful combination composed of one man of genius and several men of ability, might have governed the country for a generation had they only been able to agree . . .

'The political power of Stowe continued through long generations. There was the generation of Lord Cobham, then that of Temple, George Grenville and Pitt, brothers and brother-in-law, constantly at variance . . . Then when they disappear a new generation comes on the scene – a Temple not less turbulent and active than his uncle and predecessor, with his brother William Grenville, destined through the long years to be Secretary of State, and to succeed his cousin as Prime Minister; finally that cousin, William Pitt.

'Then that generation passes. The head of the house is now Marquis of Buckingham. He has in the House of Commons men such as Wynn, and Phillimore and Fremantle more or less fit to sit on the front bench; he has his brother, Lord Nugent; perhaps a dozen all told. In 1821–22 there are negotiations conducted by the Duke of Wellington and Lord Londonderry on the one side, and by the Marquis of Buckingham and Charles Wynn on the other as between two independent states. At last the treaty is made. Buckingham is made a Duke, Wynn is made a cabinet minister, places are found for other members of the party, and in exchange their votes are given to Lord Liverpool, the Prime Minister . . . It is the last transaction of its kind in our annals.'

The Grenvilles had been prominent in the Whig cause for nearly two centuries. Now, suddenly, they were Tories.

Sir Charles Bagot wrote, 'I am glad the Grenvilles are taken into the Government, and (for Grenvilles) they come tolerably cheap. I see no objection to a Dukedom for the head of the Grenville family, but I see many in giving it to the actual blubberhead who now reigns over them.' But the Duke was an honest man – once he was bought he stayed bought.

OUR CURIOUS PEERAGE

It is time to consider what it meant to be a duke for in the early 19th century they exercised a power and influence quite out of proportion to their number, general ability or character. Although there were only thirty of them, they all had seats in the House of Lords and were mostly leaders of groups of other peers and of members in the Commons.

Of all the political institutions in this world few have been as colourful as the House of Lords, and even in this day and age the Queen's opening of Parliament is unique for its blaze of scarlet and gold and diamonds, whilst the assembled peers in their ermined robes take us back to the pageantry of the Plantagenets or even earlier.

Dukes were of course the highest grade of peer, and in descending order there followed marquesses, earls, viscounts and barons. Whilst there were barely forty marquesses there were hundreds of barons. There still are.

But in addition to the peerage that made up the House of Lords, there was a courtesy peerage, for the eldest son of a duke or a marquess usually took by courtesy his father's second title, and other sons were styled Lord Edward, or Lord John and so on. None of these could sit in the Lords until they actually succeeded, or were granted a peerage in their own right. They could, however, sit in the Commons, and indeed a very fair proportion of the Commons consisted of sons of peers as we shall see. It was all so English and so confused that even Englishmen were pardoned for not knowing whether the earl of so and so, perhaps a cabinet minister, had his seat in the Lords or in the Commons, or whether he was an earl in his own right, or just a duke's eldest son or grandson.[7]

But what every Englishman did know in the 19th century was

---

7 The attached table shows how the system resulted in a man during his lifetime being known by several different titles.

that the possession of a title of any kind usually meant great power and wealth. Britain was governed by a most powerful oligarchy, and north Bucks was no exception to the general rule.

Brough, the writer, summed it all up when he wrote in 1850:

My Lord Tomnoddy is thirty-four,
The Earl can last but few years more.
My Lord in the Peers will take his place:
Her Majesty's councils his words will grace
Office he'll hold and patronage sway;
Fortunes and lives he will vote away;
And what are his qualifications? – ONE!
He's the Earl of Fitzdotterel's eldest son.'

Yet such is the inconsistency of the English character that everybody loved a lord, even if 'as drunk as a lord' became a much quoted axiom.

From 1822 onwards there were three dukes within a morning's ride of Bletchley. There was His Grace the Duke of Buckingham and Chandos, likewise His Grace the Duke of Bedford, and then His Grace the Duke of Grafton.

Nearly every duke was a knight of the garter by what he regarded as hereditary right, for as Lord Melbourne said (when he was Prime Minister) 'I like the Garter: there's no damned merit in it.' Each of our local dukes owned thousands of acres and had an enormous income. Each of them could control several seats in the Lords and several seats in the Commons.

The Duke of Buckingham himself controlled the rotten borough of Buckingham with its thirteen voters in no uncertain manner, and he also had in his pocket an additional Buckingham-shire county seat and the tiny borough of St Mawes in Cornwall with its two members and eighty-seven electors. Added to this, the Duchess of Buckingham and Lady Mildmay owned the two seats at Winchester, and other relatives and friends controlled about twenty-five seats.

In short he influenced enough seats both in the Lords and the Commons to shake any government. He exercised the power without many scruples. He had much influence in deciding the route of the London and Birmingham railway, for whilst the family loved canals, they were very much against any part of the ducal estates at Stowe or elsewhere being overrun by steam, and so the line came through Fenny Stratford and Wolverton, as we shall relate later. Wolverton would never have become a great railway centre if it had not been for the proud and powerful first Duke of Buckingham.

The new Duke was so pleased with his honour that he decided to place in Buckingham church a large east window of stained armorial glass. We have seen earlier the exuberance of the Tudors when it came to coats of arms, but this exceeded everything. In the top centre portion was the royal coat of arms, but below this and almost twice the size of the royal arms were the ducal arms duly emblazoned, and an inscription that takes some believing. In the side windows were the arms of George, Marquis of Chandos (his eldest son) and Earl Temple respectively, surmounted with the seals of the borough and county, with still more family crests running around as a border. The inscription recorded that the window was presented by 'the Most High, Most Mighty and Most Noble Prince Richard Duke of Buckingham and Chandos, Marquess of Chandos and Buckingham and Earl Temple of Stowe, Marquess of Buckingham, Earl Temple and Viscount and Baron Cobham'.[8] Pride could hardly go further. No one had ever created him a 'Most High, Most Mighty and Most Noble Prince', but he was quite certain he was one. All that the worshippers in the church could see when they looked towards the altar were the blazing coats of arms. Only by peering hard could one discern below the window a copy of Raphael's *Transfiguration*.[9]

8 For illustrations see Harrison's *Historical Buckingham* pp49 and 54.
9 Sheahan p237. For portrait of Duke see *Official Baronage of England* I 264. Forty years later the Duke's grandson, the third Duke pulled down the east window and built a new Chancel. What became of the window is a mystery, but the Rev. John Elkerton, former Vicar of Buckingham, relates that before his day it was stored in boxes in the belfry.

ARISTOCRATIC STYLING

As we have seen a great deal of confusion has been and will be caused to historians and the reading public by the quaint English custom of a man taking another name when he succeeded to a peerage, achieved a peerage, or even when his father went up in the peerage. Below we give an indication as to the name changes of four succeeding individuals of the Grenville family between 1797 and 1861;

Full name	Boyhood title	Later known as	Final title
George Temple-Nugent-Grenville 1753–1813	George Grenville Esq 1753–79	2nd Earl Temple 1779–84	1st Marquess of Buckingham 1784–1813
Richard Temple-Nugent-Brydges-Chandos-Grenville 1776–1839	Richard Grenville Esq 1776–84 Earl Temple 1784–1813	2nd Marquess of Buckingham 1813–22*	1st Duke of Buckingham and Chandos 1822–39
Richard Plantagenet-Temple-Nugent-Brydges-Chandos-Grenville 1797–1861	Richard Grenville Esq 1797–1813 Earl Temple 1813–22	Marquess of Chandos 1822–39	2nd Duke of Buckingham and Chandos 1839–61
Richard Plantagenet-Campbell-Temple-Nugent-Brydges-Chandos-Grenville 1823–89	Earl Temple 1823–39	2nd Marquess of Chandos 1839–61†	3rd Duke of Buckingham and Chandos 1861–89

* Closely involved in canals.
† Closely involved in railway matters from 1840 on.

2 The Power of the Peers and the Squires

During the whole period through which the Dukes of Buckingham, and their sons the Marquesses of Chandos, held sway there were other dukes and marquesses and earls around who also influenced to no inconsiderable degree our local history, and it might be argued that at certain periods the Dukes of Grafton or the Dukes of Bedford, had as much power as the Dukes of Buckingham. All lived within a dozen miles of Bletchley.

Successive Dukes of Grafton, who owned great estates in Northamptonshire and Suffolk, had a great mansion at Wakefield, near Potterspury in south Northants. They were constant visitors to Stowe in its days of glory since the six miles between the two estates could be covered in half an hour. Of these Dukes of Grafton, the third Duke, Augustus Henry Fitzroy (1735–1811) became the nominal head of the Chatham administration in 1766 and actual Prime Minister when Pitt retired two years later. He was a dull host, and a distinguished French visitor, Francois de la Rochefaucauld, complained when he visited him in 1784, 'Dinner is the most wearisome of English experience, lasting as it does from four to five hours. The first two are spent in eating and you are compelled to exercise your stomach to please your host.' An added cause of dismay was that the dishes seemed to consist mostly of boiled or roast meats.

The next Duke, George Fitzroy, who succeeded to the dukedom in 1811, like his father exercised much political influence, and was a colleague of the younger Pitt. He controlled six parliamentary seats in Suffolk and Norfolk including two at Bury St Edmunds where there were only thirty-seven electors, and Thetford where there were even fewer. Like all his predecessors the Duke felt entitled to the Garter, but when he was finally offered it in 1834 he refused it 'because he thinks himself too old to pay the fees of £1,000'. He was then 74.

The Duke of Grafton owned most of Potterspury, Paulerspury, Whittlebury, Passenham, Deanshanger, Blisworth, Stoke

Bruerne, Roade and Grafton Regis, all in south Northants, but much of the domestic shopping from Wakefield was done in Stony Stratford, and ducal influence was not decreased by the gift of a brace of pheasants or partridges to leading tradesmen and members of the professional classes. Indeed, it could be said that a whisper from the Duke's steward was as good as a command.

THE DUKES OF BEDFORD

Just over the Bedfordshire border at Woburn was the great Whig family of the Russells, Dukes of Bedford, Marquesses of Tavistock, and so on.

Their dukedom began in 1694. By 1771 when Francis Russell became the fifth Duke, they had acquired great estates[1] in Bedfordshire and London. He bought part of Bow Brickhill in 1792 and a great part of Wavendon. It was he who built Russell and Tavistock Squares in London and so augmented the already great wealth of the family. His brother John who succeeded in 1802 was a Quaker, and rebuilt Covent Garden. He was 'a plain unpretending man' who had been MP for Tavistock (one of the family's pocket boroughs) like so many of his ancestors. His son Francis, later the seventh Duke, represented Bedfordshire from 1818 to 1832 when he became a peer in his own right as Baron Howland, so that when he succeeded to the dukedom in 1839 he was already in the House of Lords.

The Woburn estate, already vast, reached its maximum in 1842 with the purchase of the Ampthill estate, and a little more land in Bucks with the acquisition of most of Bow Brickhill and part of Little Brickhill. In all the Duke of Bedford now controlled 37,186 acres in Beds and Bucks – some of the fairest land in all England – and of these nearly 4,000 acres were in Bucks.

For years the Russells had owned the pocket borough of Tavistock, where prior to 1831 the greatest number of electors was twenty-seven, and the Duke nominated its two members, since he owned all the freeholds in the borough, and even after 1831 it still returned two members with a voting list of less than 400. It often occurred that both members were Russells. Bedfordshire before 1831 returned two members and one was usually a Russell, and for Bedford itself a Russell often occupied one of the

1 See Lipscomb, and also Godber, *History of Bedfordshire* p301.

two seats. They also had influence in Cornwall where the tiny Borough of Camelford with thirty voters and two members was a borough in the Duke's pocket until he sold it in 1812 for £32,000.

Thus with half a dozen members of Parliament still directly under their control, and half a dozen relatives or more in the House of Lords (it depends of course how far back you trace the relations) the Dukes of Bedford were a political force.

THE MARQUESSES AND EARLS

As with the dukes, so with the marquesses and earls – the next ranks in precedence. James Cecil who was created Marquess of Salisbury in 1789 owned thousands of acres in Bucks including practically all Calverton and Beachampton. He too became a KG.

The Cecils had come into the Calverton and Beachampton estates by marriage. Grace Bennett (widow of Simon Bennett) who was 'a miserable wretched and covetous person' had a charming young daughter Frances, who married James, Earl of Salisbury in 1683, and when Grace Bennett was murdered by a Stony Stratford butcher in 1694 the estates descended to the Cecils.

In 1782 Parliament passed an Enclosure Act setting up Commissioners to survey the parish of Calverton with the west side of Stony Stratford and to make an Award. One hundred and thirty acres were already enclosed, but the remaining 1,720 acres took five years to allocate. The full story of this is told in the *History of Stony Stratford*, p149 *seq*. In the result the Marquess of Salisbury was awarded 1,120 acres in Calverton and the Stony Stratford Mill.

Hardly had the new fences been erected and the new roads laid than almost everybody wanted to sell, and in 1806 the Salisburys sold both manors of Calverton and Beachampton, the manor of Calverton including the manor house and 309 acres.

The greater part of the land was acquired by Lord Carrington (later the Marquess of Lincolnshire), the Earl of Egmont, and a local banker Mr Oliver, but the manor and its lordship was bought by Mr Selby-Lowndes who already held the manors of Winslow and Whaddon. Whaddon Hall was the family seat and Whaddon Chase their playground.

This Lord Carrington later acquired much of Drayton Parslow (1820), Hanslope and part of Mursley and became in a few years one of the largest landowners in Bucks. The family controlled six parliamentary seats including the snug pocket borough of Wendover with two members. Smith was the family name.

EARLS

At Milton Keynes village and Ravenstone, were estates which had belonged to an earldom for a century. Daniel Finch, Earl of Winchelsea and Nottingham inherited both manors in 1682. His family was politically of the first importance, for it was related to no fewer than fourteen members of the House of Lords and had the power to nominate some twenty members of the House of Commons, and the group there numbered thirty-one members, all high church.

When Daniel II succeeded his father in 1730 to the earldom of Winchelsea and Nottingham he himself had already been an MP for twenty years, knew all the ropes, and exercised only a little less influence. On his death in 1769 the title passed to his nephew, George Finch, who although he lived until 1826 never married, but had an illegitimate son of whom he was very fond. At his death, whilst the titles and some estates went to a distant cousin, he left the manors of Milton Keynes and Ravenstone to his middle-aged natural son, George Finch of Burley Hall (Rutland). The Finch's continued to hold both Ravenstone and Milton Keynes for over a century, but as a bastard branch of the family never exercised the power and influence of their great ancestors, though they produced several MPs.[2]

Any county votes there were in Milton Keynes or Ravenstone before the Reform Act or indeed afterwards were at the command of the Finch family.

Another family with extensive local interests was the Verneys of Claydon. There are many books by the Verneys and about the Verneys which give the family history in detail. In short the second and last Earl was a Member of Parliament for Buckinghamshire from 1768 to 1791. Since his earldom was an Irish one, he had no seat in the Lords and so could represent his own county in the Commons. But his death without issue did not diminish the

---

2 The outstanding memorial to the Finch family is in Ravenstone Church, where Heneage Finch, Earl of Nottingham, Lord Chancellor in 1675, and his wife are commemorated in a large black and white marble monument that is overbearing. Illustrated in *RCHM* ii 46, and Pevsner *Buckinghamshire*, Plate 25. In 1914 Mr Wilfred Finch of Burley Hall, Rutland, succeeded to both manors.

Verney influence for a younger branch of the family, mostly baronets, represented Buckinghamshire or north Bucks almost continuously from 1832 to 1918. They were well known in every village or town as tireless Whigs or Liberals.

Yet another earl with local influence and interests was the third Earl of Egmont, who, as we have seen, bought up a fair portion of the Calverton Manor in 1806. He was the elder brother of Spencer Perceval who became Prime Minister in 1809 and was assassinated in the House of Commons in 1812. A close relation of the Earl of Egmont was Lord Arden, who acquired the advowson of Calverton Church in 1806, rebuilt the church in 1818, and built a new rectory (now the Old Rectory) in 1820, and appointed his son, Charles George Perceval, as rector in 1821. Both were also interested in the establishment of the group of almshouses near the church in 1830. From Lord Arden the patronage descended to the Earls of Egmont, who were still holding a century later.

Apart from the dukes, marquesses, earls and viscounts there were a few barons. One of these was Sampson Gideon, son of a Jewish capitalist and financier who raised millions for Walpole's government. He bought much of Mursley and was created Lord Eardley in 1789. Soon after his death in 1824 Mursley was sold to the Selby-Lowndes.

Why did these peers exercise so much power when we consider their sometimes mediocre abilities? We have seen that land and inherited pocket boroughs and peerages gave power, but there was another reason.

The psychoanalysts tell us that character and ability are 80 per cent heredity and 20 per cent environment. Whatever some of the sons of the aristocracy might lack in hereditary talent they could make up in 'environment', for the finest tutors and the best schools and colleges in the land were at their disposal. They never had to pass an entrance exam, and somehow, if they stayed the required number of terms, they were awarded degrees. Then came the 'Grand Tour', and off they would go with tutor or more congenial companions to visit France, Bavaria and of course Italy, and then they would come back to rule England. Meanwhile the training had made the best of whatever brains they had.

The political influence of the land was immense. As late as 1870 400 peers were reckoned to own over one-sixth of the whole surface of the country.[3] In Bucks one-fifth was held by a dozen peers, and in Bedfordshire the Duke of Bedford alone owned one-eighth of the whole county.

The mass of the country was content to leave government in their hands so long as prosperity rose, taxes fell, free trade remained sacrosanct and Britannia ruled the waves. Only one in five male adults in England and Wales had the vote, and they loved aristocratic candidates and their 'influence'. As many as half the parliamentary seats were not contested at all, and there was practically no party feeling or organisation as we know it today. Members were independent, unpredictable and often disloyal.

Whole counties took their political colour from their leading 'magnifico'. Why, as Professor Gash pertinently observes, should Bedfordshire have been Whig, or Buckinghamshire Tory unless it was because the Duke of Bedford was the one and the Duke of Buckingham the other?[4]

In all this aristocratic rule the clergy (Church of England, of course) were the junior partners. Not only had they the vast influence of delivering sermons to large congregations, but they were nearly always on school trusts, and gave addresses to their schools once a week, and they also became JPs. The Enclosure Awards had often given them large grants of land in lieu of tithes, and usually they were the second largest landholder in the parish. Again not infrequently the parson was a younger son or a nephew of a peer or a squire, and had thus a double interest in the maintenance of the status quo.

So, by the time we have reckoned how many local manors were held by dukes, marquesses, earls, viscounts or barons, who were mostly absentee landlords operating through a bailiff or a steward, there would seem to be little room left for baronets, knights or esquires. Let us glance at a list of manors (or indeed parishes) controlled by the peers of the realm, and then look at those where there were local gentry in residence:

Parish or Manor	Owner
Beachampton	Marquess of Salisbury until 1806, and then Lord Carrington, Lord Egmont and Lord Arden
Calverton	
Stony Stratford West	

3 Blake *Disraeli* p273.
4 Professor Norman Gash *Politics in the Age of Peel* p185.

Parish or Manor	Owner
Drayton Parslow Hanslope Mursley (part of) Moulsoe, etc.	Lord Carrington from 1820
Milton Keynes Ravenstone	Earl of Winchelsea and Nottingham until 1826
Stantonbury	Earl Spencer
Stoke Hammond	Duke of Norfolk until 1820
Bow Brickhill Wavendon (part of)	Duke of Bedford
Deanshanger Whittlebury Potterspury Grafton Regis Yardley Gobion, etc	Duke of Grafton
Stowe Wotton Underwood, Dadford, many other manors, and much of Buckingham	Duke of Buckingham and Chandos
Mursley (part of)	Lord Eardley until 1824
Mentmore	Baron Meyer de Rothschild until 1874, then Earl of Rosebery, KG (son-in-law)
North Marston Swanbourne Hardwick	Fremantle family. T. F. Fremantle created Lord Cottlesloe in 1874

THE SQUIRES OR LANDED GENTRY

However great the influence of the peers, and it was indeed

tremendous – there was a second echelon of landowners who exercised power on the spot. Whilst the peers owned one-fifth of Bucks and Beds, at least three-fifths was owned by the landed gentry which included baronets, knights and squires, who occasionally got into Parliament, or became sheriffs and JPs, and who had much influence over the voters within their territories.

In our area we had a score of such squires. If anyone owned 1,000 acres of land, or even 500, the whole world combined to call him a gentleman, and if the lordship of a manor went with it then he was one of the county's élite. Consequently as the old families died out, or became bankrupt, new moneyed men from the city came in, lawyers, doctors, merchants and so on, who quickly strove to accommodate themselves to county standards and knew that the stables were the real heart of any country estate.

Those moneyed men of the city of London who had bought local manors turned to their new responsiblities with eagerness, and since many were lawyers they often found ways and means of enlarging their active scope.

THE ESQUIRES

In one field, that of title and precedence, they found of course that the possession of great estates did not give them an historic title or a place in the House of Lords. Lords of the manor were not lords of that kidney. Sometimes they were baronets and sometimes knights. But there was one title that the monarch did not necessarily grant, that of esquire, which had a most honourable origin. In Roman times it was the custom for an equites or knight to have a 'scutarius', one who bore his shield and his arms, who attended him in peace and war. The French picked up the word centuries later, converting it into 'escuyer', and when the Normans conquered England the eldest son of a knight, or some other young relative, was given the position and the title. He was thus a cadet for knighthood, and he ranked immediately below a knight bachelor.

In the middle ages 'esquire' (or 'armiger' – one entitled to bear arms) was the customary description of holders of knights fees who had, as William Harrison wrote in 1577:

> 'the port, charge and countenance of a gentleman: he shall for money have a coat of arms bestowed upon him by the heralds (who do many gay things), and thereunto being made

so good cheap be called esquire, and reputed for a gentleman ever after.'

Camden writing a little later distinguished four classes entitled to be called esquire:

1. The eldest sons of knights, and their eldest sons.
2. The grandsons of peers, and their eldest sons.
3. Esquires created by royal letters patent, and their eldest sons.
4. Esquires by office such as JPs and others who bear office under the crown.

But already there was a certain elasticity, and some of our local worthies, long before Harrison or Camden, described themselves as esquires whether the College of Heralds approved or not. The first 'esquire' mentioned in our local records was George Longueville in 1419 (he owned half the manor of Wolverton). A little later we have John Edy of Beachampton and Stony Stratford from 1453 onwards describing himself as 'armiger' or 'esquire', and as such he alone in Stony Stratford could wear shoes with toes up to two feet long. Others caught the idea, and so we got our squires.

By the 18th century it was a recognised thing that every lord of the manor or large landowner, unless he had a hereditary title should be addressed as 'Squire'. He was a real power in the locality and in the county. He was expected to become a JP, and occasionally a Sheriff. He and his sons were also practically entitled to commissions in the local yeomanry. As a JP he helped to fix county wages and of course to dispense justice. As we shall see later when it came to rick burning or agricultural rioting he and his colleagues would condemn the malefactors to death or transportation. Thieves were punished by lashings at the cart tail. As JPs also they were responsible for roads and bridges and a score of other activities.

In Queen Elizabeth's day JPs were 'esquires by office'. When the reform of local government took place from 1888 to 1894 all chairmen of Urban and Rural District Councils became ex-officio magistrates and consequently 'esquires by office'. Since these chairmen changed frequently few could keep track as to who was an esquire or just a mere mister. Tactful tradesmen now began the practice of addressing every good customer as 'Esq.', and so now we have all become esquires. But in the early 1800s to be a squire was to be a member of a formidable class exercising power and justice in the name of the King.

Of all our local squirearchy the senior in lineage and tradition were the Lovetts of Liscombe Park, Soulbury. Their ancestors had held Liscombe Park since about 1304. It is estimated that until the Park was sold in 1907 there had been over twenty generations of Lovetts there. It was the only family left in north Bucks of undisputed male descent from late Norman times. The last squire but one, Captain Phillip Lovett, became sheriff in 1863. In 1960 there were still Lovetts living at Liscombe Lodge, but at the Park the Bonsors held sway.

By comparison with the Lovetts of Liscombe Park, the Duncombes of Great Brickhill were late-comers, for they only acquired the manor round about 1549. The family provided its share of sheriffs from 1618 on, and when on 4 March 1824 Philip Pauncefort Duncombe became sheriff he ordered a handsome brand new carriage, and in this, drawn by six beautiful horses with two footmen up behind and two more following on horseback, he went to welcome the judge Baron Graham, at Aylesbury. It was a glorious thing to be a sheriff!

The Knapps of Little Linford and Shenley and the Uthwatts of Great Linford came later into our area, the Knapps in 1684 when a successful city lace merchant bought the manor of Little Linford and three years later one of the Shenley manors. They provided sheriffs in 1767 and 1858 and JPs in every generation. As for the Uthwatts of Great Linford, their ownership of the manor dated from 1702. They provided sheriffs in 1726, 1755 and 1831, and JPs all the time.

Another family of squires, the Selby-Lowndes, originated a little later than the Uthwatts. We have referred to them extensively in Volume I, so all we will add here is that they were masters of the hunt and loved their port.

The Roses of Little Brickhill were less talked about, possibly because their greatest distinction was won overseas. In 1794, when Little Brickhill belonged to the Duncombes, the young Frances Duncombe married Sir George Henry Rose, and her dowry was the Little Brickhill Manor. He was a diplomat and MP for forty-six years (in those days it was possible to combine such conflicting interests because Parliament only met for a few months each year). It was he who was the main mover in the enclosure of the manor in 1796, and the Enclosure Award is splattered with the name of

Rose over hundreds of acres. He died in 1855 having held the Little Brickhill Manor for sixty years.

His son, Sir Hugh Henry Rose, born in 1801, was a soldier and a diplomat, and won the title of Lord Strathnairn and Jhansi in 1864 for his services in the Indian Mutiny and after. Strathnairn's services in the Crimea and India made him a popular hero, but his fascinating and adventurous life story cannot be told here. He was Little Brickhill's greatest son – even though he was born in Berlin – and spent his old age in London! He died in 1885 unmarried, so the manor eventually passed to the Finlays who held it for half a century.

These then were some of our squires, lords of hundreds, sometimes thousands of acres, with their home farm and a dozen or more other farms which they let out to tenants. They were land ownership personified. Villages for miles around knew all about the squire and his relations, and the gossip from the servants' hall percolated to every pub and over every back garden wall.

All over the county were the large and lovely houses of the squires. From Gayhurst to Winslow Hall these great mansions overlooking thousands of acres were a visible sign to all as to where the power lay.

There was a sardonic saying at the time that the fool of the family went into the church. Since the nobility and local gentry owned most of the advowsons (or right to select the parson for their local church) it followed that many parsons were handpicked by the squires. At that time clerical incomes were normally sufficient to allow them to hunt, to send their children to first class schools and to employ curates to help with the parish work. Nevertheless the system produced many saintly men devoted to their parishes.

Up to 1840 north Bucks had no counterpoise to this combination of squire and parson. There were no great industrialists, no great towns with independent burgesses, there were no trade unions, and only a feeble Chartist movement. The only hope for those destined to be the labouring class for ever was in the Christian faith, which taught that humility in this life would bring great rewards hereafter. Meanwhile all touched their caps to parsons and squires. Railwaymen never acquired the habit.

And yet in the seemingly settled community where everyone knew his place there were odd movements.

The first was the infiltration of Jews into the great manors. Land could be bought: no one had to prove English or Christian descent. The Jews had money: they lent to the impecunious squire, and foreclosed in good legal form.

All over Bucks this leaven was working. Most of its lands were handy for London, and from the City there came the Rothschilds, the Disraelis, Sampson Gideon and many others. They became MFHs, they became sheriffs, they became MPs.

THE HUNTS

We have seen that most of the squires were JPs, and so met every few weeks at local petty sessions, or at Aylesbury. But there were other and more joyous occasions when they met almost *en masse* for one of the oldest of all sports. Adjacent to our area used to be the Salcey and Whittlewood Forests and the Whaddon Chase, where kings and knights and squires had chased the running deer or the sly old fox since Norman times.

Around 1700 all this began to be regularised. Adjacent land-owners would form a hunt, set up kennels and allow anyone to join in provided certain rules were kept and certain subscriptions paid.

Possibly the first hunt in our area was the Grafton, the master being either the Duke himself or one of his near relatives.

The Grafton country around 1750 was extensive. It included the whole of Whaddon Chase and most of south Northants, including Towcester and Brackley, with Whittlewood as the heart of it all. It was the Grafton which showed the world how to kill foxes. The kennels were at Wakefield Lodge near Stony Stratford. The old (second) Duke was a very keen huntsman, but the outstanding name of the next period is that of Tom Rose, born in 1750, and huntsman to the third and fourth Dukes for fifty seasons. He was a most colourful personality with a rattling 'holloa' that awakened the dead. At 75 he still rode to his hounds with his white locks streaming beneath his black cap.

The fourth Duke took on Tom Rose's son, Ned, and after him George Carter – immortal names in the history of the hunt – who 'halloed' the Grafton hounds on to death or glory – and it was usually glory. In the latter years of Carter's reign the music in Whittlewood forest was second to none. Forty minutes was the span vouchsafed to a fox. No pack in England stood in higher repute than the Grafton when hunted by Carter and his aides.[5]

It was whilst the fourth Duke was still hunting (i.e. before 1838) that the Grafton acquired one of its most spectacular followers, 'Adam Sherwood, a Stony Stratford chimney-sweep sportsman, who materialised at each meet costumed "to kill". With a dilapidated chimney-pot hat, green smock frock and corduroy breeches, he wore a worsted waistcoat with scarlet ground and foxes' teeth round the front instead of buttons, Mounted on an old pony, he was the cynosure of all eyes. From a flask consisting of two glass bottles welded together at the lower ends and containing, on the one side, gin and, on the other, brandy, he dispensed hospitality to all his friends. From long experience he had acquired an uncanny knowledge of foxes and their habits. Such was his assurance that he would not hesitate to sum up the day's hunting and tell the huntsman where he went wrong. On the appearance of fresh foxes he made the wood ring with his view holloa! The Duke consistently humoured him, and once, on being told by Sherwood that a black fox had been spotted, replied, "Out of compliment to you, Adam,".'[6]

Adam continued his fox hunting for ten years after the Duke died in 1844, and he was still advertising his services as a chimney sweep in 1853.

Somewhere round 1750 the Selbys of Wavendon took over the Whaddon Chase which included much of north Bucks. They were joined by the Lowndes of Whaddon and Winslow, and in 1783 the Selby-Lowndes of Winslow Hall took over the mastership. We have already recounted some of their prowess and horsemanship (Vol I, pp261–63).

In 1842 the Duke of Grafton handed over to Lord Southampton (another Fitzroy), but things did not go well, and in 1862 he sold the pack to William Selby-Lowndes. The sixth Duke now took over the Grafton, but it was his brother-in-law, Colonel Edward Douglas-Pennant of Wicken (later Lord Penrhyn) who bought a new pack. But it was not until the 1880s under the mastership of the locally popular second Lord Penrhyn that the Grafton really came into its own again.

5 *Fore's Guide to the Hounds of England,* 1849.
6 These and other delightful memories of the Grafton Hunt are to be found in *Fifty Years' Fox-hunting,* by J. M. K. Elliott (born on the Grafton estate). Edited by his son, E. K. Elliott, 1900. See also *The Royal Fitzroys,* Bernard Falk, 1950.

Oscar Wilde has described the hunt as 'The English country gentleman galloping after a fox – the unspeakable in full pursuit of the uneatable', but in truth it was generally beloved by all, and when the hunt met at a traditional meet on Boxing Day, crowds turned out to admire the hounds, the horses and the scarlet coats that went back to the days of Marlborough.

When on a good day with either the Grafton or the Whaddon Chase the hunt really got going, it was like the cavalry charge at Balaclava – hell for leather. Fences were taken blindly. The joy of the chase negatived any sense of direction or self preservation. It was glorious to be going – and if by grace and chance one was in at the kill the day was worth an age without a name.

Anybody could hunt if he contributed about £30 a year – but there were often reduced rates for farmers which ensured their goodwill. Always and at any hunt one could see the superbly mounted gentry or city capitalists, and following, on not quite such excellent mounts, local farmers and their sons and daughters who were seldom in at the kill. The annual Hunt Ball was the social event of the year, but we have no proof that Adam Sherwood ever attended one.

TRUSTEES

But there were a few villages which had no personal squire, where the estate had passed years ago to a college or a trust.

Possibly the most remarkable was Wolverton, where in 1714 Dr John Radcliffe by his will left a great deal of property to University College, Oxford, for founding medical travelling scholarships and so on. His Wolverton estate was put at the disposal of his executors to use as they thought best, and the income was mainly used in building the Radcliffe Observatory, Hospital and Library at Oxford, and in enlarging St Bartholomew's Hospital in London.

There is an excellent copy of the portrait of the doctor in the Radcliffe School at Wolverton, showing him in a formidable long-bottomed wig and looking exactly what he was, a most redoubtable 18th century personage who could rebuke princesses and queens with warmth and candour. It is also related that when he looked at William III's swollen ankles he remarked that he 'wouldn't have his legs for three Kingdoms'.

The Radcliffe Trust, well and truly administered over the

centuries had been a fine example of careful husbandry. But here, as at Willen where another doctor, equally redoubtable and an even greater scholar, Dr Richard Busby had left the entire manor to university purposes, there was no resident lord of the manor to be seen hunting, shooting or fishing, or administering justice from the local bench. The same applied to Newton Longville, which had been in the hands of New College since 1441. The college bursar or his representative would be welcomed on his rent collecting tour, and was always courteously treated, but he never became a JP or a Master of the Hunt. It was unthinkable.

In the other parishes the squires had a great influence not only locally but throughout the county. Every family has its fascinating history, but much as we would like to delve into their various records we must limit our curiosity to one family over a single generation, so in a later chapter we give the story of the Duncombes of Great Brickhill and Water Eaton, and we must let that chapter speak for generations of squires in north Bucks who for centuries, in a very privileged position, by and large served their parishes and their county well.

The death knell of the old order was sounded when death duties were first imposed in 1894–96 of up to 8 per cent, and which increased very steeply during the next half century. The result has been that few of these old estates remain today – they have been taxed out of existence or taken over by the Milton Keynes Development Corporation. Instead of the local squire we now have the local officials, growing in number every year. And many places on the Justices' bench have been taken over by railwaymen and respectable ladies.

Nevertheless, at the time this volume opens (1800) and for at least a generation after, the power in North Bucks was held by peers and squires, and there was growing resentment against so much power being held by so few. Buckinghamshire smiths and shoemakers, and agricultural paupers, were not going to put up with it much longer.

3   Reform and the State of the Poor

It was evident that although the aristocratic system with its attendant squires and tenant farmers and limited electorate had brought us safely at last through the Napoleonic wars, it was in urgent need of reform. Indeed there were many long before, like Pitt around 1780, who were considering it seriously, but the excesses of the French revolution, particularly the Reign of Terror in 1793–94 frightened many with fears of mob rule if anything like democracy was granted.

But by 1820 the reformers found a new champion, the young, enthusiastic and squeaky-voiced Lord John Russell (1792–1878), the third son of the sixth Duke of Bedford. Like many of his uncles and cousins he became a member of Parliament for a rotten borough (Tavistock) at twenty-one and was soon a keen student of the writings of William Cobbett, and a strenuous advocate of parliamentary reform.

William Cobbett (1762–1835) was a farmer and journalist who rode around England and wrote with exceptional perspicuity on agricultural and political subjects, describing the widespread poverty. He reached the conclusion that there would be no improvement until Parliament itself had been reformed. He blamed the aristocracy for causing the distress by selfish legislation, and demanded a change in the character of government. 'There is', he wrote, 'in the men calling themselves English country gentlemen something superlatively base. They are, I believe, the most cruel, the most unfeeling, the most brutally insolent . . . they are the most base of all creatures that God ever suffered to take human shape.' It is hard to disagree with him, but there were fine exceptions.

Another writer who made men think was Sir Frederick Eden, chairman of the Globe Insurance Company, who in 1797 published a formidable three-volumed work on 'The State of the Poor' and in it he gave this example of one of the Duke of Grafton's tenants who lived at Roade:

'Richard Walker was a thirty-six year old labourer, married, with a daughter of nine, three boys aged seven, six and three, and a one-year-old baby. His pay as a labourer was £20 a year, but he got breakfast and beer free. Three of his children went to the lace school, Richard paying for their education and "thread". They earnt about 6d a week. Richard was honest and industrious, and by ringing the church bell twice daily he earnt another £1.6.0 a year. He also picked up a pound a year as a barber and by digging graves at the Baptist chapel. At harvest the whole family, bar the baby, collected corn worth about £3.10.0. Thus the total family income was about £27 a year. It is not surprising that there was nothing to spare, for Richard's expenses came to £27.16.2 not including fuel at 50/-. His rent, 8/- a year, which shows that he must have been living in a very cottagy cottage, was very low, for most other labourers were paying 1/- a week. However hard Richard Walker and his family worked there was never a penny over for a frippery or a celebration of any kind.'

The same conditions applied more or less to all labourers working for the dukes, the earls and other landowners in our area. But had Richard Walker died, whilst his widow might have had a small pension from the Duke, all she would have been entitled to was half a crown a week from the overseers of the poor and a shilling per week for each child.

Eden's investigation included conditions at Stony Stratford, of which he wrote:

'The inhabitants are common tradesmen, innkeepers, and lacemakers. The latter consist entirely of women: they earn from 6d to 1/- a day. The poor are maintained in a work house. There are now 11 persons in the house. Meat is allowed 3 days in the week. 18 regular pensioners receive in weekly allowances, £1.11.0 (about 1/8d per person). In all about £210 p.a. is spent on the poor.'

At Yardley Gobion the average outdoor relief was 2s 1d a week.

It was not only Lord John Russell, William Cobbett and Sir Frederick Eden who wanted parliamentary and Poor Law reform. There was Jeremy Bentham, the great philosopher, who argued that the duty of a government was to produce the greatest happiness for the greatest number; there were the new hard thinking captains of industry, a formidable middle class, who wanted Parliament to listen to industry; and perhaps above all there were the great Whig leaders, who thought and said it was scandalous that six boroughs in Buckinghamshire should have twelve members for about 2,000 voters, and mostly bribed at that, whilst Birmingham, Wolverhampton, Sheffield, Manchester and Leeds had not a member between them.

The philosophical or political desire for reform was now emphasised by agricultural distress. During the Napoleonic wars farming had flourished, helped greatly by improved crop rotation and agricultural machinery. Farmers became rich, and then extravagant. Landlords raised the rents, which were doubled and trebled. In some parts between 1790 and 1814 they were quadrupled, but with the price of wheat at over £5 a quarter farmers could cope, and many became, in their own eyes at least, gentlemen farmers who never lifted a pitchfork or mucked out a byre.

But in the next decade wheat prices fell and so did all other agricultural prices. They fell again and yet again until by 1830 wheat was down to £3 a quarter, and there now came periods when the tenant farmer simply could not pay his rent. He cut down his labour force when he could, and great distress was caused. Pauperism increased rapidly. Even before this landlords were reducing rents by 10 to 25 per cent.

Bucks was one of the first counties to give the protests a destructive force. The spirit that had animated Henry Heriot of Bletchley to protest against manorial services in 1377, that had led Christopher Carne and others to protest against enclosures at Wolverton in 1583, that had led so many to withhold ship money in 1634 was now alive again, and in December 1830 there were curious outbreaks of violence throughout the county that looked and indeed were alarming. The forces of discontent were widespread, but unco-ordinated and spasmodic. In addition to the Chartists and trade unionists, there were those who thought out and developed the 'Captain Swing' outrages.

Normally, when these sort of movements occur, north Bucks sits placidly by, ruminating and pondering, until very late in the day it gets up, gives a shove, and the day is won. Somehow it got mixed up with the 'Captain Swing' riots. Before we describe these local protests let us have a look at the condition of the agricultural worker. There was no doubt about it that he was poorly paid and overworked when in employment, but when he was out of work, and a large proportion were, his condition was one of misery. One-seventh of the adult population of Bucks were paupers: their only relief was by the Poor Law administered by local overseers elected parish by parish. These poor relief scales varied slightly from year to year, but in general they were roughly (1829–32): Man and wife, 5s 6d plus 1s for each child up to 9s 6d. Single men over 20, 4s a week. Widow 2s or 2s 6d, plus 1s for each child.

Yet harsh as these rates seem there were many paupers (or unemployed) who would not work, particularly in Stony Stratford. Farmers and shopkeepers resented paying poor rates at 21s in the pound over the year for them.[1] As a partial solution ablebodied men were let out to farmers at 4s a week and the parish paid the balance. But pauperism increased. After all, if a married man with four children could get 9s 6d a week for not working, why should he work ten or even twelve hours a day for an extra sixpence a week? But the widow's allowance was not enough to keep body and soul together.

'Poor Law charity scrimped and iced
In the name of a cautious statistical Christ.'

Thieving and poaching helped to fill the gap, and legal gathering of berries and nuts closed it a bit more. Young hawthorn shoots (nicknamed bread and cheese) were palatable too, and nettles were boiled as a vegetable. During harvest time all would go out to glean, and Eden says that 'A good family will glean as much wheat as will serve them in bread for a year'. But those in work were also in competition for these products of the fields and hedges, and even they sought Poor Law support in addition to the low wage of 10s a week. In 1830 the English farm labourer relied on the Poor Law for 15 per cent of his income. Only at the long hours of harvest time was there a chance of augmenting the minimal income, for then they could earn 2s a day with breakfast and beer.

The labourer was not only desperately poor, he was oppressed, helpless and almost hopeless. The slightest sign of protest was treated with a shocking severity, and the petty thieving when dis-

1 Gibbs *Buckinghamshire Local Records* Vol III.

covered was punished by public lashings at the cart tail, on market days in Aylesbury – men and women alike.

More serious thieving was punished draconically. In 1801, when Henry Bennion was convicted of stealing a sheep from John Phillips of Great Brickhill, the Aylesbury Assizes sentenced him 'to be hung at the usual gallows' in Bicester Road. There were many such cases.[2]

Nothing was more natural than that the submerged minority should rebel. But how to do it and not be caught? 'Captain Swing' found an answer. The line of action was by night-time activity in the burning of ricks and the smashing of machinery. Of the new machines possibly the most hated was the threshing machine which had been invented in 1792 and by now was to be found on every large farm. In 1810 Mr Kitelee of Castlethorpe had one which cost as little as £50, which with one horse, three men and a boy, could thresh 6 quarters of corn in a day at a tenth of the previous cost. But the protests were not only against the new agricultural machinery that took bread out of men's mouths, but also against the burdensome tithes that ruined farmers, or at any rate prevented them from paying better wages, for many of the farmers too were now on subsistence levels.

By 1822 rick burnings were common – there was one at Stony Stratford, and many more in the eastern counties. Threshing machines were also destroyed. In 1828 (April) there was scarcely a night without depredations around Stony Stratford.

Discontent broke out into ugly, but seldom murderous forms. First a letter signed 'Captain Swing' or just 'Swing' was sent to the squire or whoever had introduced a new threshing machine or drill, on these lines:

'This is to acquaint you that if your threshing machines are not destroyed by you directly, we shall commence our labours. Signed on behalf of the whole: SWING.'

Ricks were then burnt, machines smashed, mobs sometimes hundreds strong, paraded yelling 'Bread or Blood', from village to village making clear their needs. Often the action would be organised in a local pub or two: often the leaders were the shoemakers or smiths, who carried the sledge hammers for the machine smashing, but most of the rioters were paupers, dangerous men because they had nothing to lose.

2 Gibbs *op cit.*

THE BUCKS HUSSARS

It could be asked what the police were doing whilst all this was going on. There was no police force as we know it today, only parish constables elected annually, with a chief constable at places like Newport and Aylesbury, and to these could be added temporary special constables. But their powers and courage were limited. The real arm of the law when civil commotion occurred was the part-time yeomanry, and in the case of Buckinghamshire this was the Bucks Hussars, raised in 1794 by the Marquess of Buckingham, officered by his nominees, and which had a minimum strength of about thirty-six officers and 400 men in eight troops, but could be up to 1,200 men in twenty-one troops. Two of these troops were at Buckingham and there would usually be one at Newport Pagnell and possibly another at Fenny Stratford and at Stony Stratford. They were light cavalry with swords and sabretaches, and their uniforms, which varied about every decade, were always a sartorial joy. Ideal to get married in. Each man had to provide himself with a suitable mare or gelding of not less than 14 hands: but his uniform was provided by the county.

In 1814 the Marquess of Buckingham, who was enormously fat, volunteered to take the Bucks militia to the Peninsula War. Wellington had already crossed the Pyrenees, so permission was given to them to proceed to Bordeaux, but they arrived the day after the peace treaty had been signed. In Bordeaux the Marquess paraded his battalion with pomp and circumstance at morning and noon. The inhabitants looked with awe on the Duke and his fellow officers, whom they described as 'les boeufs-gras Anglais' (English fat stock beasts) – but the militia found the local wine and brandy too much for their stability, and Wellington ordered them home without delay.[3]

From 1822 to 1827 the Colonel was the Duke of Buckingham who as we have seen in a previous chapter had mighty ideas of his own position, powers and prerogatives. Philip-Duncombe-Pauncefort-Duncombe was a captain as was Matthew Knapp of Linford. It will be understood that to mobilise even a troop of fifty volunteers for action was a somewhat complicated affair, and by the time they had got their orders, their uniforms and their horses, the rioters would have dispersed and were innocently

3 Gronow *Reminiscences and Recollections 1862–66* p333.

going about their lawful occasions. Occasionally, however, a riot or a commotion would be prolonged and the yeomanry be just in time to catch and arrest stragglers.

In 1827 some of the yeomanry were disbanded, but those around Aylesbury and Buckingham were retained and it was these who were used in the 1830 troubles. In November, as Gibbs records, 'the yeomanry under the command of Lord Chandos were called out but at many places where they marched about there was a good deal of yelling at them.'

MORE RIOTS

In November and December 1830 north Bucks was alive with incident. There were riots, fires and risings all over the county, especially at High Wycombe. On 1 December threshing machines were smashed and burnt at Little Brickhill and Fenny Stratford, on the 3rd the disturbances, mainly over wages, had spread to Olney and Stony Stratford, on the next day to Newport Pagnell: on the 9th to Fenny Stratford and Brickhill again. The local yeomanry were now called out. One of the troopers was James Cole, a Newport baker. Similar disturbances were happening around Aylesbury, in Bedfordshire and south Northants, and many other counties in the South East.[4] Riots now occurred in Bletchley, Wolverton and Newport Pagnell, and incendiary fires at Nash and Wavendon.

The law now stepped into action headed by the Duke of Buckingham, 'our most High, most Mighty and Most Noble Prince' who was also Lord Lieutenant of Bucks. To him and others one of the most alarming symptoms was that some of the JPs seemed to sympathise with the outbreaks, and therefore those brought to justice might well go free. The government's solution was to appoint Special Commissioners to try a thousand 'Swing' cases, and they sat at Winchester, Reading, Dorchester and Aylesbury. At Aylesbury they sat for four weeks in January 1831, trying 126 cases. Others were tried by ordinary County Courts, but there was little softness here. In Bucks 163 cases in all were tried. Forty-one cases were acquitted, forty-six were jailed, forty-four were sentenced to death, thirty-two were sentenced to

4 See *Captain Swing* by R.J. Hogsbawn and G. Rude, 1969. Also *The Times* 13 December 1830.

transportation.[5] Meanwhile at the Bucks Quarter Sessions for Epiphany 1831 a special vote of thanks to the Yeomanry was recorded.

Now at last public opinion began to be expressed. There were many protests at the severe sentences. In the result only three were executed and other death sentences were commuted to transportation, thirty actually arrived in Tasmania. Some of the finest men in Bucks were thus exiled as convicts. It is true they were guilty of rick burning or machine breaking, some simply of theft, but in sober justice it must be asked what other form of protest had they? Public meetings (even if any of them were orators) would have been cleared off by the Yeomanry, Peterloo in 1819 had shown how the yeomanry could use their sabres against people attending a meeting.

From no other comparable movement, neither from the Luddites (1811–18), nor from the Chartists (1838 on) nor from the trade union 'conspiracies' was such a bitter price exacted. What happened to those transported is described in the book *Captain Swing*. In Australia they were treated as dangerous convicts. For the slightest misconduct the men could be sentenced to twenty-five or fifty lashes. A few, after serving their seven to fourteen years' sentence returned home, working their passage before the mast. The Tolpuddle martyrs have become British left-wing heroes. The 'Swing' protests of our village Hampdens who suffered greatly, have found little praise amongst our county historians.

REFORM

The unrest added fuel to the cry for reform. Something was very wrong with the country. The wealthy were growing wealthier, and were ostentatiously building more and more palaces and halls: the poor were growing poorer. Only a representative parliament free from the power of the peers could find the solution.

Nonconformists, friendly societies, and an ever growing body of reformers now forced the change. There were meetings all over north Bucks. What the workers and the reformers wanted was summarised in six points:

5 Details are to be found in the Assize Records, now in London, but I have not had time to study them fully.

Universal suffrage
Vote by ballot
Annual Parliaments
Payment of Members
Abolition of the Property Qualification for the vote
Equal Electoral Districts

As for the labourers, they wanted an increase of wages from 1s 6d a day to 2s 3d.

Fortunately the old Duke of Wellington now ceased to be Prime Minister for in 1830 with the death of George IV a general election was held – and soon, in November, Lord Grey – a Whig and a reformer – became Prime Minister. A few months later (March 1831) Lord John Russell introduced the Great Reform Bill – not a very democratic measure, but one which castrated the rotten boroughs, gave representation to the great cities, and in rural areas such as north Bucks gave the vote to substantial tenant farmers.

The open ballot with its accompanying intimidation however remained. The power of the aristocracy was not destroyed – only moderately modified.

Let us have a look at the political situation as it was in Buckinghamshire in 1831. The population was then 147,000 of whom about 40,000 were adult males. Of these about 34,000 had no parliamentary vote, even though Buckinghamshire county and its six boroughs returned fourteen members of Parliament. (Today, with a population of 600,000, it has five.) But even these fourteen seats were not evenly allocated, for we find that:

Buckinghamshire county:	2 members, 4,000 electors
Buckingham borough:	2 members, 13 voters[6]
Aylesbury borough:	2 members, 1,050 voters
Wendover borough:	2 members, 140 voters
Wycombe borough:	2 members, 170 voters
Amersham borough:	2 members, 150 voters
Marlow borough:	2 members, 600 voters

Thirty years before the Reform Act, in 1802, Aylesbury had only 450 electors. Bribery was open and shameless. After an enquiry the constituency was enlarged to include not only the

6 But although the Charter of 1684 laid down that the bailiff and twelve aldermen should vote, only eleven ever seem to have got to the poll. See *Stockdale's Peerage, 1831,* and *Parliamentary Representation in England*, Philbin, 1965.

borough, but the three adjoining 'hundreds' and the number of electors raised to 1,000 in 1804. The ballot of course was not secret and once again Aylesbury was a pocket borough even though the pocket was deeper.

But even this is not the end of the reckoning for in Buckingham borough the thirteen voters were all aldermen, and the Duke of Buckingham approved the aldermen. All were under engagement to resign if they did not vote as the Duke wished. The members returned in the 1826, 1830 and 1831 elections were General Sir George Nugent, Bart, (a cousin of the Duke), and Sir Thomas Francis Fremantle, Bart, a nominee of the Duke. In the county election one of the nominations was the 'absolute right' of the Duke of Buckingham whilst seven other large landowners nominated the other. Consequently there was seldom an actual election. In the three elections of 1826, 1830 and 1831 Richard Plantagenet-Nugent-Grenville-Chandos-Temple, 'commonly called the Marquess of Chandos', was nominated by the Duke of Buckingham, and the Honourable Robert Smith, by the others, and the two were duly returned.

Important towns such as Newport Pagnell had only a score of voters, who voted in the county elections. Entire parishes had no vote at all, or at best were represented by the squire and the parson.

Not unnaturally the clamour for reform was insistent and vociferous, and to the everlasting credit of the Russells of Woburn they gave it a leadership which was ultimately successful. It was Lord John Russell, now an experienced MP who helped frame the first Reform Bill, and who introduced it into the House of Commons. One of the interesting points about the whole issue was that the opposition of the House of Lords with all its pocket boroughs and other influences was only overcome when William IV made it clear (on constitutional advice of course) that he was quite willing to create any number of new peers with reforming zeal to get the Bill through. The prospect of peers becoming two a penny was a more appalling prospect to the dukes and earls than any other, and they echoed Clough's words:

'Let thought and commerce trade and learning die
But leave us still our old nobility.'

The Bill passed, but it fell far short of the ideals either of the Russells or the Chartists. Let us see how it affected Buckinghamshire.

Changes Produced by the Reform Act of 1832

Over the country as a whole the Reform Act abolished fifty-six rotten boroughs including St Mawes (owned by the Duke of Buckingham). In Buckinghamshire it abolished the four seats at Amersham and Wendover. Thus 143 seats were available, half of which were conferred on industrial centres such as Birmingham and Manchester, whilst others went to improve county representation. Buckinghamshire county was one that secured an extra seat.

But the old rotten borough of Buckingham was not abolished – it still retained its two members, though now the parishes of Maids Moreton, Thornborough, Padbury, Hillesden, Preston Bissett, Tingewick and Radclive were added to the old borough, so that the number of electors was raised from a dozen to over three hundred.

In the result the new set-up left Buckinghamshire with eleven members instead of fourteen, and the eleven were distributed as follows:

		Voters
Buckinghamshire county	3 members	6,000
Buckingham borough+parishes	2 members	360[7]
Aylesbury borough+parishes	2 members	1,050
Marlow borough	2 members	700(?)
Wycombe borough	2 members	300(?)

The Act did more than redistribute the constituencies, it widened the franchise, so that in the boroughs a £10 occupier was entitled to a vote, and under the famous 'Chandos Clause' carried by the Marquess of Chandos, son of the Duke of Buckingham, county tenants who occupied tenements of a yearly value of £50 were also entitled to the vote. Thus every large shopkeeper, every successful professional man, and every substantial farmer might now be registered as a voter.

The New Register

Somebody now had to register both new and old voters, and Parliament put this duty on the overseers of the poor, who of course, were active in every large parish. Anyone could apply to be included on the electoral roll, anybody could object. The

7 Sheahan p228.

sheriff of the county was charged with the responsibility for seeing that everything was finally in order, and the Sheriff for Bucks in 1831 was Henry Andrewes Uthwatt, Esq, of Great Linford. He had a busy time.

In the church chest at Stony Stratford are the claims of all those sixty or more householders in Stony Stratford who wanted to be put on the register. It included such names as Worley, Dickens, Elstone, Goodridge, Odell, Hillyer, and so on, some of whose descendants reside in Stratford to this day. There appears to have been only one objection – a Mr Edward Joyce of Newport Pagnell objected to the inclusion on the Stony Stratford list of the Revd Charles Kipling, who was then Vicar of St Giles. Possibly he had a vote elsewhere.

Newport Pagnell, the largest and most important town north of Aylesbury, (though Buckingham was still politically more important), now had 120 voters, and the lists here included names like Bull, Coales and Lawman. Olney had eighty voters and Bletchley forty-six. But there were only eight polling places in all Bucks – Aylesbury, Amersham, Bletchley, Brill, Buckingham, Newport Pagnell, Wycombe and Slough, and polling lasted several days.

Everybody was now geared up to the General Election of 1832. The political power of the dukes and earls had been clipped – but only clipped – and even as late as 1911 the *Encyclopaedia Britannica* could write: 'It is a very common experience for younger sons of Peers to be selected as candidates for parliament, even though they may appear in no way the equals of other men. They have been brought up to the business, and therefore adapted to it by heredity.' The truth was that our democracy loved to have an aristocratic tinge. It made them feel respectable.

In counties such as Bucks and Beds the landowning aristocracy was still supreme, and the inclusion in the electoral lists of tenants at will (of £50 annual rent) as well as a few copyholders and lease-holders, perhaps tended to increase the power of the landlords. There was still no secret ballot, so that every lord of the manor knew how his tenants voted, and every townsman could find out how his shopkeepers had voted.

Anyway the Act was hailed as a tremendous step forward. One result of the Act was that responsibility for forming ministries or creating peers passed from the King to the senior ministers. In the

next century hundreds of peers were created, and Buckinghamshire got its fair share.

The election of December 1832 naturally threw up some new
members, mostly Whigs. Among these was the 31 year old Sir
Harry Verney of Claydon. He was actually born a Calvert, son of
Sir Harry Calvert, a very capable general, and inherited the
baronetcy from him in 1826. But when a year later he inherited
the Claydon estate from his cousin, Mrs Verney, he changed his
name to Verney, and under that ancient name represented Buckingham borough in Parliament almost continuously until the old
borough was at last disfranchised in 1885, and he then became the
first member to represent the new division of north Bucks. Of his
abilities and actions we shall have much to say later on.

The age of direct political bribery and corruption was passing,
that of skilful benevolence or propitiatory actions was coming.
Parliamentary candidates or members became 'patrons' of everything from fat stock shows to cricket clubs. The Verneys really
knew the constituency, and it is small wonder that they represented Buckingham or the wider Buckingham division for fifty or
sixty years.

Property was still the passport to influence and power. The list
of voters now included every little man of property in every
market town and village. To be on the voters list was to be publicly registered as a successful man. The landless, the labourers,
and industrial workers like the smiths and the shoemakers were
rigidly excluded from the ballot. As far as the House of Commons
was concerned they were the mob, and even the Russells thought
twice before enfranchising them. As for the women – whoever
would think of giving a woman a vote? Nobody did!

Registers of voters were now made publicly available, and it is
from these that we can check how the new franchise affected the
male population. Great Brickhill for example then had about 700
inhabitants of whom about 200 were adult males, but in 1844 only
twenty-four of these had the vote – all of whom either owned
freehold land or occupied a house and/or land over £10 in value.[8]

POOR LAW, 1834 ON

The new reformed Parliament took two years before it made any

8 In 1960 Great Brickhill, with a population of about 700, had 354 voters.

great changes in poor relief, and many doubted eventually whether the changes were for the better. In 1834 outdoor relief, which had existed for 300 years or more, was abolished, and the old and infirm were now sent to workhouses. The idea was that for every union of a dozen or more parishes there should be created buildings holding from 200 to 300 inmates where they would be looked after, and if possible set to work. The first was erected at Winslow – a red brick building with room for 250 – whose catchment area included Shenley Brook End. The next, in 1836, was at Newport Pagnell, in Tickford End, with room for 274, which cost £7,000, and which gathered in the destitute of forty-five parishes, including Shenley Church End.

In the same year the Potterspury Union, which included Calverton, Stony Stratford, Wolverton, etc, built the Yardley Gobion workhouse.

For nearly 100 years the poor old men and women, destitute and forlorn, who could not find a place in almshouses were sent to one or the other of these three Union workhouses – grim buildings in which there was little tenderness and often less efficiency: old couples were separated, they were allowed none of their former furniture. When the workhouses were full, which was often, the staff, willing as they might be, could hardly cope. Orphans too were sent to these institutions, and Dickens' description of the sordid conditions could well have originated in our locality.[9]

They were governed by a board of guardians, democratically elected, and democracy did a harsh job. Oddly enough the guardians' powers included setting up water supplies.

There was another kind of workhouse, the casual, as at Old Stratford, where acknowledged tramps, often able bodied, could spend a night or two in return for a modicum of work. It was estimated in 1836 that the cost of maintaining the poor had been reduced by 45 per cent.

Possibly the most scandalous case of the poor being deprived of their rights was at Bow Brickhill-with-Caldecott where the Enclosure Award of 1794 allocated 400 acres to the poor. In 1844 the local lord of the manor, the principal farmers, the rector and

---

9 In Newport workhouse about 30 per cent of the inmates were children, mostly orphans whose number varied from thirty to forty, and illegitimate children who were about twenty to thirty in number.

solicitors obtained an Act of Parliament entitling them to sell sixty acres for £500. The land was sold at that price, just over £8 an acre, but the poor got nothing, since the legal fees for this one transaction came to just £500. Fortunately the rest of the land was laid out as allotments 'cultivated by the poor of the parish', and the poor retained a little of their old rights.

Meanwhile the former poorhouses in places like Stony Stratford were rented out, and usually became dreadful slum quarters which stank lousily.

It was not until 1865 that there was any great change of approach in dealing with the poor. The Union Chargeability Act of that year abolished the old rule that any pauper, no matter how long his or her residence in a parish, must be sent back to the parish of their birth the moment they were chargeable to the rates. Instead a twelve months' residence qualification was substituted. There were therefore no more 'Settlement Certificates' given by the overseers, and labour was now free to go where it wished in search of work. The constables of Little Brickhill and Stony Stratford at last lost their fees for carting 'cripples' from parish to parish. But the Unions, or workhouses, still remained grim institutions.[10]

The harsh treatment of the poor lay not only in the hearts of workhouse masters or guardians but in those of the ratepayers, many of whom thought poverty disreputable and catching. When the enlightened Thomas Taylor of mustard fame (see chapter 10) managed to arrange for a heating system and a children's playground for the Newport Pagnell workhouse (Renny Lodge) in 1880 he found himself unable to get re-elected to the board of guardians. 'Expensive Guardians' were unacceptable to the voters. By contrast, the chairman of the guardians, the economical Francis Coales, was rewarded 'with a handsome clock and a purse of 100 guineas by grateful ratepayers on his retirement in 1884'.[11]

Yet there were occasions when even the guardians had a heart. At Winslow in July 1908 James Rhodes, a 60 year old inmate, asked to see the guardians. When he came before them he asked for a black coat and waistcoat, light trousers, a bowler hat, a

10 For much more about these workhouses, and the hardships and the love affairs that happened in them, see *The Nineteen Hundreds* by S. F. Markham, pp126–29.
11 Information from Mr A. Fleming.

pair of light boots and a trowel. Even Oliver Twist couldn't have asked for more! Rhodes had noticed that in a cottage near the Union there lived a woman of about 56 years of age, who apparently smiled not unfavourably upon him. He felt that he could not go courting in corduroys and hob-nailed boots. As for the trowel, he was a jobbing gardener by trade, but bad times and rheumatism had brought him to the workhouse, but with the trowel he would work when he could. The board could do nothing officially, but had a whip round, and James Rhodes courted and won the lady of his choice.

It was not until the 20th century that the Unemployment Insurance Acts and the Old Age Pensions Acts began to produce a solution to the question of the poor. The closing of the Yardley Workhouse, or the White House, as it was called, in 1925, and the improvement of Renny Lodge in 1948 into a modern hospital for the aged were indicative of the change that had come over the social conscience of England.

Friendly Societies

Once again we have run too far ahead with our history in order to complete a tale, and once again we must go back to pick up forgotten threads so that the story shall have more depth. We have seen that among the formidable forces agitating for parliamentary reform in a legal manner were the Friendly Societies.

The French Revolution had led our successive English governments to clamp down strongly on all sorts of secular associations for fear that revolutionary republican movements might blossom and spread with insurrectionary violence. Yet even the most reactionary government did not feel that it could suppress the Friendly Societies.

As early as 1793 there were possibly 200 of these little societies in Bucks, and it is equally probable that a few of these had been in existence for a century or more, but it was not until the Government in 1793 required their registration at the County Quarter Sessions that we can be certain of their existence. Even then, since these were all private societies there was some reluctance to give any information to the Crown. These early societies or clubs were often associations for convivial purposes at an inn with a natural impulse to assist members of the group in time of trouble, mostly bereavements; and the earliest benefits were given for the death of one of the members or his wife, or for sickness and old age.[12]

Often one of the basic rules was that every member should attend, properly attired, the funeral of a deceased member.

When the Government ordered the registration of these Friendly Societies in June 1793 they asked for no particulars of the origins of the clubs, but only for a list of their rules and their principal supporters. Within the next eighteen months about twenty clubs in the area now covered by Milton Keynes and adjacent villages were registered, and it is from the lists of these now at the Bucks Record Office at Aylesbury and from Laurance Wulcko's researches that we build up the pattern of their activities by referring to one or two of the earliest registrations.

In the July Quarter Sessions of 1794 we find among others, Friendly Societies at Calverton, Stony Stratford, Fenny Stratford and Wolverton.

The Calverton Friendly Society met at the *Shoulder of Mutton*, the Stony Stratford one at the *Crown* in the Market Square, but further records of the Calverton club seem to have disappeared.[13] A year later the Fenny Stratford Friendly Society, which met at the *Crown* in the High Street had its rules confirmed. Both the Stony Stratford and the Fenny Stratford clubs had their rules printed, which was unusual. A few years later (1800) the Fenny Society moved to the *Swan Inn* and was then known as the Old Friendly Society. It was in 1795 too that another Fenny Friendly Society is known to have been registered, this one meeting at the *King's Head* or at the church in Fenny Stratford, and what brings this to our particular notice is that Dr L. C. Gent was one of its officers. Under the revised rules of 1828 he was appointed surgeon and apothecary to the society and was to receive 2s from each member every feast day (or birthday) and 2s from each member who sought his advice. This was by no means a light fee for men earning less than 12s a week.

It was in 1794 that the Wolverton Friendly Society was registered. The odd thing about it is that whilst some meetings were held in the vestry of Old Wolverton Church, as was very

---

12 See Laurance M. Wulcko's *Some Early Friendly Societies in Buckinghamshire*, 1951, and *A History of Stony Stratford*, 1948, p126 and *The Nineteen Hundreds*, 1952, pp88–90.
13 The Stony Stratford one was transferred to the *Swan Inn* in 1870 and was dissolved in 1880.

right and proper, others were held in the *Plough Inn* at Stony Stratford, so that it seems possible that at this time Old Wolverton had no public house of its own. Another interesting point was that the secretary was the Rev Edward Cooke, rector of Haversham, who was the great friend of Lipscombe and supplied him with much material for his monumental history of Bucks. Lipscombe died in poverty: Cooke didn't.

A few years later Cooke helped to start up the Haversham and Castlethorpe Friendly Society (1811) which held its meetings in the church vestry until 1846 at least. The trustees around 1822 included well-known names such as Richard Kitelee, Gentleman, of Castlethorpe, and the Rev Henry Longueville Mansel of Cosgrove.

Newport Pagnell must have had a succession of Friendly Societies, but the only one of which we have a note was the Society of Good Fellowship, which met at the *Plough* and was registered in 1800: when it had fifty-two members. Very seldom indeed did membership of any local society exceed 100 in these early days.

FEMALE FRIENDLY SOCIETIES

The earliest local Female Friendly Society of which we have a record was that at Stony Stratford, established in 1803, and registered a year later. We have continuous records of this for nearly a century, for it was not dissolved until 1898 when it had thirty-nine members. Of these twenty were living outside the town. At the time of its dissolution the society had £1,026 in Consols and cash, quite a considerable sum in those days. The assets were distributed among the members. Its rules, as revised in 1818 and 1843, are to be seen in the Bucks Record Office.

In Fenny Stratford a Female Friendly Society commenced in November 1805, and its rules were approved by the Quarter Sessions in 1811 and 1818, when it had fifty-four members of whom thirty-one were illiterate.

It is probable that in their early days these Female Friendly Societies consisted entirely of lace workers.

It is difficult to describe today the wonderful influence of these societies. They were usually kindly societies whose great aim was to help sick or fallen members and their families. There was a tremendous atmosphere of Christian helpfulness, and also one of modest pride in their very considerable achievements. Unfortunately there was occasionally, but only very occasionally, a weak or uncertain treasurer. However, by and large they were well administered and a remarkable feature of an England that has passed.

As the years went on the number of societies increased, and so did their helpfulness. Soon they were providing hospital services, as well as sick pay and burial benefits. All this with remarkably little fuss or bother, and without numerous officials, and indeed without anything but a mildly benevolent approval from Whitehall or the county.

The great weaknesses of these societies were their limited numbers and their lack of actuarial knowledge. As time went on both of these were remedied by linking up with country-wide organisations like the Manchester Unity Independent Order of Oddfellows (founded in 1810). Soon other great country-wide societies appeared such as the Ancient Order of Foresters (1834), the Hearts of Oak Benefit Society (1842), and the National Deposit Friendly Society (1868). These stronger societies now began to revel in great banners, sashes, medals, aprons and other regalia. These banners were not of the modest size now favoured by the British Legion or the Women's Institutes but vast affairs sometimes 10ft by 8ft, very beautifully painted, and which took a team of strong men to manage in a wind.[14]

Side by side with all these were the newer railway Provident Societies. The Wolverton branch had a membership of 3,750 in 1910. The next strongest local society was probably the National Deposit with a membership of about a thousand. All of these provided sick pay, and the phrase 'on the Club', which is still current, indicated that a member was enjoying one of the benefits he had subscribed for.

In addition to these many societies, there were the Provident Dispensaries. At Wolverton, for example, there was the Wolverton and Stantonbury Dispensary, run by Dr Charles Miles, which for the sum of 1s per family per month provided medical attention and medicine without further charge, whilst at Stony Stratford, the Provident Dispensary, established in 1866 alongside the Cottage Hospital on the Green, had a similar system. Nearly

14 For further details and an illustration see *The Nineteen Hundreds* by S. F. Markham, pp88–91.

every working-class family in the area belonged to the one or the other of these dispensaries; but most of the tradesmen and well-to-do were the direct private patients of the doctor of their choice.

The Provident Dispensaries, however, did not cover hospital services, and to secure these it was necessary to belong either to a Friendly Society or to a Hospital Association. Then, as now, no doctor ever refused to go to a bed of sickness or to an accident because the patient was not duly enrolled with the appropriate formalities. Throughout the whole of the local press of this period, around 1860, there is not a single case of sickness or accident refused the appropriate medical or hospital service. But there were cases of vagrants dying in barns who were often nameless.

The hospitals were then, of course, all under the voluntary system, and were mainly financed by endowments and by the collections which took place. Annual hospital fêtes in every town and village became some of the sunniest features of the social calendar.

4   Roads and Bridges, 1800–35

FOR centuries the problem of how to maintain roads and bridges had baffled everybody, and as we have seen the 18th century governments had tried to solve it by creating turnpike roads where the traffic using the roads had to pay tolls which went mainly to the upkeep of the roads. Our most important step in this direction was probably the creation of the Hockliffe-Two-Mile Ash Turnpike by an Act of Parliament in 1706. It was the first local act of its kind, but by 1800, after nearly a century of effort, with tolls amounting to £1,000 a year at Two Mile Ash and about £600 a year at Hockliffe, the 14 mile stretch of road was still a problem. Indeed it could be said that the road was mostly an unmetalled right of way – often quite wide – and it was left to the coachman or horseman to find the easiest going between the ruts and the large puddles. Strenuous efforts were made to get the local parishes to play their statutory part, and again and again from 1800 on the inhabitants of Little Brickhill, Great Brickhill, Soulbury, Bletchley, Simpson, Loughton, Shenley, Bradwell and Calverton were indicted at the Quarter Sessions for not repairing the highway.

The Watling Street, one of the nation's busiest thoroughfares (though no one travelled unless they absolutely had to) was nearly always in a state of acute disrepair. From Shakespeare's grumbling ostlers to local MPs in the 1800s everybody was annoyed by the appalling state of the road between Little Brickhill and the bridge over the Ouse at Stony Stratford.

But neither the Turnpike Trust nor the parishes mentioned earlier had any business with the Watling Street as it passed through Stony Stratford; nor with the bridge and causeway over the river Ouse. The old High Street was in a mess. Tradesmen had built extensions into the street, impeding pedestrians, the road was unpaved, gutters spouted on to the cobbled pavements, and the local Bridge and Street Charity was quite unable to cope.

The powers that be decided that the only remedy was an Act of

Parliament. Nothing less would shake up the old town. In 1801 a comprehensive Act sequestered the town's road charities, ordered their properties to be sold, and laid down a series of regulations which upset not a few shopkeepers and others.[1] 'The Stony Stratford Local Act' of 1801 was, as its preamble says, for the purpose of:

'Paving, Cleansing, Watering, Lighting and otherwise Improving the Streets Lanes and other Public Passages and Places, within the Parishes of Saint Giles and Saint Mary Magdalen . . . and for removing and preventing Encroachments, Obstructions, Nuisances and Annoyances therein; and also for repairing the Rampart Road or Causeway from the said Town, to the Bridge over the River Ouse, and for repairing the said Bridge; and likewise for selling certain Charity Estates situate in the said Town, and in the Parishes of Calverton and Wolverton . . .'

The Act appointed commissioners, some of the most reputable citizens of the town, and invested them with:

'all present and future Carriage Ways and Footways, and the aforesaid Bridge, and also the Gravel within the several Streets and Lanes, and all Lamps, Lamp Irons and Posts.' They were given power 'to dig, get and carry away, any stone, gravel or sand' within the distance of two miles of St Giles' Church. They could compel anyone to take down any 'Sign or other Emblem used to denote Trade or Occupation, Posts, Penthouses, Porches, Show Glasses, and Show Boards projecting into the said streets or lanes.'

They could also compel all owners of property in the High Street to have spouts running down the walls and under the flag stones that were to be fixed as a pavement.

The commissioners or trustees were also vested with the extensive properties of the Bridge and Street Charity and the Handchurch Charity. They were to sell all of these and invest the proceeds as follows: two-fifths were to be expended on the prompt repair of the bridge, causeway and streets, and three-fifths to be put in government securities, and the interest yearly used to augment the principal until it reached the original amount. Then the commissioners might purchase real estate!

1 For a detailed description of the Hockliffe–Two Mile Ash turnpike 1790–1807 see the article by G. K. Tull in the *Milton Keynes Journal of Archaeology and History*, No 1, 1972.

The final sentences of the Act give the commissioners power to prosecute anybody who:

'put, drove or placed, on any pavement, any wheel, sledge, wheel-barrow, or horse beast or cattle, or shall kill, slaughter, singe, scale dress or cut up, any Cattle, Swine or other Beast in any of the said streets, Lanes, Public Passages or Places, or shall set, place, or expose to sale, and Goods Wares or Merchandises, whether upon the Footpaths or Carriage ways, or shall hang up or expose to sale any Matter or Thing upon any Flap, window or otherwise, so as to obstruct or incommode any passengers, or if any person shall make or assist in the making any Fires, commonly called Bonfires, or set fire to, or let off or throw, any Squib, Serpent, Cracker or Firework within the said Town, every Person offending in any of the said cases shall be fined ten shillings.'

The Act gave no power to the commissioners to levy a road rate or to raise any funds by means of a toll. It placed quite a burden on their shoulders.

The new commissioners themselves soon found that they had no light task. The sale of the properties of the old Bridge and Street Charity and the Handchurch Charity resulted in a gross sum of £6,510 (of which the sale of the *Cock Inn* produced £900), but of this £700 went in legal and other fees.

Their first order (1802) was 'That application be made to the Gentlemen and Farmers in the neighbourhood to employ their Roundsmen in picking up large Pebbles, and that the Treasurer be authorised to pay a reasonable price for such pebbles.' The High Street was then 'Pitched in the Middle with Pebbles', the pavements were flagged, and small cobble stones laid between the flags and the sides of the houses. 'Pitching' consisted of tipping a load of pebbles or gravel into the road, raking them over, and leaving the carriages and wagons to complete the work by rolling them in.

Nobody liked the Act, and as so often has happened in north Bucks in the past, a stolid unco-operative resistance began to be felt. It was the ship money attitude all over again. And where the King could not prevail in 1634–38 Parliament could not prevail in 1802. By the autumn of that year stubborn resistance had increased to such an extent that no fewer than twenty-two meetings of the commissioners were called, but the requisite quorum of five never appeared. In 1804 there were fourteen meetings adjourned, and so it went on for ten more years! Parliament, very vexed, appointed more commissioners, and regular meetings at last were held.

The new Bridge and Street Commissioners had no easy job to make ends meet. The spendable income was only about £100 a year, which barely sufficed to keep the thoroughfare in repair, in spite of low wages and costs generally.

By 1815 all the interest was spent and £620 was borrowed locally to enable 'pitching and paving' to continue. In this year iron railing over the bridge was painted with 'iron coloured paint consisting of white lead, and Linseed oil coloured with lamp black'. The old humpbacked bridge then consisted of three main arches and two little ones over the river (as is shown in our illustration in Volume I, p320), but there were a dozen smaller arches or culverts under the causeway. The six stone causeway arches nearest the bridge were now bricked up for added support, the road widened, and the other arches repaired, and a footpath made. A series of large stepping-stones was also fixed for use in time of flood, the last of which could be seen in the Memorial Garden on the Green until recently. All this cost £118, and created additional hazards from floods.

In 1818–19 the commissioners spent £114 for gravel, masonry and labour. According to the 'Paving Commissioners' a/cs' the average weekly wage of each of the four labourers employed was 9s, whilst 'Elmes boy' was paid 3s per week, but they had in addition to this an item recorded as 'beavers for the men at one Pint per day each man'.

The records relate many complaints that people were wheeling their barrows on the pavements, or permitting their swine, asses, and other beasts to wander about the streets. Shopkeepers were exposing their wares for sale on the pavement and so hindering pedestrians. John Wells was then appointed 'Informer' and told to bring evidence against those who thus violated the Act.

By 1823 the invested moneys of the trust had reached £6,510, and it was decided to buy an estate as the Act directed. They bought the Manor Farm at Loughton (144 acres) for £6,357, and let it for a rental of £245 to a Mr Gallard. It was a bad bargain, for the farm cost them £300 in repairs during the next few years and Gallard was a poor tenant in a poor agricultural period.

Floods at this period were very frequent: the meadows along the Ouse occasionally looked like a raging sea; cattle and horses were drowned and haystacks swept for miles. On 8 November 1823, one particular flood came well over the causeway and even over the bridge. The 'Crown Prince' coach on its way to Northampton met another coach on the unfenced causeway; each naturally gave way a few inches to the other, but those few inches tilted the 'Crown Prince', and the current was such that the coach overturned. The passengers were extricated, but one of the horses was drowned. It says much for the ingenuity of coachmen of those days when we recall that by the next morning the entire coach with its load of luggage, was extricated, another horse found, and all the passengers resumed their journey. No wonder the churches prayed for travellers with great sincerity: in fact they included them with prisoners and women in childbirth.

During the next ten years there are constant references to the purchase of gravel for pitching, but no matter how much gravel was pitched, the road never seemed to be in a good state, and matters were not helped by the floods. This, of course, was the heyday of the coaching era, and the Watling Street was one of the busiest roads in the country. From time to time the commissioners considered other methods of surfacing the road, including that of laying stone setts, but always they were limited by their income.

How bad our local roads were may be gathered from a quotation from the Rev St John Priest's work entitled *A General View of Agriculture in Buckinghamshire*, 1810:

'The bye roads of Bucks are extremely bad, some of them dangerous and cautiously to be used; they have ruts so deep, that when the wheels of the chaise fall into them, it is with the greatest danger an attempt can be made to draw them out, nay, instances may be produced where, if such an attempt be made, the horse and chaise must inevitably fall into bogs. The difficulty in finding the way from Fenny Stratford to Whaddon (through Water Eaton) was such that without a guide I could not have surmounted it. From Winslow to Wing there was no less danger, and had it not been now and then, for a colony of gypises, I might have been obliged in more than one instance to have taken refuge in a milking house for a night's lodging.'

Good roads or bad roads, the military had to cope, and whilst the officers could ride and the men march through our clayey adhesive mud, other steps had to be taken to get officers' baggage and regimental impedimenta (including wives and children) over the country roads. The regiments had little transport of their own, so wagons would have to be impressed en route. The farmers and millers did not like the job, it was poorly paid and very risky. On 10 October 1821 the Quarter Sessions at Aylesbury announced increased rates for such carriage 'due to the present price of Hay and Oats'. Their advertisements show clearly what types of haulage vehicles were then in use, for the new rates were:

'the sum of Four Pence, in addition to the sum of one Shilling for every Mile any Waggon with five horses, or any Wain with six Oxen or with four Horses and two Oxen shall travel.

The sum of three Pence, in addition to the sum of nine Pence for every Mile any Cart with four Horses shall travel. And the sum of two Pence in addition to the sum of six Pence for every Mile any Cart or Carriage of less than four Horses shall travel.'[2]

It can well be seen that a wain with six oxen, laden with a ton or two of goods, did not help to settle the gravel or pebbles on the road.

In summer the dust was astonishing, and it was to master this that in 1826 the Stony Stratford Road Commissioners bought their first water cart, at a cost of £26. To get the cart from London to Stony Stratford cost nearly 30s in tolls.

By now the bridge was 'in a very imperfect state of repair', not to say unsafe, but the trust was again in financial difficulties; consequently they sought parliamentary powers to erect a toll. Meanwhile, Parliament had created a Parliamentary Commission to improve the Holyhead Road, and its chairman, Sir Henry Parnell, MP, ordered the clerk to the Stony Stratford Commissioners to appear in London and to give an account of their stewardship. It appears that the Holyhead Road Commissioners proposed to take action to compel the two Stony Stratford parishes, and the Street and Bridge Charity, to make an immediate and effectual repair of the thoroughfare. Sir Henry Parnell met the townsmen at a joint parish meeting on 19 February 1828, the

2 Advertisement in the *Northampton Mercury*, 10 November 1821.

results of which were so unsatisfactory that Sir Henry ordered legal proceedings to be instituted against the parishes to compel them to put their streets in repair – and he estimated that £3,000 would be required for the purpose. Local alarm can be imagined, and the parishes and the charity sent their solicitor, Mr J. F. Congreve, to London in May to see both Sir Henry Parnell and the celebrated road engineer, Mr Thomas Telford.[3]

Apparently Sir Henry Parnell spoke with some heat of the state of the road at Stratford. Congreve presented the local case, which was that the income of the charity was not sufficient for the magnitude of the repairs and again asked for parliamentary power to set up a toll bar and for the trust to borrow money. In June Congreve went up to London again, but, as he records, 'nothing was done'. But his bill for the two journeys came to £18 11s 2d, of which 'Coach hire to and from London' came to £2 8s 6d, and his expenses in London £4 5s 6d.[4]

In 1831 the Postmaster-General was still complaining that the bad state of the road at Stony Stratford was hindering his posts. The farm at Loughton was now mortgaged, and the commissioners were feeling pretty glum.

THE NEW BRIDGE

In 1833 there came an unexpected accession of help: the clerk of the peace for Bucks, Mr Acton Tindal, summoned the commissioners and trustees to meet the local magistrates at the *Cock Inn* on 4 November 'to consider proposals for relieving them of all future liability to repair the Bridge'. Tindal's proposals were that in return for £900 from the trustees, Parliament should be asked to take down and rebuild the bridge and erect a toll, and then relieve the trustees from all liability for the bridge in future. The trustees' reply was that since all the funds were for the use of the town, and not for the Northamptonshire half of the bridge, they declined to comply with the proposals! Parnell was now really angry, but the town was saved from his wrath by the action of Charles Markham, the clerk of the peace of Northamptonshire, and his colleague for Bucks, Mr Tindal, who now called another meeting (1834) with the magistrates at the *Cock Inn,* and announced that the two counties had decided to rebuild the 'narrow,

---

3 See *History of Stony Stratford* pp158–59.
4 Details from papers in the church chest at St Giles' Church.

incommodious, and decaying bridge' and that they would promote a Bill for this purpose in Parliament.

Stratford welcomed the idea of a new bridge – at someone
else's expense – but was shocked at the idea of a toll being placed
upon it, and within a few weeks both Stratford parishes had
created a petition to Parliament against the toll.

The last straw to the burden of the old bridge was the passing
over it of a heavy train of wagons from London to Birmingham,
which were carrying machinery for making plate glass. The bridge
broke under the last wagon, which fell down between the arches
of the bridge. It was not extricated until forty horses had been
gathered together, which, with an amazing system of harness and
ropes, succeeded in dragging the wagon up the hill to Old
Stratford. Something had to be done quickly now; an Act of
Parliament was rushed through (1834), authorising a new bridge,
towards which the town had to pay £735. Work on the new
bridge and causeway was commenced almost at once. It is
interesting that the Act described the bridge as being in the
parishes of Calverton, Wolverton, Passenham, Cosgrove, and
Furtho, which is surely a record. It was decided to raise the level
of both bridge and causeway by several feet.

The work took a year, and on 25 July 1835, the present bridge
was opened to traffic with a pleasant little ceremony – but local
rejoicing soon changed to grumbles when it was found that a toll
gate and toll house were also erected, which remained *in situ* for
twenty years. The local tolls were put up to auction every now
and then, and in 1852 they were let to a Mr Cockerill for £584.
There were great rejoicings when, in 1857, the bridge toll gate
was abolished, and an ox was roasted in the Barley Mow field.

Meanwhile a meadow on the opposite side of the High Street,
known as Bridge Foot Close was acquired in 1838 by a brand new
company called 'The Stony Stratford Gas, Light and Coke
Company', which also took over the stone-mason's yard where
much of the work on the new bridge had been carried out, and
proceeded to erect the first gas works in the locality. Up to this
time the only illumination in the town was by means of candles or
oil lamps. There were no street lamps. Within a few months the
older part of the town was lighted by gas, but gas fires or stoves
were, of course, quite unknown in the town until half a century
later.

Stony Stratford had got a new bridge, a fine road and town illumination. It faced the future lightheartedly. Parnell after his frustrating time with the town became a cabinet minister and was created Baron Congleton in 1841. As he had Irish connections it is probable that he often travelled through the old town, but there is no record that he ever stopped at the *Cock Inn* again.

Meanwhile other parts of the Watling Street were having detailed attention, and once again our local parishes adjoining it were strongly of the opinion that as this was a great national road the burden of its upkeep should not depend on small villages like Shenley or Loughton or Little Brickhill.

And now came Telford and Macadam and the other great road-builders who had learnt how to prepare and surface a road so that it would stand up to quite formidable traffic. In 1828 the trustees of the Hockliffe tolls followed Thomas Telford's advice to widen and level the road at Fenny Stratford, to reduce the rise at Rickley Hill, and to re-align the Little Brickhill – Fenny Stratford part of the Watling Street.

As for the other roads, mud, and clayey mud at that, was their foundation and often their surface. Floods made many of our local roads quite impassable at certain times.

Sometimes a little progress was made by private endeavour, for as Sheahan wrote about Simpson:

'Thirty years ago [ie, around 1830] it was, in appearance, one of the most wretched and miserable villages in the county. During a great portion of the winter time the main road was generally impassable without wading through water three feet deep for a distance of about 200 yards. But chiefly through the exertions of Mr. Charles Warren the road has been raised 3½ feet; and the handsome villa residence of this gentleman with its tastefully laid out pleasure grounds, summer houses, grottoes, rock work, fountain, fish pond, etc., sets the place off to great advantage. There are also several other genteel houses here.'

Every house, not only in Simpson, even the humblest cottage, had a stout boot scraper just outside the front door. Many still have.

About this time a turnpike was erected near Debb's Barn, along the Stony Stratford–Wolverton road, and the turnpike house was also a little sweet-shop kept by two old women.

Persons living at Cosgrove now found that in order to drive a horse and trap to Wolverton station – one mile distant as the crow flies but three by road – three tolls had to be paid at 6d each – one at *The Dog's Mouth* along the Northampton road, one on the Stony Stratford bridge, and now the third along the Wolverton road.

Telford and others did a great job in improving our roads, which from about 1820 were fit to carry all but the most awkward traffic. This, coupled with improved springing of vehicles, gave rise to the finest period of the stage-coach era, which has been so romanticised, and deserved to be.

The two great local roads were the Watling Street, and, branching off from the Watling Street at Hockliffe, was the Newport, Northampton, Leicester and Nottingham Road, which was quite important. In 1824 Hockliffe welcomed about 200 commercial stage-coaches a week, of which 112 came on to Stony Stratford and 92 went on to Newport. By 1830 these figures had increased to 468 a week at Hockliffe, of which 280 came on to Stony Stratford and 188 to Newport.[5]

In addition to these there were a dozen coaches weekly from Buckingham to Bedford, and hundreds of private coaches and lighter vehicles. There were also the great lumbering wagons and strings of pack horses, which were still used for distribution from canal wharfs. To cater for this growing traffic there were inns, taverns and ale houses. Fenny Stratford was seldom a recognised stop for stage-coaches and only had a dozen licensed houses, but Stony Stratford, a very popular stop, had a score, and Newport Pagnell still more.

The Royal Mail and the stage-coaches generally were the swiftest means of disseminating news, whether by distributing the few newspapers like the *Northampton Mercury* (from 1720) or *The Times* (from 1788), or by word of mouth. Often word of mouth would precede the journals, for when the news of the battle of Trafalgar reached London in October 1805, many stage-coaches started off with it before the printers had time to set up the type. The coaches proclaimed good news by a jolly display of flags and bunting; bad news was symbolised by black streamers or funeral plumes.

5 *Pigot's Directories*, 1824 and 1830.

Interest was intense therefore when on 23 October the coaches arrived at Hockliffe, Fenny Stratford, Stony Stratford and Newport Pagnell not only bedecked with the gayest colours to celebrate the great victory by the British navy over the combined French and Spanish fleets, but with the funeral plumes signifying the death of the nation's great hero, Lord Nelson, at the very moment of victory. Such happiness and such sorrow were hard to combine.

The church bells as usual relayed the news, and the peals for the victory were interspersed by the mournful tolling of the funeral bell. England hardly knew whether to rejoice or weep. For the moment gladness supervened.

'GREAT PAUL'

Telford had succeeded in making the Watling Street a passable route, but lack of upkeep over the next decades resulted in serious mishaps. In 1882 a firm at Loughborough had completed the splendid bell 'Great Paul' for St Paul's Cathedral. Neither railway nor canal could manage such an awkward package. It was 9ft high, 10ft in diameter at its base, and weighed 17 tons. It was decided to send it by road, and it was estimated the journey could be done in a week. But half way between Fenny Stratford and Little Brickhill it got 'mired up'. It took three days before enough horses, traction engines and great cables could be organised to get it up Little Brickhill hill. The youth of Fenny and all around enjoyed the spectacle.

Another problem remained for years, the problem of swirling dust in dry weather. Tar spraying was tried and found good, but the local gas works did not produce enough tar to meet anything like the demand.

Meanwhile the turnpikes on the Watling Street were abolished in 1868 and others a few years later, the responsibility for the upkeep of the roads being thrust back on the parishes. But remedial legislation was under way and by 1888 with the setting up of the County Councils the responsibility was firmly undertaken by the Government.

A few years later tar became available in quantity due to the setting up of petroleum refineries. The coming of the motor car helped the highway engineer, and bitumen (mineral pitch or asphalt) was much better than wood or coal tar for the purpose.

We have gone too far ahead with our story, and now we go back half a century to consider the origins of a development that completely altered the whole transport pattern of the area. Barely had Telford finished the re-aligning and re-settling of the Watling Street than rumours began to spread that a great railway was to be built from London to Birmingham. Everybody knew that the shortest way from London to Birmingham was along the Watling Street as far as Weedon, so it was expected that the new railway would come through Fenny Stratford and Stony Stratford.

Others with better maps were certain that the best way was from Tring and then through Buckingham, and the great George Stephenson, now in his formidable 50s, agreed with them.

5 The Coming of the Railways, 1831–60

THE Grand Junction Canal had been in existence for barely thirty years when it became obvious that it might be challenged by a railway running along practically the same route. The success of the Stockton and Darlington Railway, opened in 1825, and the Liverpool and Manchester Railway, opened in 1830, set afoot innumerable schemes for other railways, one of which was the London and Birmingham Railway. The route of this railway might have paralleled the line of the Watling Street or might have taken approximately the line of the Grand Junction Canal, or an even more direct route through Buckingham, but whereas the great landowners had welcomed a canal, there was much opposition to a railway, both on the grounds of noise and of smoke.

The newly formed London and Birmingham Railway company had as its engineer-in-chief Robert Stephenson, and the powerful secretaries were Richard Creed and C. R. Moorsom. The board of directors had few difficulties in deciding that the line should run from Camden Town through the Tring gap in the Chilterns. It was more difficult to decide the route from there north-west not only because the Ouse had to be crossed, but also because the Northamptonshire uplands created certain tunnelling and other problems. They first entrusted the task of selecting the route to Richard Creed, the company's secretary. On 4 July 1831 he reported:

'Looking towards Birmingham from Ivinghoe there is a breadth of high land lying between Leighton Buzzard on the East, and Aylesbury on the West, which extends north-westerly to the Ouse and presents formidable obstacles to a Railway. In the direction, therefore, of one or other of those towns it should be carried, and certainly the fertile vale of Aylesbury with its wide spread expanse of level ground, affords great inducement to look at it – Mr. R. Stephenson having besides called my attention to this point. I proceeded thence on the road to Buckingham, by the high grounds of

Whitchurch, Wing and Winslow, I extended my observations sufficiently to the westward to ascertain where the levels most favourable for our purposes were to be found.

'Having examined the ground thoroughly on both banks of the Ouse west of Buckingham, and satisfied myself as to the direction the Line should take, I followed it to the town of Brackley . . .'

So Creed's report was broadly in favour of a line from Tring to just north of Aylesbury, then to Whitchurch, Winslow, Buckingham and Brackley – the most direct line to Birmingham. But the board were now much influenced by outside pressures, including that of the powerful Duke of Buckingham, who would not have the line anywhere near Buckingham or through any of his properties.[1] It will be remembered that the Duke of Buckingham not only owned Stowe but most of the land running south from there to Wotton, and he had enough influence in Parliament to hamstring any scheme of which he did not approve.

The board of directors sought other advice, and although George Stephenson had himself favoured the Buckingham route, his son Robert, who was commissioned to do the second report, came out with other ideas. His long report from Leighton Buzzard dated 21 September 1831, included the following points:

'The Surface of the Country from London to Birmingham may be regarded as consisting of a series of basins or low districts, separated from each other by considerable ridges of Hills.

'Our object was to cross the low districts at as high a level and the Ridges of Hills at as low a level as was consistent with the other considerations that governed us *viz* – Directness and cheapness.

'The low districts or basins that we have just alluded to include the low Land in the neighbourhood of Leighton Buzzard which is connected with districts of a similar level in the direction of Fenny Stratford, to Stony Stratford thence to Stoke Bruerne where it terminates, and is succeeded by the valley of the Nene in which Northampton is situated . . .

'. . . The only situation however where Tunnelling will be required to any extent is near Cashiobury and through the

---

1 Vernon and Bonner, *Buckingham* p109.

high ground between Kilsby and Crick – In other situations when Tunnelling is likely to be adopted, they will scarcely exceed 300 yards in length when the Character of a Tunnel almost vanishes.'[2]

So it was decided that the line should be through Leighton Buzzard, Fenny Stratford, Stony Stratford and Castlethorpe. Later on an adjustment was made taking the line two miles east of Stony Stratford through Wolverton, which may well have been the best point for the Ouse viaduct.

The railway did not arrive without more difficulties and struggles. The Bill authorising the construction of the line passed the House of Commons in June 1832, but was then rejected by the House of Lords. The amended Bill was re-introduced in the Commons in October, and after months of negotiation and debate received the Royal Assent on 6 May 1833. By 1835 the plans were complete and were included in another series of Acts of Parliament. These confirmed powers to build a great viaduct over the Ouse at Old Wolverton, a tunnel at Blisworth, and branch lines from Bletchley to Oxford and to Bedford and to make a great central station at Wolverton.[3]

The company now bought just over 8 acres of land from the Radcliffe trustees at Wolverton. It was tucked in the bend of the Grand Junction Canal which naturally produced wharfing facilities of great value, but the only road access was the twisting and narrow Stony Stratford to Newport road. Other landowners along the route had to be dealt with, and there were scores of these, from the great nobles to the little Simpson Charity Trust, but by October 1836 even the latter was satisfied.

As with the canal, the crossing of the Ouse created real engineering problems. It was only accomplished by building an embankment nearly $1\frac{1}{2}$ miles long and 48ft high in the midst of which was a viaduct 660ft long of six principal arches, and 57ft above the river. Hard by this embankment to the west was to be the new Wolverton Station.

Meanwhile hordes of navvies, who were paid about £1 a week,

2 I am grateful to Mr R. Ayres for drawing my attention to these reports, and for much else in this chapter.
3 Both Roade and Northampton had been considered in this connection. For a more detailed account see Miss Moira Courtmans' excellent thesis on 'Wolverton: A Study in Urban Geography', which she prepared for her MPhil degree at London University in 1960.

descended on the neighbourhood, and the villages of Bletchley, Loughton and Wolverton learnt new swear words, while the local publicans were delighted. The biggest labour camp was at Denbigh Hall, a notorious spot where the new railway was to cross the Watling Street, and which was to be the terminus whilst the viaduct over the Ouse was completed and the Kilsby tunnel to the north finished.

There was a touch of the bizarre in the setbacks in building the Wolverton embankment. The highest portion slid sideways when it was almost ready for ballasting. It was laboriously rebuilt, and then proceeded to catch fire. The spontaneous combustion of alum shale containing sulphurate of iron was the cause. Half a mile to the south-east the line had to cross the Grand Junction Canal. The canal company had fought the Bill tooth and nail in Parliament, and had protected itself by insisting that the waterway should not be obstructed, even for an hour. In order to complete the embankment for the main railway-crossing Stephenson and the contractors had to transport half a million cubic yards of earth from cuttings to the south, across the canal over a temporary bridge that was ready by Christmas 1834, to the embankment on the far side. He managed it in spite of a great row with the canal company.

VERNEY AND STEPHENSON

It was around this time that Sir Harry Verney, the second baronet (1801–94), who had represented Buckingham in Parliament since 1832, formed a lasting friendship with both George and Robert Stephenson.[4] The Stephensons were of course anxious that the railway Bills should get through Parliament with the minimum of opposition or even of amendment, and young Verney became a parliamentary railway apprentice. Whilst others were learning to build railways or to design locomotives, he was learning the more subtle science of achieving the possible in terms of railway legislation: whilst the Stephensons could cope splendidly with the newest of technical problems Sir Harry Verney could help with the problems of land acquisition, rights of way, personnel problems in their widest sense, and, negotiations with other companies.

4 *The Verneys of Claydon* edited by Sir Harry Verney, 1968, p253.

Far more surprising was the fact that the second Duke of Buckingham and Chandos now became keenly interested in railways, and invested quite a lot of money in them, whilst his son, the Marquess of Chandos, as he was known from 1839 to 1861, was a railway enthusiast. Soon these two and Sir Harry Verney were thinking up a railway of their own, 'The Buckinghamshire Railway', which would add a spider's web of lines in our vicinity. But this we must leave to our next chapter.

DENBIGH HALL

The line from Euston to Denbigh Hall, near Fenny Stratford, was officially opened on 9 April 1838, and that from Birmingham to Rugby the same day. The railways board had foreseen the need for a road link between Bletchley and Rugby and so the temporary terminal was at Denbigh Hall, where the old Watling Street (A5) stretched its muddy and potholed way, instead of being at Wolverton. Bletchley was then described by a contemporary as 'a small miserable village where those disappointed at getting on from Denbigh Hall must not expect to find accommodation, even for their dog'.

Indeed the area around Denbigh Hall resembled a race course or a fair, where booths took the place of shops and crude timber structures or tents took the place of houses. There were coaches, horses, post boys and mud everywhere. Since the railway planners expected the line between Bletchley and Rugby to be completed in six months nobody put in adequate sanitation, laid good streets or erected anything but the flimsiest stables. The appalling centre of all this was *Denbigh Hall Inn*, which, as we have seen in a previous volume, had a dreadful reputation for murders, robbery and bawdiness. The landlord, Thomas Holdom, now converted the parlour into a coffee room, the bar into a parlour, the kitchen into a bar, and the stable into a kitchen. Tents provided bedrooms by night and dining-rooms by day.

In the London Midland & Scottish railway publications *A Century of Progress*, issued in 1938, and *The Track of the Royal Scot* there are these references to Denbigh Hall:

> 'Denbigh Hall Inn witnessed the closing scenes of the glorious cut-throat epoch of the stage-coach. Denbigh Hall Station was for the time being very important and the station hotel very inadequate. Hence booths, tents, hutments, were run up

and the newspapers were filled with gibes at the pretentious name of the hospice . . .

'Irishmen who worked on the construction of the railway were billetted in the camp, and drunken brawls were common; the gypsies also made a sort of Hampstead Heath of the place and made money out of the railway traveller who of necessity had to break his journey there owing to it being the first terminus of the railway.'

To escape from these surroundings one had to have a seat in a coach or omnibus. Regular stage-coach services organised by the railway met most trains, and took four and a half hours to get to Rugby (34 miles) via Stony Stratford and Towcester. They had the character and reliability of years of organisation and service. But since nobody knew how many passengers would be arriving by any given train, or whether they wanted to go on to Rugby, Northampton, Newport Pagnell or even to stay the night in Fenny Stratford, the occasional clamour and chaos can be imagined.[5]

Other coach companies catered for those who wanted to go anywhere but to Rugby. Some of these were:

'The Commercial'	for Nottingham through Stony Stratford and Northampton
'The Railway'	for Newport Pagnell via Fenny Stratford
'The Banbury & Buckingham'	to both towns
'The Rocket'	for Lichfield and Tamworth via Newport Pagnell
'The Lincoln'	to Lincoln through Stony Stratford and Northampton
'The Boston'	through Newport Pagnell and Spalding
'The Times'	for Derby and Nottingham via Stony Stratford
'The Brilliant'	for Sheffield via Stony Stratford

Places in these were limited, and often seats went to the highest bidder.

It will be seen that most of the coaches went through Stony Stratford or Newport Pagnell. For these two market towns and for Fenny Stratford too it was the last six months of the great

---

5 For more information see A. E. Griggs' *In Railway Service*, 1972.

stage-coach era. In Stony Stratford the number of stage coaches per week dropped from 280 in 1835 to 12 a week in 1844, and even in Newport which had no railway as yet, the numbers dropped from 188 a week to 30 in the same period. It was not only inns which suffered, but also farriers, wheelwrights and blacksmiths. But there were slight compensations, for the old posting houses or inns now bought light one-horse carriages known as flys and proudly advertised that their 'Flys meet every train'. Some of the better ones provided horse omnibuses to meet the more popular trains, and for sixty years or more they still needed a few ostlers and coachmen, but the hotel rooms no longer had stage-coach passengers staying overnight.

In August 1838 at the half-yearly general meeting the railway directors reported that:

'A large and immediate outlay is needed in the goods department, but also for some additional accommodation in the passenger department. The central station for engines and goods at Wolverton, the goods stations at Birmingham and London and on the line, ought not to be delayed . . . The difficulties of Wolverton, Blisworth and Kilsby have been successfully overcome. A single line of rails is laid from end to end of the line, and the engineer-in-chief has reported that the opening of the whole line may be expected in September.'

By September 1838 the double track of cast-iron rails was laid along the full 112 miles, and the L. & B. Railway was complete. The opening celebrations for the first through-train were gay and elaborate. Robert Stephenson, George Carr Glyn, the L. & B. chairman since 1837, Captain Moorson, the company secretary, and all the directors, rode to Birmingham in grand style. Processions, parades, speeches, bands, flags and bunting, fairs and the firing of cannons and all the paraphernalia of noisy celebration which was the English way of rejoicing, were met or seen at every station. The local inhabitants and passengers had a great day. The navvies and labourers might have had greater cause for celebration had not Robert Stephenson sternly discouraged the directors from paying any kind of cash bonus to them. 'If I may express an opinion on the matter, I think it unnecessary,' he wrote to the secretary. 'A few barrels of beer and something to eat – say 50 rounds of beef – placed at different points where men are employed (and under the control of the police) would be more congenial with the idea of a treat to the men.' 'It would also,' he emphasised, 'be the least expensive.'[6]

The success of the London and Birmingham Railway was almost instantaneous. It provided travel twice or three times as fast as the best stage-coaches, and at two-thirds the price. It was possibly as comfortable. Even some of the sounds were agreeable. for instead of the clip-clopping of horses there was the accelerating chuff-chuff that settled into a rhythmic d-d-d-der or d-d, d-d, according to which line one was on. And the trial of sleepless nights was almost eliminated. Another development was the daily milk train, which took the milk and butter to Watford and London, and was one of the factors which led to the change from sheep farming to dairy farming in the neighbourhood.

Railways dominated the industrial layout of England. Every company soon had its distinctive coat of arms and company colours, and in so far as elongated boxes can be beautiful, railway carriages became resplendent in their superb livery created by the finest craftsmen in the world.

Meanwhile on 10 November 1835 Sir Harry Verney, then in his early thirties, called a meeting at the *White Hart Inn*, Aylesbury, for the purpose of promoting a railway to join the county town with the London and Birmingham Railway at Cheddington. Somehow he managed to raise enough money, and to get parliamentary sanction to start the job in April 1838, and on 15 June 1839 the line was opened and leased to the L. & B. Railway at a rent of £2,500 a year. This short branch, only 7 miles in length, was a great success, the passenger receipts for the first half year totalling over £5,700. Sir Harry was greatly encouraged.

WOLVERTON WORKS

We have seen that in 1836 the L. & B. Railway decided that since Wolverton was about half way between London and Birmingham it would be the best place for a central engine works where locomotives could be serviced and repaired in the most modern shops equipped with the most modern machinery. In August 1838 the report of the directors of the L. & B. Railway stated that the central station at Wolverton ought not to be delayed. Work was already in hand to a plan of crude simplicity. Broadly there was to

6 *Great Railwaymen* pp27-28.

be a great engine shed, almost as large as a cathedral, where reserve engines could be kept in steam and those which were giving trouble (and there were many) could be serviced.

In the great shed itself in addition to room for thirty-six engines were to be an iron foundry, smithy, boiler yard, hooping furnaces, iron warehouse and various machines worked by a steam engine. From this, across the main line, was to be access to the wharf on the canal, which was also a goods warehouse. Around it on three sides were to be scores of tightly packed terrace houses, and north of the canal was the actual passenger station with lavatories and a confectionery stall. Access to the station was from the Old Wolverton road near the present Park entrance. Schools were to be built near the great engine shed and a new access was to be made from the east to terminate in a barred gate near the schools. (This later became the Stratford Road.) A little later Whishaw reported in his monumental *Railways of Great Britain*, 1842: 'Every engine with a train from London to Birmingham is changed at Wolverton Station, which answers the double purpose of having it examined and of easing the driver and stoker. We consider even every fifty miles too great a distance for an engine to run without examination'.[7]

But as the first trains stopped at Wolverton to change engines and comfort the passengers it was realised that whilst the great engine shed and its workers could cope with their side of affairs the little passenger station had neither enough lavatories nor cups of tea to satisfy the throngs that wanted all comforts within ten minutes. The decision was rapidly taken to build a bigger and better passenger station just south of Stratford Road, and this became a national pride and joy. These new refreshment rooms and kitchens, opened in November 1840, had a sunken ice house where ice could be made available throughout the year. There was only one other such ice house for miles and miles around, just off the Jaywick at Cosgrove, which can still be seen.

Owing to the kindness of Mr G. W. C. Tew, MA, CEng, Works Manager of British Rail Engineering Works at Wolverton, we are fortunate in being able to reproduce, in simplified form a plan of 'Wolverton Station', drawn up in 1840 by Binns and Clifford with proposed additions. It will be seen that the great engine

---

7 He also gives a detailed engineering account of the Works.

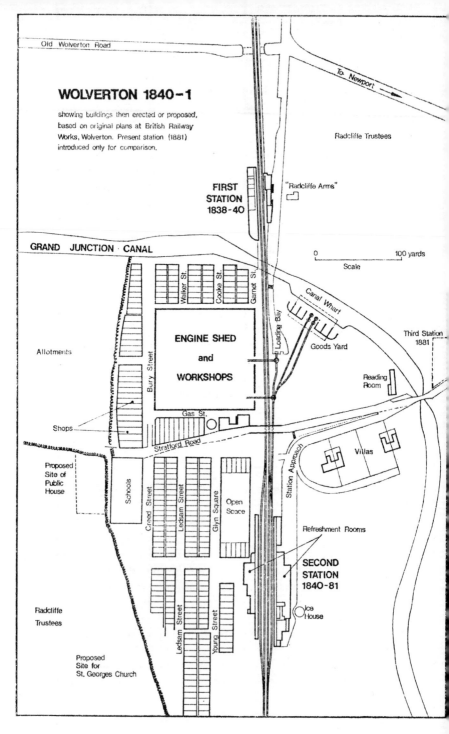

WOLVERTON 1840-1

showing buildings then erected or proposed, based on original plans at British Railway Works, Wolverton. Present station (1881) introduced only for comparison.

Old Wolverton Road

To Newport

Radcliffe Trustees

FIRST STATION 1838-40

"Radcliffe Arms"

GRAND JUNCTION CANAL

0   100 yards

Scale

Walker St.

Cooke St.

Garnet St.

Canal Wharf

Loading Bay

Goods Yard

Third Station 1881

ENGINE SHED and WORKSHOPS

Allotments

Bury Street

Reading Room

Gas St.

Shops

Stratford Road

Station Approach

Villas

Proposed Site of Public House

Schools

Creed Street

Ledsam Street

Glyn Street

Open Space

Refreshment Rooms

SECOND STATION 1840-81

Radcliffe Trustees

Ledsam Street

Young Street

Ice House

Proposed Site for St. Georges Church

Shed (now the Brake Shop) was the dominant feature of the station, and that it was surrounded on three sides by the workmen's houses. On the fourth (east) side, running almost due north and south, was the double railway track, which widened to four tracks at the new refreshment rooms. On the other side of the tracks were four superior type houses for 'Clerks'.

Also on the east side of the line can be seen a strange structure between the canal wharf and the main line. This was the shed where the wealthy could have their personal carriages loaded on to a wagon as we see in the Osborne illustration, but there were very few who wanted to use this facility.

As yet there was neither church nor chapel, but both were being thought about. There was however a reading room which could be used for services as well as for dancing or for whist drives. Old Wolverton Church was only half a mile away, but the local vicar had little sympathy for railwaymen.

There was no shopping centre, but in Bury Street there sprang up a dozen shops including the post office. As for public houses, in addition to the *Locomotive* at Old Wolverton (now the *Galleon*), which was later owned by the canal company, there were soon the *Radcliffe Arms* (1839) and the *Royal Engineer* (1841). This set-up lasted several years with the addition of St George's Church (1846), the vicarage, a Wesleyan chapel, and another hundred houses.

EARLY RAILWAY TRAVELLING

Among the best commentaries of the period is Osbornes' *London & Birmingham Railway Guide* published in 1840. We have seen how in 1812 the Grand Junction Canal was written up by John Hassell and we quoted freely from this entertaining work. Comparably, in 1840, E. C. and W. Osborne of Birmingham published their guide, with illustrations by Samuel Williams, from which we now take a few extracts. Among the regulations were:

Passengers are allowed 100 lb in luggage, each extra pound one penny.

Carpet bags and small luggage to be placed under the seat opposite that which the owner occupies.

Smoking is strictly prohibited both in carriages and on stations. If a passenger persists after a second warning he will be immediately removed from the Company's premises and forfeit his fare.

No gratuity under any circumstances is allowed to be taken by any servant of the Company, including Porters.

Ten minutes are allowed at Wolverton Station where a female attendant is appointed.

Any passenger wilfully cutting the Lining, removing or defacing the number Plates, breaking the Windows, or otherwise damaging a Carriage shall be fined Five Pounds.

As we can see in our illustration, gentlemen were allowed to take their own carriages and horses with them. The charges were:

Carriage from London to Wolverton: 35s Horse 30s
Carriage from Wolverton to Birmingham: 25s Horse 30s

Trucks were kept at Wolverton and other main stations on which the carriage could be loaded. Persons travelling in their own carriage were charged second class fares.

These early trains were uncomfortable. Everybody complained of the cold and of draughts. There was neither heating nor lighting. Wealthier travellers carried rugs and replaced their toppers with caps. Second class coaches were open at the sides, and had holes in the floor to let out rain water. The seats were just narrow bare boards. Third class passengers were in roofless, seatless trucks (sixty to a truck maximum) until 1844 when Parliament ordered that they should at least have a roof.

In March 1839 the London & Birmingham Railway produced a poster time-table for 'Wolverton Central Station, Newport Pagnell' which had an office at the Swan Hotel, Newport Pagnell.[8] There were seven 'Up' and seven 'Down' trains each weekday, and fewer on Sundays.

8 See *Records of Bucks*, 1972, p158 for a facsimile of the poster. *Bradshaw* for October 1839 records that 'mixed trains' stopped at Bletchley.

An early mail train as depicted in Osbornes' 'London and Birmingham Railway Guide' 1840. The Bury four-wheeled engine was typical of those serviced at Wolverton for many years.

Trains	Leave Wolverton for London	Arrive in London
Mixed	6.45 am	9.45 am
Mixed	10.10 am	1.30 pm
Mail	11.30 am	2.30 pm
Mixed	4.15 pm	7.30 pm
First Class	6.00 pm	9.00 pm
First Class	7.00 pm	10.00 pm
Night Mail	2.40 am	5.45 am

It will be seen that it took three hours by the fastest trains to get to London. The first stop for several trains was Leighton Buzzard, for there was no proper Bletchley Station for years. As time went on the daily number of trains increased, as did the speeds, so that successive time-tables showed more and more improvements. All tables made allowance for the difference in time, there being no Greenwich time – thus 12 noon at Euston was 12.03 at Wolverton and 12.07 at Birmingham, and each station went by its own legal local time.

There was another development at Wolverton in 1838 in which the Marquess of Chandos played a part and probably benefited. There was a need for Buckingham (and of course Stowe) to get the mail as quickly as possible. The first Mail arrived at Wolverton at 12.10 pm and there was now a Royal Mail stage-coach from Buckingham to meet it. The Mail Coach (horsed) actually left Banbury at 7 am, reached Buckingham soon after 9 am, and Wolverton Station about 10.30 am, well in time to catch the 'First Up mail' to London at 11.30 am.

After picking up the London mail it returned through Stony Stratford to Buckingham and on to Banbury (29 miles). This service continued until 1850 when the Buckinghamshire Railway was built, as we shall see in our next chapter. This particular Royal Mail was possibly the last stage-coach seen in Stony Stratford.

We must now return to Osbornes' *London & Birmingham Railway Guide* in which the authors describe (page 138 on) the thrilling journey from Euston Grove, to Birmingham. We pick up the narrative at Fenny Stratford.

'Fenny Stratford is a village situated on a slight ascent. The canal runs at the lower side of it; and at the bottom of the valley is a brook called the Old River. The valley of Fenny Stratford is exceedingly fertile, and the neighbourhood delightfully picturesque.

'The high road from London passes from Fenny Stratford towards Stony Stratford, at a place called Denbigh Hall, which name leads most people to expect an elegant mansion, park, etc: this expectation ends in disappointment; for the traveller, on enquiring where is Denbigh Hall, has pointed out to him a mean looking beer shop, situated by the side of the bridge by which the line crosses the road. This beer shop had its custom so much increased during the progress of the works, from the number of ever thirsty men that were working in the neighbourhood, that the owner found it to his advantge to open nearly all the rooms in his house for the use of his customers, who consisted principally of that class of men called navvies. These constitute a race of Englishmen almost as distinct from the rest of their countrymen as the gypsies; they are men of perhaps, the finest physical structure, and most daring courage to be found in any part of the globe; and to this is superadded cunning.

'Prior to the completion of the middle portion of the railway, there was a temporary station erected at Denbigh Hall, and the passengers were forwarded from thence on coaches and omnibuses to the Rugby Station; the temporary wooden erection is now entirely removed, and the train dashes by its site. To the right, Brickhill with its church is conspicuous on the hill top, and to the left a long view of the road up towards Stony Stratford may be taken . . .

'On the right is the village and church of Bradwell, and close to the line is a quarry, from which materials have been taken to construct the neighbouring embankments: Just after this, the train stops at the grand central depot of the company at Wolverton. This Station is an extensive establishment, and will probably give rise to the formation of a new town; the engine house, which is 112 yards square, is on the left, and the booking offices on the right side; upwards of fifty cottages belonging to the servants of the company have already sprung into existence. A stall at which confectionary is sold, is permitted at this station. Just beyond the station, the road from Newport Pagnell to Stony Stratford is crossed by a bridge, from which (Old) Wolverton Church is observable amidst the trees, about half a mile off. Stony Stratford is a market town, two miles on the left of the station; it consists principally of one street, situated on the parliamentary road from London to Holyhead, and contains about 1700 inhabitants. Owing to the great thoroughfare, there is considerable traffic carried on; but the only manufacture is that of bone lace; the market is held on Friday, and there are several fairs in the year.

'Four and a half miles to the right is the town of Newport Pagnell, one of the largest in Buckinghamshire. The main street is well built, but deficient with respect to a good pavement and lighting. The manufacture of bone lace used to give considerable occupation to the inhabitants of this town; but the competition of Nottingham machinery has caused the trade to decline: the manufacture of paper gives a good deal of employment. Annual races were re-established here, after an intermission of forty years, in 1827, and are now regularly held every August.

'Just after the train has crossed the bridge over the road, we arrive upon the great viaduct over the Ouse, which consists of six large central arches, and three small terminal ones at each side, making in all twelve arches. To the left, the canal is carried over the Ouse on a viaduct. A little onward, on the same side, the village of Cosgrove stands upon a hill, the church visible above the trees.

'The valley of the Ouse being crossed by a high embankment, we enter the Castlethorpe Cutting, and then find ourselves upon another embankment over a wide valley, with the spire of Hanslope Church standing conspicuous to the right; the valley is of a luxuriant nature, consisting of pastures filled with cattle, rich corn fields, and here and there a farm house, with its orchard and other rural appendages. Hanslope steeple was thrown down by lightning in 1804, on a Sunday evening in June; fortunately the church was empty, and no lives were lost: the spire has been rebuilt in the original form.'

By 1840 the railway company had built sixty cottages for the servants of the company in Wolverton. These tightly packed red-brick houses had little of the aesthetic attraction of the old thatched cottages, but they housed railwaymen's families which had their own hierarchic ranking. A signalman, a fireman, a trimmer or a platelayer could live in adjacent houses, but it was recognised that a signalman was superior to a platelayer, and that an engine driver was Mercury's representative here on earth.

Railway directors (who always sported a gold medal pass on their watch chains as everybody knew) were potentates whose claims to near divinity were unimpeachable. In every railway town streets were named in their or other senior railway officials' honour. Creed Street, Glyn Square, Ledsam Street, Young Street and Bury Street in their day housed the near élite of Wolverton railwaymen.[9]

Bury retired under a cloud of bankruptcy in 1846, but continued to live at the parsonage house at Great Linford. He was associated with the firm that made many 'Bury' engines for the L. & B. Railway. He was replaced as Locomotive Superintendent in 1847 by J. E. McConnell, who was to raise Wolverton to great heights of industrial efficiency.

Wolverton was now developing fast, and in 1844 Dr Lipscomb, the historian, could write:

'This gigantic station may justly be considered one of the wonders of modern times. The land which a few years ago was coloured with rich crops is now overspread with extensive premises and streets.'

In 1846 the London & Birmingham Railway was merged with several northernly lines to form the London and North Western

9 George Carr Glyn was an early chairman of the L. & B. Railway and became the first Baron Wolverton in 1869. The family continued to provide directors until the railways were nationalised in 1947.

Railway. The Marquess of Chandos (MP for Buckingham 1846–57) now became keenly interested in the new group, and was its chairman from 1853 to 1861. The Marquess had simple tastes, and lived economically. He created much comment by becoming an efficient railway chairman. Peers were not supposed to be good at this sort of thing. During that time not a decision was taken regarding Wolverton or Bletchley which did not have his consideration. His influence was great, and extended into ministerial circles.

THE SECOND DUKE OF BUCKINGHAM AND CHANDOS

Chandos's position was at once strengthened and weakened by the bankruptcy of his father, the second Duke, in 1847, who had succeeded to the title eight years earlier and was a prodigious spender. Whilst some of his difficulties may have been caused by investing in railways, there were other factors which materially contributed, including the lavish entertainment of royalty.

In 1840 the dowager Queen Adelaide came to Stowe by way of Wolverton where she was regally welcomed. All Buckingham was excited, and on the Market Square a triple arch was erected which carried the ambiguous sentence 'God Help Queen Adelaide'.

In 1844 when the Duke's eldest son, the Marquess of Chandos, came of age there were huge and expensive celebrations. Beer for everybody and champagne for the elect, and three pounds of mutton for every poor person in Buckingham and Aylesbury.

The apogee of all this spending was when he persuaded Queen Victoria and Prince Albert to visit Stowe for several days in 1845. As the plans were finalised the bailiffs were in, but the Duke got them to don the ducal livery and act as extra footmen during the visit. The Queen and Prince Albert arrived by train at Wolverton. Here they changed into a cheerful coach to drive through Stony Stratford and Deanshanger to Buckingham escorted by a glittering troop of Bucks Hussars. Stony Stratford was brilliantly *en fête*. There were no fewer than five triumphal arches erected in the High Street, with mottoes from 'God Bless the Queen' to just 'Hail Victoria'. The banners of the Friendly Societies, not just bits of bunting but really elaborate banners, with 10ft poles and streamers, added more animation. Even Deanshanger, then a trifling village too small to have a church, had a triumphal arch, and a rustic band welcomed the royal cortege there. The reception at Stowe was magnificent and costly.

It was a Grand Party. It was not only the Queen and the Prince Consort who were guests, but also the Prime Minister, Sir Robert Peel, the Foreign Secretary, Lord Aberdeen and other cabinet ministers and local peers. Among the untitled fry was Benjamin Disraeli and his unconventional wife. 'The whole scene' wrote Disraeli to his sister on 20 January 'was sumptuous, and a great success for the Duke'. But it was cold and nearly everybody shivered.

For Disraeli it was also a success, for the Queen met him in private for the first time and listened to him with curiosity.[10]

What with the fantastic cost of the party and some imprudent land speculation on borrowed money, the Duke became bankrupt. Disraeli said of him that 'he had the talent of inspiring ruffians with enthusiasm, of charming creditors and of taking swindlers in'. But the ruffians, moneylenders and swindlers caught up with him at last and in 1847 the Duke fled to the Continent owing possibly a quarter of a million pounds – an enormous sum now but sixty times more valuable then. In 1848 there was a forty-day sale of the 'priceless' furniture and art of Stowe which realised £77,000 and was sufficient to mollify his creditors. Other sales of books and land followed. His wife divorced him in 1850.

When the second Duke of Buckingham fled to the Continent in 1847 his railway interests were taken over by his only son, the Marquess of Chandos, who as we have seen, had just come of age. In 1850 the Marquess had the satisfaction of seeing the first part of the 'Buckinghamshire Railway' opened and in October 1853 he became chairman of the LNW Railway in place of George Carr Glyn. A year or two later he refused a cabinet position, preferring to continue his railway activities.

Railway Accidents
Meanwhile Wolverton Station was becoming famous. We have already noted that the new station had quite large refreshment rooms and lavatories to meet all requirements. For most trains Wolverton was the first reasonable halt after leaving Euston three

10 Lee *Queen Victoria* p161.

hours earlier. In the refreshment rooms a matron and seven young ladies served everything from gin to sandwiches; Banbury cakes and lemonade were in great demand, coffee was more popular than tea, and brandy more popular than either gin or sherry. Fortunately we have a contemporary record of Wolverton at this time (1850) from Sir Francis Bond Head, a colonial governor and an author of distinction:

'We will now conduct our readers to the Station and town of Wolverton . . . It is a little town composed of 242 little red-brick houses . . . three or four tall red-brick engine-chimneys a number of very large red-brick workshops, six red houses for officers, one red beer-shop, two red public-houses, and, we are glad to add, a substantial red schoolroom and neat stone church, the whole lately built by order of a Railway Board, at a railway station, by a railway contractor, for railway men, railway women, and railway children; in short, the round cast-iron plate over the door of every house, bearing the letters L.N.W.R., is the generic symbol of the town. The population is 1,405, of whom 638 are below sixteen years of age; indeed, at Wolverton are to be observed an extraordinary number of young couples, young children, young widows, also a considerable number of men who have lost a finger, hand, arm, or leg. All, however, whether whole or mutilated, look for support to "the Company" . . .'

At this time the accident rate for railway servants was high and indeed the average of sudden deaths yearly for personnel throughout the country was around 700. Trains, although few, would bump into other trains, or leave the rails of their own accord; wholly unauthorised persons would cross the line head down like Chinamen. Even the railway staff at Wolverton preferred to dash across the tracks rather than use the overhead crossing. Again, suicides were always trying out new methods. The Blue Bridge at Wolverton became a favourite spot for those who wanted to jump straight down in front of a train. Shunting too had its terrors, and to be a shunter or a goods train guard or brakesman, with the annual death toll of one in 400, meant that one had joined a suicide squad. The greatest causes of accidents were defective couplings and personal errors. On 5 June 1847 there was a horrible accident at Wolverton. Apparently a pointsman on duty at the Blue Bridge switched the mail train from London into the goods siding, where it crashed into some coal wagons. The engine and the first four carriages were almost undamaged, and the driver and passengers only bumped around, but seven people in the fifth carriage were killed and many injured. Bernard Fossey the pointsman said he had mistaken the express for a goods train. Signalling was still in its infancy. Added to all this were the consequences of an impure water supply. For a time the company used canal and well water without discrimination. Dr Rogers, the resident MO was 'overwhelmed' by cases of skin diseases, liver disorders and pulmonary trouble. In 1848 more than 120 cases had to be sent to the Middlesex hospital. Typhoid and diphtheria were later added to the ailments. It was not until years later that a better water supply was inaugurated.

Our contemporary record now continues:

Wolverton's Refreshment Rooms

'The refreshment establishment at Wolverton is composed of: A matron, seven very young ladies to wait upon the passengers, four men and three boys do., one man-cook, his kitchen-maid, and his two scullery-maids; two housemaids; one still-room maid, employed solely in the liquid duty of making tea and coffee; two laundry-maids and one baker's boy, one garden boy. And lastly, "an odd man".

'The young ladies are awakened exactly at 7 o'clock, in order that their première toilette may be concluded in time for them to receive the passengers of the first train, which reaches Wolverton at 7.30 a.m. From that time until the departure of the York Mail train, which arrives at about 11 o'clock at night, these young persons remain on duty, continually vibrating at the ringing of a bell, across the rails (they have a covered passage high above them, but they never use it) from the North refreshment-room for down passengers to the South refreshment-room constructed for hungry up-ones. By about midnight . . . they are all enabled once again to lay their heads on their pillows.

'In the refreshment-room these youthful hand-maidens stand in a row behind silver urns, silver coffee-pots, silver tea-pots, cups, saucers, cakes, sugar, milk with other delicacies . . . On the arrival of a train, the confused crowd of passengers, simultaneously liberated, hurry towards them with a velocity proportionate to their appetites . . . Considering that the row of young persons have among them only seven right hands, it is really astonishing how they can in the short space of a few minutes manage to extend and withdraw them so often – sometimes to give a cup of tea – then to give an old gentleman a plate of warm soup – then to drop another lump of sugar into his nephew's coffee-cup – then to receive a penny for a bun, and then again threepence for four "lady's fingers".

'It is their rule as well as their desire never, if they can possibly prevent it, to speak to any-one. At each end of the buffet, close to a warm stove, there is the rapid uncorking of innumerable black bottles of what is not inappropriately called "Stout", inasmuch as all the persons who are drinking the dark foaming mixture wear heavy great-coats, with large wrappers round their necks – in fact, are very stout. The excellent matron, who has charge of these young people, who always dine and live at her table, with honest pride declares that the breath of slander has never ventured to sully the reputation of any of those who have been committed to her charge.

'(Postscript. Notwithstanding the everlasting hurry at this establishment, four of the young attendants have managed to make excellent marriages, and are now very well off in the world.)[11]

Among the young workers at Wolverton Works at the time was the teen-aged Hugh Stowell Brown earning 8s a week. Later, when he was famous as a Baptist minister in Liverpool he wrote that although there were now 500 men working in the workshops, 'the majority of them lodged in the villages around'. He described Stony Stratford as having a market place full of grass, and 'we railway folk were looked upon with much disfavour there'. He adds that his fellow 'station men' spent 'not less than a hundred pounds in the public houses every Saturday night'.[12] One public house enjoyed the name of *Hell's Kitchen*. It was lit with scores of candles – and was notorious for its singing, quarrelling, swearing, thumping, and the clatter of mugs and glasses from every room. Stowell Brown reports that the talk inside or outside the pubs was

11 From *Stokers and Pokers*: or, *The London & North-Western Railway* (1850), by Sir Francis Bond Head, Bt.
12 Autobiography by H. S. Brown, edited by W. S. Caine, 1887.

profane and beastly in the extreme, and that the men (who included Welsh, Scottish and Irish) had very little political intelligence although it was a time of great agitation about Chartism and Free Trade. Most of them were unable to read or write. Hours of work averaged 58 a week.

Some of these 'station men' were expert poachers, but the inexpert were caught by gamekeepers and hauled up before the local magistrate, who was often the parson from Old Wolverton, and was greatly disliked. He was one of the local fox-hunting clergy, who mumbled the services, and had almost empty churches.

These moral problems came before the railway board. Something more was needed than just a school and a reading room. By now they decided that the company should build a church in 'New' Wolverton itself on land given by the Radcliffe trustees, and even before the church was built (1846) they appointed its vicar, the Rev George Weight, who by sheer force of character soon began to appeal to the better elements among the station men and their families. He started evening classes for boys and girls, encouraged the foundation of the Mechanics Institute. He was as Stowell Brown said, 'a thorough evangelist and a capital preacher'. He was no teetotaller, for when he gave a banquet in 1851 the supplies included 'ham, tongue, ribs of beef, lamb, pastry, 18 gallons of pale ale and 24 bottles of wine'. It cost £13. Such a man was deservedly popular.

But his gift of a party was far surpassed by that of the company itself. Both Weight and the company had helped to create a Mechanics Institute a few years earlier. It had not been quite the success hoped for, so the company decided to have a soirée celebrating the Institute's anniversary in December 1849. One thousand five hundred guests were invited to a tea party at 6 pm. For such a gathering the large engine shed had to be cleared of locomotives in the course of construction or repair, of machinery and impedimenta. It was brilliantly lighted with gas 'which at every corner was twisted into stars and crowns, initials and cornucopias'. All the columns and joists were festooned with evergreens and there were flags everywhere. Since all this sounds quite unbelievable we reproduce elswhere a picture from the *Illustrated London News* of 29 December 1849 which confirms the account.

The speeches were long – but all emphasised the splendid

relations between the company and the men. Eventually the speeches ended, and dancing commenced shortly after 10 pm and went on 'until we know not what hour in the morning'. Possibly it was parties and speeches like these that helped to change the minds and hearts of the town, for Wolverton soon became one of the most law abiding and moral towns in all Buckinghamshire. Gradually the Irish, Welsh and Scots either went home, died off, or succumbed to the combined pressure of wives, children and neighbours, to live exemplary lives.

Wolverton worked to a new rhythm, and the Works hooter gave the tempo.

EXCURSIONS TO A PRIZE FIGHT

But before this calm settled there was an event which made national news and which materially upset for a few days every railway official at Wolverton Station. Just before the advent of the railways, bare-knuckled prize fighting was the sport of princes. The pugilistic art had the warm support of the Prince Regent who was anxious to put down duelling as a solution to quarrels, and so the noble art of self-defence was encouraged. The 'fancy' or the 'prize ring' was at its zenith about 1830 but then began to degenerate. Prize fights became gathering places for the scum of a region – and such fights were only determined after scores of rounds when one contestant or the other was completely insensible – or dead. Parliament now banned what had become not only a brutal and murderous sport, but the occasion of public uproar. Consequently contests had to be arranged by stealth – but somehow the railway companies knew and ran excursions from all over England to the nearest station to the scene of the contest.

In 1841 the Championship Belt was held by Ben Caunt who had beaten W. Thompson (better known as 'Bendigo') in a somewhat dubious fight. Bendigo was anxious for his revenge, and in April 1845 it was announced that police or no police the fight would take place for a purse of £200 a side – a small sum, but the betting was soon of Littlewood proportions.

Ben Caunt was an ugly giant of a man, 6ft 2in and 17 stone, but he could train down to 14 stone. 'Bendigo', the nineteenth child of a poor but ferocious Nottingham woman, was a cocky fellow of 5ft 9in and a thorough ruffian. He was the darling of the Midlands and Caunt was the hero of London and all around. Their managers agreed that the fight should be at a place half way between London and Nottingham, so they chose the demure and self-respecting town of Newport Pagnell, or the nearest 'safe locality'.

The London & Birmingham Railway immediately put in hand plans for excursions from London, Manchester and Nottingham to Wolverton. On Sunday 7 September 1845 Bendigo and his party arrived at Wolverton and went on to the *Swan Inn* at Newport. The Chief Constable for the Newport Hundreds promptly informed Bendigo that he had a warrant to arrest anybody breaking the peace. On Monday Caunt and his party travelled from London to Wolverton by train, and choosing the best accommodation in the area put up at the *Cock* in Stony Stratford. On the same day hordes of excursionists arrived at Wolverton from Nottingham, Manchester or London, and most walked to Newport. The Nottingham men had all brought 'Nottingham twigs' (cudgels) with them, and seemed to be a para-military formation. Between Newport and Stony Stratford any miserable dossing place in a barn was let at exorbitant prices – and the owner of any broken down old rattletrap charged a sovereign a head for the journey of a few miles.

On Monday evening Caunt's manager suggested that since the Chief Constable seemed such an obstinate wet blanket, the fight should take place at Whaddon, four miles south of Stony Stratford just outside the Chief Constable's sphere of influence. From here they could move to Northants or Oxfordshire if need be. Bendigo's friends reluctantly agreed.

Meanwhile the prize ring commissary or master of ceremonies, with his cart full of gear, made his plans and on Tuesday morning, 9 September 1845, he set off from the *Cock* at Stony Stratford to Whaddon. A crowd of 5,000 followed him and at Whaddon the Nottingham squads arranged the ring and arena. But now the police interferred again. The Buckingham magistrates were determined to prevent the fight.

And now a superb solution was discovered. Five miles west of Stony Stratford was the sleepy village of Lillingstone Lovell which had only just been transferred from Oxfordshire to Bucks, and a mile away was the Northants border which was quite unprepared to resist invasion. Lillingstone Lovell was also the site of a previous championship match for the same reason, so that old hands knew all about it. It had been transferred to Bucks in 1844, but only for local government purposes, and not for police purposes. So off the commissary, his Nottinghamshire squads and thousands of spectators (now reinforced by fresh arrivals from Wolverton) went to Lillingstone Lovell. A 20ft square ring was erected. Around it was a 12 yard deep 'inner ring' which only the élite were supposed to occupy. But of course the crowd had other ideas and the disorder was immense, but there was not a constable in sight.

At last the two fighters, in knee breeches and stripped to the waist, the referee, umpires and seconds, were all ready. The fight began. We cannot describe it round by round as the television commentators love to do, for there were ninety-three rounds! Both men were battered almost into insensibility. Their hands looked like masses of jam. In the midst of pandemonium the referee gave the match to Bendigo, a decision that was hotly disputed then and long afterwards.[13]

The mob now streamed off to Wolverton, thirsty and bloody minded. Every pub on the way was sold out. At Wolverton the railway officials closed the iron gates against the disorderly mob until their trains arrived. It is doubtful if anyone could have protected the refreshment room damsels against some of the demands of the mob!

The whole event put the sporting world in an uproar but all agreed that it was a disgusting and disgraceful exhibition. Newport Pagnell, Wolverton, Stony Stratford, Whaddon and Lillingstone Lovell had seen some incredible sights and even the publicans did not like the crowd.

Since then Lillingstone Lovell has been a pattern village of the utmost good behaviour. Most visitors who go there now are ecclesiastical enthusiasts who admire the 13th century church with its 15th century brasses which are worth seeing. As for Bendigo, he became a revivalist preacher.

We have a scanty record of another prize fight locally when according to Gibbs (Vol IV) one took place in 1847 between Nobby Clarke and Tom Paddock at 'Sutfield Green', Stony Stratford. This was an open tract of land just over the Northamptonshire border at Puxley. The stakes were for £50; 'Nobby' lost,

13 I am indebted to Mr R. Ayers for drawing my attention to *The Victorian Underworld* by Kellow Chesney, from which much information has been garnered.

D

and was taken into custody. Paddock went on to become champion of England in 1855.

It was around this time, 1814–57, that the elegant and amiable Rev Loraine Smith was rector of Passenham. He was a great lover of the ring and probably helped to promote many minor fights. In 1868 the railways were prohibited from carrying people to a prize fight. Fisticuffs died out and the new boxing championships with gloves came in under the Marquess of Queensbury rules that year. Never again was Wolverton deluged with fans of the fancy and in fear for its females.

Education and Housing in Wolverton

In 1851, 775 men were employed at Wolverton Works. At the top of the tree were the superintendent and the engineer-in-chief with four 'overlookers' and nine foremen. The rest were mainly craftsmen and apprentices. There were thirty-two engine drivers and 119 labourers. The LNW Railway was the largest single employer of labour in north Bucks.

Top railway wages at this time were 42s a week for engine drivers – the peak of many a lad's ambition. To be an engine driver in those days was to be ranked with the great, and to drive an express train was an honour and a glory that only astronauts can feel today. The discipline was harsh and the hours long, as with astronauts, but no engine driver would willingly give place to another for the triviality of a meal break. Fitters received about 38s a week, and firemen 24s 6d a week, permanent waymen about £1 a week, but others averaged about 17s a week: all of which contrasted with the agricultural labourers' 11s a week.

Wolverton and Bradwell never had to complain about the swift aggravation of wrongs that wanted righting such as sweated labour, shanty towns, or the exploitation of young children. Industrial expansion came to Wolverton with a benevolent paternalism that really cared for the hundreds it employed and the thousands who depended for their health, education and even places of worship, on a board of directors led by George Carr Glyn and from 1853 by the Marquess of Chandos.

Among the growing work force were locally engaged men and boys whose ancestors for generations had worked on the land. They still thought and worked in the agricultural tradition. The directors were keenly aware that to advance smoothly there was the need to educate local youngsters up to railway standards. In 1847 a lecture room, library, reading room and music hall were authorised. We have a first-hand description of these activities and the schools in *The Railway Record* for September 1847:

> 'The schools which are very near the works, are surrounded by a small court and garden. In the centre there is a room for girls from 5 to 9 years who are instructed by a governess in reading, writing, arithmetic, geography, grammar, history and needlework. Here we counted 55 clean healthy faces. In the east wing were 90 fine stout athletic boys of various ages . . . learning mathematics and drawing, including quadratic equations, Euclid, land surveying, trigonometry and even conic sections. At the end of the building there was an infants school under the superintendence of an intelligent looking girl of about 19.'

The foundation stones of the new schools and church were laid by the Marquess of Chandos. It was reported that he gave 'a very excellent and appropriate address', but there were no local newspapers at the time and his words of wisdom have been lost.

Thus, when the company expanded its works a few years later there was a local pool of apprentice material that did credit to both sides. The eventual social changes were far reaching. This new railway work force knew little about agriculture except from grandfather's tales. For them there was no squire: indeed the only landlord was the company.

The population was now growing faster than ever before, and there arose a housing problem of acute dimensions, but the Radcliffe Trustees were reluctant to sell more land. The railway authorities built a few more houses in Wolverton, but there were never enough to meet the demand, and both in Newport Pagnell and Stony Stratford a dozen new streets or terraces were planned to house the ever-growing number of railway workers, and even as far afield as Old Stratford and Deanshanger, rows of cottages of an industrial character were now erected. The population of the area doubled within a generation, and the strain upon every sort of amenity, from schools to water supplies, can be imagined.

In 1856 the LNW Railway decided to expand the Works. So far it had been a centre for the repair and servicing of engines and tenders: now it was to become a locomotive factory and from Wolverton's own designs. The four-wheeled, inadequate Bury engines were to be gradually scrapped. In their place were to be the new 'Bloomer' engines which were to win great renown as we shall see later. As we have seen, the great engine shed and factory was surrounded on three sides by the small terraced houses. To allow for expansion of the Works some of these had to go, and before long the little streets between the engine shed and the canal, Walker Street, Cooke Street and Garnett Street, were razed to the ground.

The short 'New road' (Stratford Road) was now (1842) extended to link up with the 'Old Road', and this became one of the busiest rural roads in the county. All this created more and more housing problems and more land was required, but the Radcliffe Trustees were difficult. For ten years (1847–57) no agreement was reached with them. Something had to be done, and in 1852 the company decided to create a dormitory town at Stantonbury, where land was available. That year the company bought 15 acres of arable land there between the canal and the turnpike road to Newport and 4 acres of meadow adjoining Bradwell Brook and the road, all at £150 an acre, and about half a mile from Wolverton Station.

Within a year the company had built the first 116 houses, a public house and several shops. A church was planned and by it the associated Church Schools.[14] For years the new township was known as Stantonbury, but gradually it became better known as New Bradwell. These little houses were not the last word in spaciousness or beauty, but by contrast with some that were being built elsewhere they were little palaces. Indeed some of the worst houses ever built during the 19th century in England, were being erected in Stony Stratford, Newport Pagnell and the larger villages.

We have seen that with the opening of the railways some of the coaching and wagon inns and public houses had a sharp decline in their business. Their yards where horses had been stabled and coaches cleaned were almost empty. Throughout the entire county builders and other speculators thought it would be a good idea to build the cheapest kind of houses in these inn yards – houses so cheap and miserable that it is difficult to describe them. But generally they were in groups of half a dozen or so, tightly

14 The Church of St James was not actually consecrated until 1860. I am indebted to Miss Moira Courtman for much information about the new town.

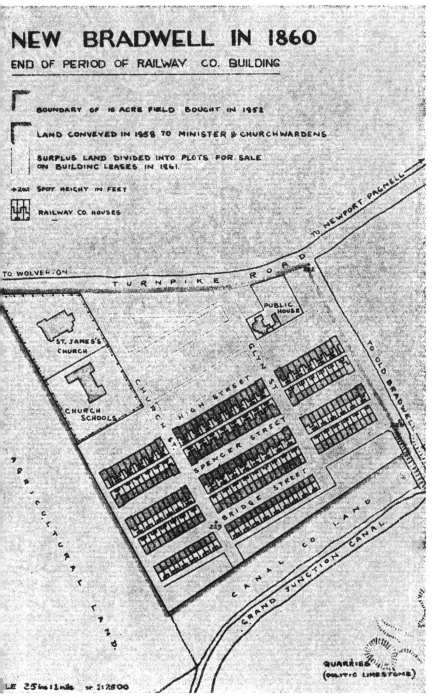

NEW BRADWELL IN 1860

END OF PERIOD OF RAILWAY CO. BUILDING

BOUNDARY OF 16 ACRE FIELD BOUGHT IN 1952

LAND CONVEYED IN 1958 TO MINISTER & CHURCHWARDENS

SURPLUS LAND DIVIDED INTO PLOTS FOR SALE
ON BUILDING LEASES IN 1861.

+202 SPOT HEIGHT IN FEET

RAILWAY CO. HOUSES

TO NEWPORT PAGNELL

TO WOLVERTON

TURNPIKE ROAD

PUBLIC HOUSE

ST. JAMES'S CHURCH

TO OLD BRADWELL

CHURCH SCHOOLS

CHURCH ST.

HIGH STREET

GLYN ST.

SPENCER STREET

BRIDGE STREET

AGRICULTURAL

CANAL CO. LAND

CANAL

GRAND JUNCTION CANAL

QUARRIES
(OOLITIC LIMESTONE)

LE 25 inches 1 mile or 1:2500

Reproduced by courtesy of Miss Moira Courtman from her thesis 'Wolverton: A Study in Urban Geography' 1968.

built on to a patch about 100ft by 14ft, and so each house covered an area (including the 'yard') of about 12ft 6in by 20ft. In the yard of the historic *Cross Keys Inn* at Stony Stratford, on a patch 100ft by 16ft, eight houses were built, one room up and one down, with a ladder for communication, and one common lavatory (which it was nobody's business to clean), no running water, and one common pump in the yard. In the *White Horse Inn* yard, on a patch 90ft by 14ft eight houses and one privy were built, each house about 14ft by 11ft. In Swan Terrace, backing the *Swan* public house in the High Street, six houses were erected on a plot 80ft by 20ft, again with only one lavatory and a single pump. Some of these houses were built with only $4\frac{1}{2}$in walls. Nearly every one of these houses was still in existence in 1919, and nearly every one tenanted in squalor, despair and disease. Not one exists today.[15]

And so by 1850 Wolverton was definitely on the map: Bletchley was only just. We must now see what led to its development.

15 Two famous Acts of Parliament, the Artisans and Labourers Dwellings Act, in June 1875, and the Housing of the Working Class Act of 1885, stopped the greedy building of large numbers of small houses crammed together, often back to back. Local authorities were given power to insist that there should be two good sized bedrooms and a small one, a living room, sitting room, kitchen and outhouses. Walls had to be a certain thickness, every house had to have a sink in the kitchen with a tap, a copper for boiling water to wash clothes, and its own lavatory. These new houses were efficient and comfortable, but not very beautiful.

6 Bletchley and the Buckinghamshire Railway

HAVING seen the London and Birmingham Railway created, and the early growth of Wolverton, we can now turn our attention to Bletchley, which up to 1847 had not even an adequate station. The development of Bletchley was in fact so gentle that between 1838 and 1847 it could be said that the railway made no impact on the small village other than scenically. Intending passengers had to go to Wolverton.

When Denbigh Hall was closed down in 1838 it was decided that no station was necessary at 'this miserable dump', and all that remained was the pub, a halt for milk trains and the signal box. But a few years later, in 1844, plans were put forward by a group of Bedford business men for a branch railway from Bedford to Bletchley and a new station in Bletchley itself.

The Duke of Bedford was one of the sympathetic figures in the new development. The intended date of opening was 20 October 1846, but a heavy rainstorm swept part of the track away near Simpson, and 17 November proved to be the formal date when the Duchess of Bedford and 'a brilliant company travelled to Bletchley and back in 30 carriages drawn by two powerful engines'. At Bletchley the band was out, the bells were rung and the locality had a day's holiday.

There was an obvious need for a better station at Bletchley, and the idea was reinforced by representations from a few local squires and farmers. In 1847 the new station, 'Bletchley and Fenny Stratford' was opened, and when, in 1850, the Bletchley-Banbury branch line was completed, five trains a day brought in passengers from along the line who often found they had an exasperating wait for their next connection. When the line was formally opened on 1 May 1850, May Queen processions helped to colour the occasions at the new stations at Swanbourne, Winslow and Buckingham. Railwaymen had already learnt how to decorate a train, and their daughters knew how to decorate a station. The effect on Bletchley village (as it still was) was minimal, for whilst it took hundreds to man Wolverton Works, and would take many more, it only took a score of men to run Bletchley junction. Indeed the population of the village rose only from 373 in 1831 to 426 in 1861, and the number of houses increased only from 83 to 97, half a dozen of which had been built by the railway.

Even up to about 1850 Bletchley, Water Eaton and Fenny Stratford were still three small separate communities. There was not a house along the Buckingham Road between Fenny and Old Bletchley save the four at the corner of Church Green Road, and again there was not a house between Old Bletchley and Water Eaton, and only a couple along the Fenny–Water Eaton Road.

We must now go back a few years and see how the Bletchley–Banbury branch originated and who was behind this and other railway developments in north Bucks. England had already entered on a period known as the 'Railway Mania', when everybody who had money or credit, and some who had not, wanted to speculate in railways. In 1846 over 272 Railways Acts were passed by Parliament authorising new lines or extending those already in existence.

It is not surprising that half a dozen new schemes emerged for lines to serve Buckinghamshire, some were supported by the Great Western Railway and others by the London & Birmingham Railway (which became part of the London & North Western Railway in 1846).

Two of the chief landowners in north Bucks were Sir Harry Verney centred in the Claydons, and the second Duke of Buckingham whose home was the great palace of Stowe, but whose territories extended south-east to Wotton Underwood near Aylesbury. They looked at their own territories in north Bucks and still further afield and decided that this railway void should be criss-crossed, first by a line from Banbury or Brackley through Buckingham to Aylesbury and Harrow and another from Oxford to Bletchley. Two separate companies were formed for the purpose. The ultimate aim was to provide two important and profitable links – the first would link up with other railways to north Wales and provide the fastest and most direct line from there to London: the second would be an important and direct link between Bristol and Norwich. The Duke became the chairman, but Sir Harry was the driving force. Others who invested in the

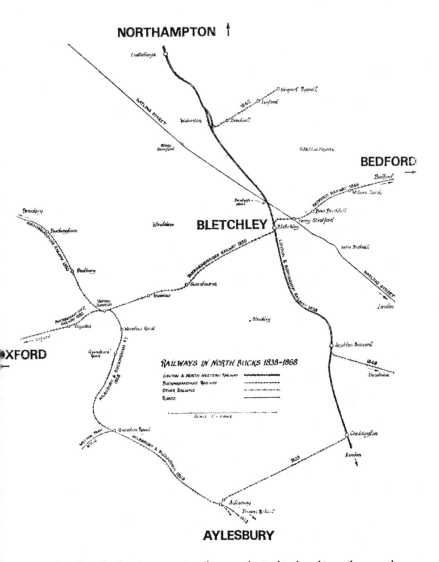

Map of north Bucks showing connections between the Buckinghamshire railways and the LNW Railway.

idea were Lord Nugent, Mr Bailey of Shenley and Mr Lowndes Winslow. They persuaded the London & North Western Railway not only to invest in the new lines, but later to supply engines and rolling stock. In the 19th century only the larger lines could afford both track and rolling stock. The smaller lines were almost always worked by the larger, as their capital was exhausted by the time the track, bridges and stations had been paid for.

The railway complex conceived by Sir Harry was quite large; it was roughly in the form of a cross the two arms of which intersected near Middle Claydon at a point later to be called Verney Junction (see map). The engineer was Robert Stephenson. The mileages involved were:

Bletchley to Banbury	31
Verney Junction to Oxford	21
Verney Junction to Aylesbury	12
Aylesbury to Tring	9
Aylesbury to Harrow	33
	106

In 1845 Parliamentary powers were obtained for the whole scheme. But within a year, at the general meeting of the Buckinghamshire Railway, the chairman Sir Harry Verney, announced that the Tring and Harrow extensions from Aylesbury had been dropped through lack of the necessary capital. So another Act was needed and obtained in 1846 to modify that of 1845. With these and other modifications the Buckinghamshire Railway went slowly ahead.

Although the Duke of Buckingham was chairman of the Buckinghamshire Railway his influence did not last for long. As we have seen, he inherited a great burden of debt from the first Duke and was compelled by the threat of bankruptcy to leave the country in 1847. His place was most ably taken by his son, the Marquess of Chandos, but Sir Harry now took on the chairmanship of the Buckinghamshire Railway. In August 1847 Parliamentary approval was given to extend the railway to Banbury. The map on page 97 shows the extent of these schemes.

But now the LNW Railway, much to Sir Harry's disappointment, refused to have anything to do with the Verney Junction to Aylesbury section as they already served Aylesbury from Ched-

SEALS OF THE BEDFORD AND THE BUCKINGHAMSHIRE RAILWAYS

Since these railways, of which the history is briefly recounted in chapter 6, mostly borrowed their rolling stock from one of the major railways, they had no insignia or livery of their own; but they had their seals, three of which are illustrated above.

That on the left is of the Bedford Railway Company (1845) which built the Bedford–Bletchley line. It shows the Bedford eagle on the coat of arms of the London and Birmingham Railway, which in turn depicts the arms of London to the left and Birmingham to the right.

The centre seal is that of the Oxford and Bletchley Junction Railway Company (1850), which displays the chained swan of Buckinghamshire.

The third seal, to the right, is that of the Buckingham and Brackley Junction Railway Company, again a part of the Buckinghamshire Railway, and again displaying the beautiful swan of Buckinghamshire.

The seals are reprinted from a page extracted from an old copy of 'The Railway Magazine', lent by George Read, of Wordsworth Drive, Bletchley.

dington which was the branch line Sir Harry had been very active in creating in 1839.[1]

In 1850 as we have seen, the Bletchley–Banbury line was completed, and the status of Bletchley as a junction greatly enhanced.

By 1853 it was evident that the Buckinghamshire Railway was disappointing its promoters and investors, and Sir Harry Verney thought the time had come to write a fairly strong letter to the Marquess of Chandos (now chairman of the LNW Railway) pointing out how that company had thwarted the Bucks railway, even though they had leased the line, provided all the rolling stock, and generally called the tune. They grumbled publicly that the Bucks railway was losing money every year. In 1853 the working expenses of the Bucks line, paid by the LNW Railway came to £35,000. Receipts were just under £16,000.

In September 1853 Sir Harry drafted the following letter to Lord Chandos, and sent it to his brother, Frederick Calvert (who had not changed his name) for his opinion:

'There are matters connected with the Bucks Railway to which I venture to solicit your attention, & in which, if on consideration you shall find that my views are correct, I hope that you will exert your influence.

'Where the railway was first undertaken, in 1845, the object was to furnish railway accommodation to Bucks both lengthways from near Willesden to Amersham, Aylesbury, Buckingham, Brackley: and also across from Oxford to Bletchley – I still think that a scheme better for the interests of the County of Buckingham, & more likely to prove remunerative to the shareholders, could not have been devised. It comprised the most direct line from Wales to London, including the shortest passage to Ireland: & embraced a communication to Wolverhampton & the whole District Southward & south Westward, as far as Bristol. The cross Line was to give railway communication across England via Oxford, Bletchley, Bedford, & eastward to Lynn & Norwich.

'On taking a retrospect of the very exciting time when the

---

1 *The Duke of Buckingham's Railways* by E. J. S. Gadsden, Bledlow Press, 1962. I am indebted to Mr F. G. Cockman of Bedford for other information about the Bucks railway. See also article by R. S. Hampson in *Records of Bucks*, 1970, pp386–92 and *Records of Bucks*, 1973.

scheme was proposed, & when many very bad schemes were proposed, I am of opinion that we may congratulate ourselves that the Bucks schemes were laid out so judiciously.

'We had the option of uniting our interests either with the North Western or the Great Western –

'After careful consideration & enquiry, those who planned railway communication for the county were of opinion that the character & business habits of those who conducted the affairs of the L. & N.W. were inferior to those of no other company, and it was decided to ally ourselves with the L. & N.W. (the L. & B. as it was then called). Maps were made, & language held, under their sanction & authority – How comes it that the language then used has failed to be carried out? We all said – railway communication strait across England will be supplied from Bristol & Oxford to Lynn & Norwich. On this promise we advanced our money – but a short gap Bedford to Sandy about 8 miles of nearly level country & land which might be had for a small sum, has been allowed to remain. Bills have been brought into Parliament, but they have never been pushed forward – in fact the N.W. Company were not anxious to obtain them – they were afraid that Bedford traffic would go via Sandy to London, instead of via Bletchley & the L. & N.W. Therefore, the interests of the Bucks Line, & the convenience of the public, were disregarded.

'And now, crowning the impolicy of the London & N.W. Company, comes the proposed line Leicester to Hitchin. Bedford was naturally determined not to remain without communication eastward. Had the N.W. given that by a line to Sandy, we would have been satisfied: but that not being supplied, Bedford is to have a line which will do to the N.W. far more injury than Bedford & Sandy could have done, and which will less efficiently help their lines – Bedford to Bletchley – Bletchley to Oxford.

'I hear that Leicester to Hitchin is to cost £3 Millions – Bedford to Sandy would have cost, perhaps, £80,000.

'At Banbury we have never formed our junction with the Oxford & Birmingham Line. I have had some correspondence on the subject with the Board of Trade, but if the L. & N.W. group really desired the junction, they ought to have directed their counsel to keep the point before the Parliamentary committees. It could not have been refused – It would have furnished to the Bucks Line narrow gauge communication with Birmingham via Banbury. Is not the Bucks Line again sacrificed, in order to bring the traffic from Buckingham, for instance, via Bletchley to Birmingham?

'The portion of Bucks railways which was of most importance, & expected to be the most remunerative, that communicating with Aylesbury N. & S. has never been made. Aylesbury is not only our County Town containing our county Institutions but it is also the best & most growing market in our part of England.

'I do not hesitate to say that I thought their not making the Line from the Bucks junction to Aylesbury so wrong, I considered very seriously abandoning all connection with the Company. I would certainly have done so had I not thought that I might thereby lessen any means of forwarding that which I have struggled so long – namely to provide railway communication for all Bucks – at this time what we have of railway is not employed as it might be – the Bedford & Bletchley & Bletchley & Oxford time tables do not serve. People are kept waiting long at Bletchley – residents near Bedford & even at Bedford prefer going to London by the Great Northern, & to Bristol or even Oxford, by the G.W., on account of inconveniences at Bletchley.

'At many of the smaller stations on our Line there is a monopoly of coals – only one sort is sold. I consider this extremely wrong. It ought to cease forthwith.

'The goods traffic of the District is not properly developed – Goods ought to be received at the smaller stations – the staple commodity of our District suffers considerably in consequence. It is well known that butter will not bear shaking – that which arrives in London with the finest, sharpest edge & corners sells the best – but the butter at Mursley & Swanbourne & Little Horwood, made close to Swanbourne Station is carried in a jolting cart to Winslow – and that from Steeple Claydon is carried by Claydon Station to Winslow. In hot weather the butter suffers very considerably. I have attended the London markets, & at several principal shops at the West End. I have seen the Butter Baskets from Bucks opened, and the Butter Boxes from Ostend, and been told by the Butter merchants that Buckinghamshire is losing the London market, not because our Butter is not the best, but because it is so shaken and does not unpack with clear, sharp edges – and I have before-stated all this to the L. & N.W. Company and I add with very great regret, to no purpose.

'In every report of the N.W. Company the loss sustained by them on account of the Bucks Company is inserted. I do not hesitate to say that I view it with deep concern. I lament extremely that any one should be a loser by supplying that which I, among others, sought to obtain.

'Capt. Huish has remarked to me more than once, "Your county does not contain the population to afford the traffic." To that I would reply that our calculations are founded on the *through* traffic, which the L. & N.W. deny to be for reasons not affecting the interests of the Bucks railway at all our termini – Bletchley, Banbury and the junction towards Aylesbury. I would remind him that our passenger traffic far exceeded expectation *until* the fatal accidents at Bicester and at Oxford – accidents for which we are as little responsible (as we have nothing to do either with the appointments or management) as if they had taken place on any other line.

'I do not like adverting to the accidents, because I know that the N.W. Company officers have deplored them as keenly and sympathised with the sufferers as heartily as any resident in the district – but when Capt. Huish adverts to our small traffic it is only fair to enquire what are the causes of it. The obvious means to restore public confidence is to double the line the whole way . . .

'I do not doubt that one of the best Lines in England remains still to be completed

> Wolverhampton
> Banbury
> Aylesbury
> Amersham
> Willesden

and the best Crop Line

> Oxford
> Bletchley
> Sandy

So long as these remain incomplete I shall not feel that my original expectations, are proved to have been erroneous.

'I have addressed this to you, My dear Lord Chandos but I care not who sees it. I am the last man to desire to find fault with your Company. I was one who always desired that our county should be connected with you in preference to any other Company, and I can never forget that in the days of railway roguery, it was the manly, bold, upright conduct of your able predecessor, more than any one other thing that saved the honour of the railway world.'

Sir Harry sent this draft to his brother, Frederick Calvert, with this footnote:

'My dear F.,

What think you of my addressing some such letter to Lord Chandos? He is to have a salary not less, I am told, than £2,000. per a.

Yrs. H.V.'

Whether the letter went in this form to Lord Chandos or not is uncertain, but what is certain is that the letter brings out very clearly Sir Harry's disappointment at the way the Bucks railway had failed to develop as part of the most direct line from Wales to London, with a cross line linking Oxford to Norwich. It also brings out his great interest in the minutia of railway administration.

The only letters in the Verney archives from Lord Chandos at this time are much briefer – almost terse.

'Euston Station
Sept 19/53

My dear Sir Harry Verney,

'I have this morning received yours of the 17th respecting a proposed line from Claydon to Aylesbury & enquiring whether "if the line be made, the L. & N.W. Co. would make working arrangements with the owners" –

In this as in any other case where the landowners & persons locally interested may form a railway in connection with this Company's lines the latter will be desirous of giving every aid in their power to the development of the traffic of the district or arising upon the new line, but I do not think the Board will assent to any thing in the shape of a guarantee which I presume would be the intention of the working arrangements you refer to –

I will however place your letter before my Board at their next meeting.

Yours very faithfully,
Chandos.'

'Wotton
Nov. 17/53

'Dear Sir H. Verney,

I have received yours respecting the excursion train from Oxford for the Xmas Cattle Show, & asking that it may stop at Claydon – which I will bring before the Executive Committee on next Thursday –

Your letters respecting insufficiency of accommodation at the Bucks stations is under consideration.

Yours very faithfully,
Chandos.'[2]

Three years later in March 1856, Sir Harry Verney returned to the attack, and the board of the Bucks Railway Company agreed with him that he should stress to the LNW Railway Company:

1: Fares between Bletchley and Oxford had been doubled by the L.N.W. Railway without the Bucks Directors being consulted.

2: Passengers from Beds to the Bucks line are kept waiting a long time at Bletchley, and the delays at Winslow are much complained of.

3: Passengers should be able to book through from Claydon to London and not have to rebook at Bletchley.

---

2 The above letters are from the Verney Archives at Claydon, and I am grateful to Sir Ralph Verney for permission to quote them. There are hundreds, if not thousands of other letters there, for Sir Harry lived to be 93, never lost his interest in local matters, and he seems to have kept every letter, every draft letter, and even draft speeches. I have chosen these as illustrative not only of Sir Harry's feelings about the Buckinghamshire Railway, but also as indicative of his relations with Lord Chandos – who was so evidently the real power in the LNW Railway until 1861.

Unfortunately all the family records of the Marquess of Chandos, and of the Dukes of Buckingham went to the Huntington Library in California in 1921 and are mostly uncatalogued.

Sir Harry died in February 1891. There is a detailed obituary notice of him in the *Bucks Herald* of 17 February of that year.

4: The Bucks train from Bletchley arrives at Oxford 7 minutes after Great Western has left. That delay costs the traveller to Torquay six hours, as the Bishop of Oxford experienced last Monday week when he went to visit his dying son at Torquay . . .

10: Lower rates of freight ought to be charged on certain agricultural produce. Manure costing a 1s a ton at Oxford costs 8s 2d per ton to send to Claydon or Winslow.

11: The public ought to be able to get coal from any colliery and have it delivered to any station, instead the Shipstone colliery have a monopoly. . .

15: The Bucks line is declared to be a burden on the L.N.W. Railway, but if the Railway was completed as planned the line will pay well.
The interests of the Bucks Company have been sacrificed to the supposed interests of the L.N.W. Railway. The welfare of the Bucks line would have been greatly advanced by consulting the Directors on local questions.'

Sir Harry was persistent. Finally, years later, he managed to get approval for his long sought Aylesbury–Buckingham line.

THE AYLESBURY AND BUCKINGHAM RAILWAY

This was the 13-mile line from Aylesbury to Claydon Junction and so linking up with Buckingham which had to be dropped after 1846 when the LNWR refused to have anything to do with it. By Sir Harry's persistence the dormant section of the Buckinghamshire Railway was revived in the Aylesbury & Buckingham Railway Act of 6 August 1860.

The Marquess of Chandos (chairman of the LNWR) became the chairman and subscribed £5,000, whilst Sir Harry became deputy chairman. It took eight years before the line was opened. Somehow or other the Marquess of Chandos, who succeeded to the dukedom in 1861, was forced to resign from the LNWR board which now refused to have anything to do with the new line, consequently no rolling stock was available. The new company was in financial difficulties, the line and the new Verney Junction (formerly the Claydon Junction) station having cost £167,000. But Sir Harry was not defeated. He got the Great Western Railway to provide two locomotives and three old carriages, and the line was opened on 23 September 1868. But the line was soon bankrupt and Sir Harry lost a considerable sum. And so did the Duke.[3]

The Act permitted the usual railway rates to be applied. Third class passengers could travel at 1d per mile. First class passengers could be charged a maximum of 3d a mile if the company provided the engine and carriage, but if the passenger brought his own coach he was charged 10d a mile if the company provided the truck or wagon and the engine. If the passenger found his own engine and carriage he was charged 5d a mile for the use of the line.

The cheapest traffic rates were 1d a ton/mile for manure, lime or road material if the customer found his own wagons and engines, and $1\frac{1}{2}$d a mile if the customer only provided the wagons. Coal, bricks, clay, iron etc, were charged $1\frac{1}{2}$d per ton/mile, or 3d per mile if the railway company provided wagons and engines. These rates lasted well over a century, for Verney Junction is one of the places passed by the Kaolin (china clay) trains from Cornwall to the potteries, and even today as one has a drink at the *Verney Arms* one can see these long goods trains thundering past.*

Possibly one of the greatest benefits from all these schemes was the cheapening of materials of all kinds not only to farmers and builders, but also to householders. The canals had done much a generation earlier, but with both canals and railways competing for the transport of minerals and other imperishables, it became possible to retail coal at 12s 6d a ton for 'kitchen cobbles' – and Sir Harry Verney could boast to his constituents that due to the Buckinghamshire Railway coal was 30s a ton cheaper anywhere between Bletchley and Buckingham, than it had been before

In all this change Bletchley was a focal point. With the opening of the Bletchley–Oxford line (May 1851) Bletchley really was important in all railway minds and in the eyes of the travelling public. In 1862 the Bletchley–Bedford branch line was extended to Cambridge, and the two great university towns were at last within a few hours reach of one another, but even the Dons had to change at Bletchley, and it was still a tedious place to wait in. In 1862 Sheahan described Bletchley as 'scattered and mean looking, consisting mostly of poor thatched cottages built in two

* 1975.
3 It became part of the Metropolitan Railway in 1891.

sections, the Green and the Town'. Most of the houses even at this late date were half timbered, with brick filling, dating mostly from the 17th century. Of these there are still a few standing in Old Bletchley. It was not until years later that the town began to increase and this was mainly due to the modernised brickmaking industry.

Within a generation the railways had changed the face of north Bucks. Bletchley from being a 'miserable dump' had become a well-known railway junction: Wolverton had jumped from a village of 400 people to a bustling thriving new town of nearly 3,000 people: New Bradwell was approaching 2,000.

More even than this, not a village in the entire area was more than $5\frac{1}{2}$ miles from a station; a passable walk in those days, and even on the smallest branches there were several trains a day. People began to think in terms of railway timetables and railway parcel rates. Country-women began to learn by heart the timing of trains and the junction connections when they went to visit married daughters and sons. Old men, or even middle aged men, talked lovingly of the old coaching days, but young men knew in a dim way that Britain had given one of its greatest gifts to the world – the steam engine. The panache and the glory of the great coaching days had passed for ever. The future lay with steam, and as we shall see in another chapter, tremendous efforts were now made to apply it to agriculture, to mills, and even to road transport. Very soon Queen Victoria would see a road steam engine that could transport three people and a stoker all along the roads from Buckingham to Windsor and not only get there safely, but get back too, under its own steam. Even in the smallest villages, like Little Woolstone there were men applying steam to farm problems and holding exhibitions at Stony Stratford to prove their value.

7 The Agricultural Scene — Great Brickhill and Water Eaton

IT is high time that we left the clamour and development of Wolverton, Bradwell and Bletchley, and the clash of the new railway age, and remembered that even with all these developments north Bucks was essentially an agricultural area where the harvest was the most important event of the year.

All around Wolverton and Bletchley were serene villages, only mildly affected by the railway mania and still almost self-contained units. The list is a long one – from the Northamptonshire border to Stewkley or Soulbury, most of them with a lord of the manor, productive farms, an ancient church, a school, a village pump or two, and a comforting pub.

To write the history of any one of these villages, with all the voluminous information now available, would fill a good book. We must select one or two only as examples and try to condense their history, during the 19th century, to a single chapter. The choice falls on Great Brickhill and Water Eaton, not because they are more beautiful or more historic than any of the others, but because they are possibly the best documented. All villages have their parish registers, churchwardens' accounts and manorial records. Most have been well written up in Lipscomb, Sheahan, the *RCHM* and *VCH*, but Great Brickhill and Water Eaton have that something more, the recently accessible papers of the Duncombe family who had been lords of the manor of Great Brickhill since 1549 and who have generously donated many family records to the County Record Office at Aylesbury for all to see. But one important and artistic document was kept back – the beautiful leather-bound manuscript *Report upon the Duncombe Estates* made in 1863, by Joseph Snowball, a most competent estate surveyor. This, with its accurate and beguiling coloured maps of the various villages and farms is a treasure. Henceforward we shall refer to it as the Report.

Before we consider a few details of this report it may be well to have a quick look at the Duncombe family and to refer to their close friendship with Benjamin Disraeli.

In 1549 the Duncombes acquired in Great Brickhill and the adjacent parishes 20 messuages (or farms), 10 tofts (or derelict buildings), 10 cottages, 1 water mill, 1 dovecote, 20 gardens, 20 orchards, 2,000 acres of arable land, 500 acres of meadow, and 2,000 acres of pasture, as well as 200 acres of woodland, and some rights over heath and common pasture. All this was confirmed by the Enclosure Awards of 1772 and on.

Around 1769 the manor of Great Brickhill descended, through daughters, to the Rev Philip Barton, rector of the parish, who had only two years previously acquired the manors of Bletchley and Water Eaton. This Rev Philip Barton however had no legal issue and when he died in 1786 he left all his estates to his godson, Philip Duncombe Pauncefort, a babe in arms, on condition that he later assumed the name of Duncombe; which he did in 1805, and he started up a goodly line of Duncombes who are still in residence in Great Brickhill.[1]

Between 1800 and 1860 many acres of land were sold to canal or railway companies so that the original estates were reduced to about 3,000 acres.

The name Duncombe has always been an honoured one in Bucks, and when our Philip Duncombe Pauncefort Duncombe became sheriff in 1824 the county welcomed the appointment. He was very immersed in politics, and when Benjamin Disraeli came on to the local scene in 1847, Duncombe extended the warmest hospitality to him, and the flashy, flamboyant newcomer, with his ringlets and exuberant clothing, surveyed the scene from Great Brickhill manor and liked it.

According to the biography of Disraeli by Monypenny and Buckle (Vol 1, Chapter III) Disraeli in 1846 was not altogether happy in his relations with his constituency at Shrewsbury, and he hoped to find a firmer seat somewhere else. The Duke of Buckingham was a friend of Disraeli and when one of the three

---

1 His son, Sir Philip D. P. Duncombe, was born in Great Brickhill 1818, married 1844, youngest daughter of Col Thos Philip Maunsell: was High Sheriff in 1855 and a DL for Bucks and Northants. Created a Baronet in 1859. His son and heir Henry Philip was born in London in 1849, succeeded in 1890, and died in 1895. From him there descended the well-beloved Sir Everard who died in 1971 at the age of 86.

county members of Parliament for Buckinghamshire announced his intention of retiring, there was some chance that the Duke's son, the Marquess of Chandos, would come forward. But when he refused, the way was clear for Disraeli's nomination. On 24 May 1847, Disraeli issued his farewell address to the electors of Shrewsbury, and the following day there appeared his address to the electors of Buckinghamshire, which of course included many farmers and prosperous business men in Newport Pagnell, Stony Stratford, Wolverton, Fenny Stratford and the adjacent villages.

It was a historic document, which Monypenny and Buckle quote almost in full. But to be very brief, in it he stressed his long connection with the county, declared his opposition to free trade, and said that he was in favour of placing the education of the people in the hands of the clergy. The Poor Law, he wrote, should be controlled by the counties, and the supervision of our parishes should not be entrusted to strangers. 'I shall support all those measures which will elevate the social and moral condition of the Working Classes, by lessening their hours of toil – by improving their means of health – and by cultivating their intelligence.'

The campaign began. In his first speech at Newport Pagnell, and again at Aylesbury, he expanded these and other points. It is doubtful if the full impact of his oratory was understood at Newport or throughout the nation at that moment, but years later he came back to these ideas. In a speech at Amersham during this 1847 election he repeated again his profession of faith in the political greatness of the county:

'It gave us the British Constitution in the seventeenth century, and it created the British Empire in the eighteenth. All the great statesmen of that century were born, or bred, or lived in this county. Throw your eye over the list – it is a glorious one – from Shelburne to Grenville. Travel from Wycombe to Buckingham, from the first Lord Lansdowne, the most accomplished Minister this county ever produced, to the last of our classic statesmen. Even the sovereign genius of Chatham was nursed in the groves of Stowe . . . And in our own time, faithful to its character and its mission, amid a great parliamentary revolution, Buckinghamshire called a new political class into existence, and enfranchised you and the farmers of England by the Chandos clause. Now let the men of the North, who thought that they were to govern

England – let them bring a political pedigree equal to that of the county of Buckingham.'

There were four candidates for three seats, but Disraeli was one of the three elected.

Disraeli was often accused of being the nominee of the Duke of Buckingham. This always made him indignant, for he was certain that he came forward at the request of leading yeomen and proprietors in the county. In Buckingham itself he sturdily maintained his independence, and that he must remain 'master of his political destiny'.

Thus began Disraeli's connection as MP for our area and other parts of Bucks which lasted nearly thirty years. In 1860 he could write that his election as MP for Bucks 'is the event of my life which has given me greatest satisfaction'.

The general election again returned the Whigs under Russell, so that Disraeli spent his time on the back opposition benches.

During the thirty years that Disraeli represented us as one of the county MPs he was often returned unopposed, as for example in 1858 when he became Chancellor of the Exchequer, but always he had to be on the alert to retain his parliamentary seat. Naturally at Hughenden, which he had bought in 1846, he had a superb vantage point to survey the south of the county, but he could count on a warm welcome any time at Stowe, for in spite of the bankrupcty of the Duke in 1847, and his flight abroad, there was still the Marquess of Chandos in residence.

When the Marquess succeeded his father as the third Duke in 1861 he gave up his railway interests and became immersed in politics again, and was a cabinet minister from 1866 to 1868 whilst Disraeli was Chancellor of the Exchequer.

Disraeli showed his gratitude when in March 1868 the Lord Lieutenancy of Bucks fell vacant. Disraeli, then Prime Minister, promptly wrote to Queen Victoria recommending the then Duke for what was then a very influential appointment:

'The Duke of Buckingham still has the largest estate in the county. Mr. Disraeli remembers that more than twenty years ago in the dark troubles of His Grace's youth telling him that he had a great mission to fulfil; and that was to build up again the fortunes of an ancient house . . . The Duke has succeeded in this noble enterprise . . . Mr. Disraeli having in his youth, and days of great obscurity, received kindness

from the House of Grenville he should feel grateful to fortune if by your Majesty's permission he was authorised to
inform the Duke of your favour . . .
'The flag waves again over Stowe, which no-one ever expected: and if your Majesty confers on the Duke the great honour
of being your Majesty's representative in this county, the
honours of the Grenville family will after great vicissitudes
and searching trials be restored.'

The Queen cordially agreed. 'No one', she wrote, 'bore his
misfortunes more nobly, or more truly deserves re-institution in
the ancient family seat than the Duke.'

THE DUNCOMBES OF GREAT BRICKHILL

The Grenvilles were not the only friends Disraeli had in north
Bucks, he had many, but warmest of them all were perhaps the
Duncombes of Great Brickhill. Young Philip Duncombe born in
1819, became his firm friend and counsellor, and indeed he could
be described as entrusted with the surveillance of the whole of
north Bucks in the Disraeli cause. Disraeli often stayed at the
interesting manor in Great Brickhill and from here visited other
houses: the more he saw the more he was impressed. In April
1857 he wrote to Lady Londonderry:

'We have been paying visits to some of my principal
supporters in north Bucks during the last few weeks: people
you never heard of before, yet living with a refinement and
splendour quite remarkable. Nothing more striking than
some English gentry, with chateaux, parks and broad
domains, greater men by a good deal than many German
Princes, and yet utterly unknown in London society: among
these one of our greatest Bucks squires, a Mr Pauncefort
Duncombe, whose home was really radiant, and contrasted
very much with Woburn Abbey, which he took me over to
see, larger, but the most gloomy and squalid palace that you
can conceive.'[2]

Duncombe senior died in March 1849 from a wound in the foot
caused by dropping a pair of scissors on it; and young Philip took
over the squirearchy of Great Brickhill and Water Eaton with
enthusiasm.

2 Quoted in Monypenny and Buckle iv 77, and Blake, 279.

Another warm friend of Disraeli's in the area was the solicitor, William Powell of Newport Pagnell, who was secretary to most organisations in the town, including the annual race meetings. He was his election agent for years, and as such scrutinised the electoral lists with an eagle eye. He organised the agricultural dinners for Disraeli year after year, but when Disraeli spoke at one of these on 14 July 1852 for well over an hour people thought it a bit much.

The Duncombe Estates

Now it is time to turn to Great Brickhill, Water Eaton and Bletchley to see how the Duncombe estates were administered, and it is now that we can give extracts from the Report on the estates prepared in 1863. By parishes the Duncombe possessions were as follows:

Parish	Area in Acres	Rents		
Great Brickhill	1,599	£2,678	2s	6d
Water Eaton	894	£1,571	0s	6d
Bletchley	418	£631	19s	0d
Fenny Stratford	151	£447	0s	0d
Dropshort Farm	49	£125	0s	0d
Little Brickhill	3	£10	0s	0d
Bow Brickhill	1	£4	0s	0d
Leighton Buzzard	3	£12	0s	0d
Soulbury	—	£7	16s	0d

So that in this area alone the Duncombes held 3,118 acres and received rents of £5,487.

The Manor of Great Brickhill

Out of the entire parish of Great Brickhill of 2,383 acres, only 444 acres were arable, mostly corn, 1,500 acres were pasture, and there were 122 acres of woods or plantations. There were magnificent pastoral and sylvan views in all directions, since most of the village is over 300ft above sea level, and the ridge itself is over 500ft. The surface is broken into bold inequalities, lofty hillocks, narrow, deep and exciting ravines, which remind one of Bavaria or Switzerland.

We know that during the Civil War this was, in 1643, the location chosen by Lord Essex as the best site alongside the Watling Street for the defence of London, and how Charles I missed the chance of driving through the starving demoralised army of Essex. In 1772 the entire parish was reorganised by the Enclosure Award. We have seen how, due to purely geographical reasons it was missed by both the canal and the railway, so that when we resume our story of the parish we have one whose base was not vastly different from that of Domesday.

It was still governed by the lord of the manor. The Duncombes now had not so much power as the early lords of the manor, for the manorial courts were dying, but in influence and moral responsibility they had more than ever before. The shrewd common sense and political sagacity of Philip Duncombe, who succeeded in 1849, had won Disraeli's admiring friendship, and when Philip Duncombe was made a baronet in 1859 no one questioned this item in the Honours List.

At this time Great Brickhill was a village of 700 or more people, and Water Eaton a hamlet of 240 souls. Both were entirely agricultural with no other industry. Eighty per cent of their adult males worked on the land.

In Great Brickhill the Duncombes had always kept the Manor and Home Farm (248 acres) in their own hands, and all woods and plantations (122 acres). The Manor and Home Farm were estimated to be worth £440 per annum, but there was no assessment of the value of the woodlands.

Apart from these, the broad acres of the manor were divided into half a dozen large farms, the most important of which were:

		Rent	Approximate Rent per acre
*Westfield Farm	247 acres	£370	£1 9s 0d
*Galley Lane Farm	237 acres	£360	£1 10s 0d
*Eaton Leys Farm	183 acres	£275	£1 10s 0d
*Ivy Lane Farm	162 acres	£235	£1 10s 0d
*Park Farm	157 acres	£210	£1 6s 8d
	986	£1,450	

* The rents were raised soon after the Report. Smith's and Knight's holdings were later merged into adjacent farms or added to the *Duncombe Arms* territory.

Smaller holdings were let at higher rents:

	Rents		Approximate Rent per acre		
Smiths Farm	43 acres	£95	£2	4s	0d
Thornton's Farm	35 acres	£56	£1	12s	0d
Franklin's (Church) Farm	35 acres	£80	£2	5s	0d
*Knights Farm	27 acres	£50	£1	18s	0d

Just outside the parish – actually in Bow Brickhill and Little Brickhill – was Dropshort Farm – the historic site of Magiovinium, the farmhouse of which had been a renowned posting house and hostelry. As the Report says 'The Farm House, formerly an Inn of importance on the old post road, is more than sufficient for the size of the farm'. It still is, for the farm was then only 48 acres. It was let at £125 a year.

Westfield Farm soon had its rent raised to £430 for as the Report says:

> 'The farm house and buildings are in excellent order, and I should think little will be required to keep them good for many years. The farm is in good condition and in general dry, though about one third of the land requires draining. The subsoil is porous, and drains at a distance of 40 to 60 feet apart, 4 feet deep, will drain the land perfectly.'

Then, and for a century afterwards, the farm was occupied by the Clements family. Church Farm is still occupied by the Franklin family.

How did the large farmers prosper? We have seen that a principal charge on the farm was the rent at about 30s an acre. Probably more important than this was the labour bill, for each large farm needed up to a dozen agricultural workers. The average pay of a farm hand in 1863 was 11s a week, so that if say eight were employed the wages bill was over £220 a year, and inevitably there were dairy maids and house servants. Then there were the horses to be tended, the ploughs and carts to keep in good order, the occasional need for better seed or more manure, and it will be seen that the outgoings could be up to £1,000 pounds a year Let us see how the most extensive farm of all, Westfield Farm, with its score of fields was cultivated. Twelve fields totalling 120

* See note on p113

acres were down to 'old grass' as the Report has it. Here would be the dairy herd or the beef cattle, possibly sheep. Some parts would be kept for hay. Sixty-three acres in half a dozen fields were producing wheat, oats or barley, mostly barley. Two fields were set to clover and one to beans to provide fodder, and the remaining three fields of just over 30 acres set to turnips with a little fallow. Fallowing was gradually being superseded by turnips and legumes. These records show that this part of Bucks was one of the last areas in England to retain fallow.[3]

Most other farms were in these proportions with an occasional field devoted to peas or mangold-wurzels, or a small orchard.

But wheat prices had been dropping since 1861 when the import of wheat from the USA and Canada came in at the rate of over 23,000,000 cwt a year, rising to treble that amount in a few years. The price per quarter dropped from 74s 8d in 1855 to 41s 10d in 1865. Farmers were equally depressed. The price of bread (best 4 lb loaf) dropped from 11d in 1855 to 7d in 1865.

The growing millions connected with the industrial revolution demanded cheap bread; they were getting it, and there began an agricultural depression that was to cause great distress throughout the whole of England. In fact the time was to come, and very soon, when some lords of the manor would forego their rents in order that farms might survive. It only needed a couple of bad harvests, or an outbreak of murrain, and farmers were in great trouble.

Apart from the large farms and the smaller holdings the Duncombe Great Brickhill estate included an inn, a smithy, a schoolhouse, various shops, six 'lodges' and close on sixty cottages. The inn, the *Duncombe Arms*, with stables and 14 acres of 'old grass' was let for £55 per annum to John Linnell, who was also a butcher.[4] The rival institution, the *Red Lion* did not belong to the Duncombes.

The thatched smithy and its cottage near the *Duncombe Arms* was let for £5 – and a smithy still flourishes nearby.* It was described as 'thatched but in good repair' with a good garden and other premises, but all told it only covered 1 rood, 11 poles. There were two bakehouses, with cottages and stables – the one 'wanting repairs' let for £26 and the other 'new built' and with a couple of acres, for £14. The one opposite the parish hall is still in use. There

* 1975.
3 Winslow was probably the last.
4 It was sold in 1946, but still continues to bear the family arms on its sign.

was a general shop let at £5 which sold everything from candles to kettles, and Charlotte Saunders had a drapery and grocer's shop and three acres, just opposite the *Duncombe Arms*, for which she paid a yearly rent of £14.

An interesting item is the list of 'lodges', rather better class houses, let at £4 a year or more and where the higher servants of the manor usually lived. A still better house was rented by Thomas Chew who was the relieving officer for the Newport Board of Guardians, registrar of births and deaths, and government emigration agent. He had 'a good homestead, 2½ acres of arable and acre of old grass nearby and a good yard', for which he paid £23 10s a year. His cottage fronted the junction of the five roads at the south of the village so that his posters advocating the attractions of Canada or other colonies must have been seen by all. The Report mentions that as the part owner of some other cottages he had 'the liberty to get rushes out of the river for their repair'.

Another feature of the estate was that seven acres either side of the Soulbury road were devoted to 'Allotment Gardens' and a dozen smaller plots of about a rood or a quarter of an acre each were let here and there. The income from this total of twelve acres was over £40, about 17s per annum per rood. This was good for the landlord but it was also good for the labourer, as he could rent a plot of his own to dig. They continued up to 1960.

Turning to the cottages, the cheapest was let at £1 a year, but it was as the Report tersely states, 'In bad order'. There are several cottages listed as 'free', which presumably were occupied by the staff of the manor.

The rents of the other cottages were as follows:

At £1 10s per annum	1	At £3 10s per annum	4
At £2 or £2 2s per annum	4	At £4 or £4 4s per annum	7
At £2 8s, £2 10s or £2 12s per annum	20	At £5 or over per annum	6
At £3 per annum	16		

It will be seen that the average rent for the ordinary working-man's cottage was about 1s a week. Rents were somewhat dearer where the houses were blue slated or tiled, but the average was a thatched cottage, and many had roses around the door. They still have.

A few had a backyard pump, but these were usually shared, and there was normally a privy, but the Report ominously notes that two cottages let for £5 and £2 12s respectively, had no privy. One wonders how they managed. Perhaps they had agreeable neighbours and took turns at emptying the bucket which was the universal accessory.

Great Brickhill has still a dozen 17th century cottages, all of which are described in *RCHM*. Some are even 16th century, with great ingle-nooks and iron casements, and chamfered ceiling beams, but most of these have been restored and altered.

WATER EATON

Whatever might be the strength or power of the Duncombes in Great Brickhill, it was even more pronounced in Water Eaton. Of its 1,016 acres the Duncombes owned 894: in fact the only land and buildings not in their hands were the strips owned by the LNWR and the Grand Junction Canal, the *George Inn*, and the nearby Green and a few acres dedicated to the poor.

Nobody quite knew who owned the Green. It is not included in the Duncombe possessions in the Report though three thatched cottages standing on it are shown. In 1973 the Bletchley UDC reluctantly took formal possession of it.

The village or manor had a population of only 240 souls, and had changed little since the Civil War. It had neither school nor church, though there was a Methodist chapel and a small school was being thought about.[5] It looked to Fenny Stratford for all its amenities except two public houses at the crossroads and three small shops.

The Duncombe's received £1,571 in rents from Water Eaton of which the greater part came from the five large farms as follows:

Belgrove's	168 acres	£272
Cowcommon	277 acres	£335
Hammond's (Slad Farm)	114 acres	£155
Goodman's	98 acres	£165
Sowland's (Waterhall)	133 acres	£210

As in Great Brickhill there was plenty of 'old grass' on each farm,

---

5 The school was actually opened in 1873 in a small building near the canal wharf.

and still a fair amount of fallow. Most of the farm buildings were in tenable order but required spouting.

Quite as important as any of these farms was the Mill and Mill House. Both were 'in tenable repair, all blue slated having undergone recent additions . . . The Mill and House windows are bad, also the house window shutters, and the house requires spouting'. Fifty-eight acres, mostly 'old grass' went with the Mill, and the rent in all was £192 per annum.

Only a short distance from the mill race, and running parallel to it was the canal which before the coming of the railway had been a busy waterway, but now with declining freights and no passengers, the two wharves, one either side of the Mill road as it crosses the canal were not exactly prosperous. The one north of the road with its stables was rented by Mellor Colsall & Company for £21 and the one south of the road by John Whitehouse, with three acres for £11. Both are described as 'beer retailers, wharfingers and shopkeepers' in a contemporary directory. The wharves were united around 1870.

In the centre of the village, across the village green from the independent *George*, was the *Plough*, 'a Public House with Brewery, stables and other buildings' with 8 acres which was let for £30. Whilst the *George* was quite an historic building, the *Plough* had only been going about fifty years.[6]

The rest of the estate consisted of about forty cottages, mostly let at about 1s a week, but three of these had shops. 'Martha Grace had a blacksmith's shop etc.' near the *Plough*, for which she paid £3 a year. Mr Jonathan Young had 'a Shoemakers Shop, thatched low and very bad' along the Stoke Road, for which his rent was only £2 a year. As in Great Brickhill six acres were devoted to allotments, and these brought in a rent of £18 a year.

It was a very settled community mostly consisting of farm labourers. Their feet were ever in the clay, their heads were never in the stars.

BLETCHLEY

In Bletchley the Duncombes owned 418 acres with a rental of £632. It followed the patterns described above, but there is more mention of 'inferior thatch' and the need for rebuilding several

6 Around 1899 it was burnt down, and rebuilt nearby. It was again rebuilt around 1966.

cottages. One item of interest is the description of the *Swan*, Shenley Road, as 'Public House not in good condition. The Wood Barn very dilapidated and requires to be rebuilt as well as the Cowshed and Piggery. The Tenant would pay more if it was put in order.' The rent was £7 per annum.

FENNY STRATFORD

In Fenny Stratford the Duncombes owned 151 acres; the principal part was the Manor Farm between Aylesbury Street and the river. 'The House is in fair repair except the kitchen floor which requires relaying. The Piggeries are close to the house and ought to be removed on account of the smell. The Cowhouse is good, barn sufficient, but a new shed required on the east side, with a shed for horses, etc.' For the 103 acres Thomas Hammond paid £280 rent.

A pregnant comment comes when G. O. Clarke is shown as renting 3 acres just off Aylesbury Street near the canal where the GPO Repeater Station now stands, for £30 10s. 'Mr. Clarke makes large quantities of bricks, etc. Puts up all his own buildings. A fresh arrangement is required.' This was land near the Watling Street and the Grand Junction Canal, and he had his own wharf. He already had since 1819 a brickworks and lime kiln on the site of the present Pulman's Press, and had a wharf of his own just off the Watling Street. He was one of Fenny's most business-like citizens, and when the Duncombes came to negotiate 'a fresh arrangement' with him, the argument must have been very determined on both sides.

In all, the large farms in Great Brickhill and Water Eaton, well over a thousand acres, were let at about 30s an acre. In Fenny, Manor Farm was let at about £3 an acre. The hundred or more cottages were let at about 1s a week.

The Duncombes held a few more acres in north Bucks, 400 acres in Warwickshire, 1,300 acres in Staffordshire, and even more in Lincolnshire.[7] From these other estates there was £1,514 in rents. In addition the Duncombes had Great Brickhill Manor in hand, as well as 122 acres of woodland, and still a few manorial dues, so that all told the income of Sir Philip Duncombe Paunce-

---

7 The Duncombe Buckinghamshire estates were enlarged by more purchases in the 1870s, but from 1946 onwards sales mainly for Bletchley's housing needs reduced the estate to about 600 acres.

E

fort Duncombe in 1863 could not have been less than £8,000, equal to about £100,000 today, and income tax was only 6d in the £.

The £8,000 a year was gross. What was left after outgoings was a much less charming picture. By the custom of the manor the lord of the manor was responsible for the church and school in the parish, for pensions for many aged workers or widows, for the drainage, repairs and maintenance of every farm or cottage on the estate, subscriptions or donations to every good cause that raised an appeal, and a dozen other outgoings such as management, minor roads, bridges and even signposting.

We have not the details of these for the Duncombe estates, but we have the figures for a century for the Beds and Bucks estates of the Dukes of Bedford. The outgoings on these were formidable. Indeed the time was shortly coming when owing to the agricultural depression the estates would show losses for years in succession.

The ninth Duke was very frank about all this, and in 1897 published his book *A Great Agricultural Estate* giving the position in great detail. These estates in Beds and Bucks were ten times as large as the Duncombe estates, in all about 30,000 acres, and the average gross annual income for the period 1856–75 was £51,300, but after the outgoings mentioned above the net annual income was £9,767. This however dropped sharply during the next decade with the continuing agricultural depression.[8]

If we apply the same criteria to the Duncombe estates we find that the Duncombes' net income would be about £2,000 a year, but as the agricultural depression deepened, and farmers sought and had to have a relaxation of rents, the net income turned into a loss some years.

When young Philip Duncombe came of age in 1869 the senior trustee may well have said to him: 'If you want to retain the estates, Philip, you'll have to marry an heiress'.

But good years or bad, neither the Duncombes nor other leading squires failed to pay the pensions, to support the charities,

8 The Duke however had great estates in Bloomsbury which were much more profitable. Disraeli in 1878 writing to Queen Victoria observed that 'The Duke of Bedford is the wealthiest of your majesty's subjects: his income absolutely exceeding £300,000 a year.' His Grace considered accumulation was the only pleasure of life, and he never retired to rest satisfied unless he could trace that he had saved that day, at least a five pound note.

churches and schools.* They had little help from the Nonconformists who had their own chapels, but the schools were greatly
helped from the rates.

The lords of the manor have played a very great part in the
history of England and often a decisive part in their particular
parishes. In their declining years of influence, whatever their
difficulties, they seldom ratted on their obligations – obligations
so heavy that few other landowners or industrial companies
could have borne and remained solvent.

Whilst the lord of the manor by the end of the century could
see his net income decline to a quarter of what it had been in his
grandfather's day, and the farmer was reduced to a co-labourer
on his own farm, the state of the farm worker remained practically unaltered, that is to say at almost the lowest possible subsistence level. Wages rose from 10s a week in 1850–60 to 11s a
week in 1860–70, and about 13s a week from 1870 until the end of
the century.

It could well be asked how any family could exist on 11s a week,
even if we add a shilling or two for the earnings of another member of the family. Naturally no such family ever kept household
accounts, but from facts that filter down through grandmothers'
tales and recollections when I was young, we may not be too far
wrong if we cast a rough weekly budget like this:[9]

Rent	1s 0d
Bread and flour	7s 6d
Meat	2s 6d
Tea, sugar and butter	1s 7d
Soap, starch and candles	4d
Clothing and shoes	9d
Beer	4d
Church	½d
	————
	14s 0½d

---

* Great Brickhill Church was restored and improved in 1867, chiefly at the cost of Sir
  Philip Duncombe, and the school was enlarged in 1886.
9 See also Rev David Davies' *The Care of Labourers in Husbandry*, 1795, and Eden's
  The State of the Poor, 1797.

Current prices were:

Beer	3d a gallon	Smock	3s 3d
Beef	3d a lb	Stays	7s 0d
Butter	6½d a lb	Candles	6d per lb
Sugar	6d a lb	Shirt	2s 8d

Milk and cheese the labourer may have had in small quantities as perquisites from the farm, and possibly wood for firing, but if milk was bought it was 1d a gallon.

It was the unbudgetable items that shook the family: the doctor's or mid-wife's bills for sickness and confinements, the funerals, the breakages or the imperative need for a wedding gift for one of the many, many relatives. Any one of these could send a family into debt – and the undertaker's bills were usually paid last.

Often of course there would be sons earning a bit, and daughters would go out into service at possibly £8 10s a year with food and lodging found. To go 'into service' was a most honourable occupation. The Duncombes and their like, most of the local parsons, doctors and innkeepers, had staffs of up to a dozen domestics, and the average shopkeeper would employ a couple or more. Usually servants were fiercely loyal to their employers, and when they met off duty they would take rank according to the status of the family they served. To be an under-parlourmaid at Stowe, Wakefield Lodge or Woburn Abbey was to have a standing infinitely above that of a barmaid or a farmer's dairymaid.

It will be seen that there was no disaster margin, nothing for the doctor, for children's pocket money, for house furniture or decoration without getting into debt. It needed the harvest bonus to get matters straight.

THE DOMESTIC SCENE

'Happy folks have no history' is an old adage with a lot of truth in it, and so it is that we know little about housewives and their daily round in our villages and small towns.

When a girl reached her middle teens, or maybe a little later, her own sense of what was now important led her to dress with a little more care and daintiness: nature supplied the sparkling eyes and roses in the cheeks, and before long many boy-meets-girl situations arose – often just after church service, or at an occasional dance, or along 'the rabbit run'. In every small town and village there was a recognised walk on Sunday evenings – usually between the church and the local, where the boys in gangs and the girls in couples would parade. It was a very useful and venerable superstition that a girl was perfectly safe if she went out with another girl. The jostling, the giggles, the more silent assessments went on, and at some future date the girl introduced the young man of her choice to her family. This was often a very decisive step, for the young man, often from a neighbouring village within walking range, was now an accepted visitor, and 'had his legs under the table'.

The girls knew that the principal reason for their existence was the reproduction of the species and they were often willing assistants. But it was the era of the strictest Victorian morality. The influence of church and chapel was great: permissiveness was unthought of; and if a girl did slip, the church was there to put a ceremonial blessing on what had already happened in the hay loft. With no contraceptives there could be no concealment, and the justices had their own way of dealing with a treacherous lover. So they were married and set up house in a cottage – at a shilling a week rent – smaller than the average home of today, with no damp course, no running water, no gas or electricity, no room for an echo even, but a lot of hope and confidence.

Passing the years quickly, by the time the wife was 30 there might well be half a dozen children. This in a two-bedroomed cottage led to a certain amount of overcrowding.

Because Queen Victoria, who was married in 1841, had nine children, many thought that this was the appropriate and even Christian size of a family, and whilst infantile mortality reduced the number by a third, the family with six or seven children was not uncommon in any village or town. Life was an alternation of pregnancy and nursing, and hard work all the time. My own grandmother on my father's side had twelve children, of whom two died young, and my maternal great-grandmother gave birth to thirteen at Newport Pagnell, of whom four died young. Industrious and curious as I was, I never completed the family tree to anybody's satisfaction, for the survivors all married and produced about eighty children between them. Grandmothers rejoiced over their grandlings: it was absolute proof that their lives had been worth while. Grandfathers were more reticent.

It was a tremendous birthrate – an era of great productivity.

Meanwhile the wife had embarked on a routine that was to last her all her life. Monday was washing day: possibly the hardest working day of the week though all were hard. Up betimes to get the copper lit and the kettle and saucepans boiling on the cast-iron grate. The great wooden trough or wash tub was then filled and in the cleanest water the few silks and the many cottons would be washed; men's shirts of tough material would have to be scrubbed. Somewhere in the sequence, sheets or counterpanes were washed and wrung out. From time to time the wash-tub or trough would be topped up, and in this final blue-brown mixture socks would be washed.

Now all had to be hung out to dry – but if the weather was wet – and it rained one wash day in every three at least, the washing was draped about all over the house to dry.

Every day had its back-breaking routine, but the old song *'Twas on a Sunday morning* made even the most repetitive chores sound romantic. All days were darning and mending days. The amount of darning was prodigious. All socks and stockings were made of wool and since walking was the only means of progress holes as large as small potatoes could appear in an incredibly short time.

In her spare time the mother, and the grandmother too, would make lace, or straw plait. Daughters, even five-year-olds, helped too.

Sunday came again, with all the children to Sunday school and church – three times a day. Sunday dinner was often the only day when meat was part of the midday meal, but nearly every cottage had a hen run and a pig sty. Egg and bacon for breakfast was so definitely English that it was unremarkable. Historians rarely mention it.

Did any of these large families ever learn to read and write or cast accounts? Well, some did, as we shall see in another chapter.

8 Chapels and Churches

IN spite of the setback that Nonconformists had at Fenny Stratford in 1710 when Browne Willis bought up their chapel and closed it, there soon began a great period for the dissenting movements, and had they been united they might well have become as strong and as powerful as the official Church of England.

But dissenters never could unite and before long in north Bucks we get not only the Quakers with their meeting houses and the Baptists with their chapels, which we have previously noticed, but also

> Particular Baptists
> Independents or Congregationalists
> Wesleyans
> Wesleyan Methodists
> Primitive Methodists
> and (later) the Salvation Army

Of all these the Baptists were the strongest. They had chapels at Stony Stratford (with a very active minister and a manse), Loughton, Great Brickhill (1812), Stoke Hammond, Newport Pagnell and other places.

The Baptist movement was greatly fostered by the dominating and energetic figure of John Heywood who was the pastor of the chapel at Potterspury from 1740 to 1778, and who preached in Stony Stratford and Towcester and a dozen villages in between. According to the Baptist records:[1]

> 'After preaching at Pury in the morning, he would deliver an evening lecture at Stony Stratford or Towcester, or some of the neighbouring villages. On these pastoral excursions he rode an old grey horse, generally, with his waistcoat open, and the long ends of his white cravat flying in the wind. His loyalty, love of literature, simplicity of heart and eccentricity

1 Quoted in Hyde and Markham's *History of Stony Stratford* p146.

of manners attracted the notice of the neighbouring nobility; the Duke of Grafton condescended to call upon him: and Earl Temple frequently invited him to Stowe . . . Soon after the accession of George III in 1760 the dissenting ministers went up to the throne to offer an address of congratulation. Mr. Heywood went too, and was recognised by Earl Temple, remaining in conversation with him whilst the address was being presented. Just as the King was about to leave, Heywood called out, "Stop, please your Majesty, stop. I have come all the way from Potterspury to kiss your Majesty's hand, and I hope I shall be allowed the honour". The King, with all that excellence of disposition for which he was remarkable, turned round and presented his hand. Mr. Heywood gave it two or three hearty kisses, adding "God bless your Majesty, and I hope you will make a good King." '

The King's reception of Heywood of Potterspury and his fellow Nonconformist ministers was outward and visible proof that Nonconformity was not only legally permissible but also socially acceptable, and during the next century the Nonconformists grew in numbers and power until they became the conscience of powerful Liberal governments. Gone were the days when Browne Willis or any other lord of the manor could deliberately pull down a chapel and persuade his fellow landowners never to allow another chapel to be built in the parish.

Naturally all such dissenters had to have Biblical justification for their dissent. It was there in abundance. From Baptism to Prayers for the Dead there were texts enough to justify polygamy, monasticism, absolute poverty and belief in the Devil and all his works. Each little sect, or large sect, had its own chosen passages and texts that required no lawyer to interpret. Each was happy that it had found the true path to salvation.

For centuries the people of England had wanted a direct appeal to God without the mediation of priests garbed like the King of Sheba, uttering the sonorous Latin rumblings of the Roman church. For centuries such attempts had been persecuted – now the people were free – free to combine in faith, hope and charity as they saw it, free to appoint their own ministers or to have none at all.

But the Nonconformists still suffered under great disabilities. No marriages could take place in chapels, and all births and deaths had to be entered in the church parish registers. Added to this, the great universities of Oxford, Cambridge and Durham were virtually closed to Nonconformists. To this ban a formidable reply was made by the remarkable Bull family of Newport Pagnell. Here around 1767 William Bull, the Congregational pastor and friend of Cowper and Newton, opened one of the first dissenting academies in England, and in 1792 another was opened by him at Olney, which lasted twenty-two years. The Rev William Cole, the Bletchley diarist, whom we have quoted freely in our first volume, looked with great disfavour on Bull and his projects. He calls Bull 'an impertinent coxcomb' and describes him as 'a tall, thin, pale faced Man, with a starched and formal Gait, a White wig combed into nice Ringlets, with a large cocked Hat and a Cane in his Hand'. Cole, needless to add, regarded all dissenters, under whatever name they adopted, as 'Enemies of the Established Church' (pp109–10). The Newport academy however continued in strength under three generations of Bulls until 1850 when the first Nonconformist colleges were opened at Oxford and Cambridge.

It was not just that Newport and Olney were places where young Nonconformists could be trained for the ministry during the week, it was also that every Sunday the 'undergraduates' visited and preached at all the villages around. Sometimes they rode: more often they walked. No local chapel, however small its numbers, was without a circuit preacher or a visiting student preacher. The zeal and honesty of these young men, and their growing knowledge of the Scriptures and of the oratorical arts, were important factors in the great growth of Nonconformity both in Bucks and Beds, where there was already a dissenting tradition going back to the Civil War and earlier. Newport Pagnell became a national centre of Nonconformity.

We must now have a quick look at some of the chapels in action.

THE BAPTISTS IN FENNY STRATFORD

The history of the Baptist chapel at Stony Stratford has been fully written up in the *History of Stony Stratford*. To parallel this we now have available (through the kindness of Mr Ron Staniford of Bletchley) the *Church Book & Register of the Particular Baptist Church at Fenny Stratford* which begins with the following:

'As this Book is intended to shew to our Posterity (and perhaps Generations to come) the beginning of the above Church, we shall begin where the Lord first began with us, to incline us to hold social meetings for Praying, Singing and reading the word of God; this was in the Winter of 1797, and on Sunday night, December 26th, 1797, Rev. Mr. Sift of Woburn (Beds) preached at Bletchley (a village near this place) at a House in the occupation of Mr. Holton, the house was duly registered . . .'

During the next four years meetings were held in various houses or in a barn at Fenny Stratford, 'many standing without'. The barn in Aylesbury Street was 'excessive cold' and the wind often blew the candles and rushlights out. It belonged to William Linnell, a prosperous baker who was the real leader of the chapel. In 1800 we get the following:

'At Bletchley & Eaton, things bore a very heavy Aspect, for in the Room where the Preaching was (but not at the very time) the Enemies of God's cause got leave to Dance there. It was not right to receive the preaching of the Glorious Gospel under a Roof where Dancing was held.'

The next year it was decided to build a church; possibly this decision was aided by the fact that:

'Our enemies who loved Darkness rather than Light have several times in the dark daubed the Styles and Gates we got over or passed through, with Night Dung and even thrown Stones.'

There seems to have been a long tradition of smearing your enemies' gates or stiles with dung to express disgust. It goes back to the days of Browne Willis or earlier. A local tribal custom!

In 1805 the first chapel (31ft × 24ft) was erected. It cost £100 and the Church Roll included eighteen names, but there were children in addition. The services were nearly always conducted by students from Bull's academy at Newport Pagnell, who were paid 'seven shillings a Sabbath'. By 1808 there were twenty-one full members but in 1809 two persons were expelled 'because they refused to obey the moral law as binding on Christians'. As one goes through this church book one is struck by two outstanding impressions. The first, that whilst the greater part of the brotherhood were poor men and women, with only an occasional prosperous shopkeeper to find a few pounds for a very special occasion, they managed to pay their way and the preacher, and to keep the chapel clean and tidy.

The second main impression is their stern censoriousness towards one another. Time and time again enquiries are made into the morals of this or that member – and usually this self-imposed discipline was accepted by all. There was a great deal of intolerance; members were brought before the church accused of immoral behaviour of many kinds, and some names were struck off almost as soon as they were put on.

A few years later in 1815 they had a permanent pastor, Mr James Crudge, but this was not a happy solution, even though the membership had risen to sixty-five, for in May 1826 we read:

'Mr. Charles Gurney (a Member of the Church) made statements to Mr. Linnell, one of the Officers of the Church, concerning Mr. James Crudge the Pastor which were of an immoral nature; and many of the Members believed said statements and in consequence thereof a Letter was addressed to Mr. Crudge dated or delivered to him at his House 30th May 1826 which was worded exactly thus:

"Brother Crudge

It grieves us much to thus attending to our Painful Duty and we know not what to do. If you wish to see either or both of us before another Sabbath we are free of access to consult at any place within five miles of or at your House: we have heard so much as we think the best way for your future welfare and the Probability of being Pastor to some other Church will be to give us Notice of leaving: for if this subject is brought before the Church we think no good but much harm may arise therefrom: but we wish not to Dictate and think no harm to Intimate.

We remain

Your Grieved Brethren

Wm. Linnell ⎫
            ⎬ Deacons"
Robt. Ping ⎭

'The Letter was accompanied with the statements in writing of what was said against his moral Character and Certifying that the said statements were signed and would be verified

on oath if necessary. Mr. Crudge thought proper not to reply as to Particulars but wrote as follows:
(Resignation Letter), June 4th, 1826.

"My Christian Friends,

As my Ministry among you has been rendered peculiarly useful, I felt encouraged in my arduous employment and hoped to have spent the remnant of my days with you, but as many ill-founded and injurious reports have been fabricated and propagated to the no small injury of my moral character and especially as many minds appear to be prejudiced against me I herewith tender my Resignation and shall not consider myself any longer your Pastor when three months from the present period shall have expired.

I am, Yours faithfully,
J. Crudge."

'After "a very secret ballot" 50 voted for Crudge's removal and 14 for his continuance. This was made known to Mr. Crudge "in a friendly way". He then sent on the 18th June his "conditional Resignation Letter":

"My Christian Friends,

I understand from one of the Officers of the Church, that you not only accept my Resignation but that you wish that my ministry amongst you to cease at the close of the next Sabbath.

Perhaps there are many Members of the Church who are not aware that when I accepted the Pastoral Office here it was upon these Conditions, 'That if at any future period we should be under painful necessity of separating 3 months Notice should be given'. Nevertheless for the sake of peace, my labours amongst you shall cease at the time you specify provided I am paid up for the two months and that the two Guineas that were deficient in the last Quarterage be made up: but if you refuse to advance for the two months I shall expect to occupy the pulpit till they are expired.

I am, Yours respectfully,
J. Crudge."

	£	s	d
Deficient last Qr.	2	2	0
Present Qr.	18	2	0
Two months	12	1	4
	£32	5	4"

'Same day (as what we call the Resignation Letter was received) we called a Church Meeting and it was agreed on as Mr. Crudge intended leaving peacefully we would if possible comply with his conditions and we did so accordingly and paid him the £32 5s. 4d. and he left us and the Town in peace (after Prayer with several of the Members) on the 17th July, 1826.'

The record for the next few years seems to alternate records of baptisms with records of suspension, dismissal or exclusion. Some of the dismissals (and a kindly word this at times) were of members who had emigrated to the USA. Most of the exclusions were for non-attendance or for 'grossly immoral conduct'. We are never told what the latter was, it may have been something really immoral or just taking a pint at the local. In spite of the high exclusion rate church membership grew. In 1836 sixty attended a church meeting, so it is fairly safe to assume membership which included several persons from villages around, had risen to about eighty, a figure at which it continued for some years.

But peace could not last long, and in March 1841 Gibbs records that at the Lent Assizes at Aylesbury there was 'a trial amongst Fenny Stratford Dissenters, being a quarrel about the Chapel Lamp', and we now have the disrespectful comment of Dr Bradbrook who wrote 'in July 1841 the dissenters at Fenny Stratford divided into two sections as a result of a quarrel. They are distinguished by the very choice appelations of "the Potato Party" and "the Cauliflower Party".'

In May, 1842 we have the solemn record in the Church Book: 'The Baptist Church at Fenny Stratford having been for some time past in a very unsociable state and the disorganised condition of the Society such as to render all discipline and order impossible, it was resolved to dissolve the existing body and to remodel the Church. It was resolved that the choice of persons should be left with Mr. Davis the Pastor and that these should constitute the New Baptist Church in Fenny Stratford.'

The purge probably took place, but the records are silent on the point. The church record book ends in 1862, and the succeeding one is missing.

In 1892 the old tiny meeting house 'being ruinous and in decay' a new church was built in Aylesbury Street with seating for 600 – the Spurgeon Baptist Memorial Church, which from that day to this has given spiritual comfort to thousands.

It is important to realise that the Particular Baptists were not so unlike other dissenting groups. All had the strict Puritan conscience, nearly all were temperance reformers, and nearly all supported the Liberal party in civil politics. They were the Nonconformist conscience of England, and they knew it.

THE WESLEYANS

The Wesleyans, and Methodists, as we shall see, due possibly to the activity of John Wesley himself in these parts, began to win more and more support and there were soon Wesleyan chapels at Fenny Stratford (1813),[2] Bletchley (1866), Simpson, Water Eaton, Woughton, Newton Longville, Great and Little Brickhill, Stoke Hammond and other places. Wesleyan Methodist places of worship were established at Wavendon and Hogsty End (later Woburn Sands), Bow Brickhill (1840), Fenny Stratford (1809) and Simpson (1842). Methodist or Primitive Methodist chapels were erected at Fenny Stratford (1866), Stony Stratford, Wavendon (both in the village and at Hogsty End), Bow Brickhill and Soulbury. Bow Brickhill somehow managed to have three chapels at one time, but it was then actually a larger community than Bletchley.[3] It would be an exhausting exercise to describe the theological differences between these shades of Methodism.

The Wesley brothers, Charles and John, who preached all over England, had a particular influence in Bedfordshire and Buckinghamshire. John Wesley, according to his diary, paid three visits to Stony Stratford. The first on 30 July 1777, was in a large barn,

---

2 It was replaced in 1911 when a larger building was erected in Bletchley Road. The old chapel became a cinema, and has recently been demolished.
3 Musson and Craven, 1853.

arranged by Richard Canham and others, but it was not large enough to contain the congregation. The barn continued as the Wesleyan chapel until 1844 when a new chapel was built in Silver Street. This chapel still stands, but is now unused, and may soon be demolished.[4] Four months later John came again, to a large and attentive congregation, but he wrote, 'I fear they received little good, for they need no repentance'. Two years later he came again, preaching under an elm tree in the Market Square which stands to this day. The town's affection for the old tree is such that although it is now rotten within and pollarded above it has survived all efforts to remove it for parking space – which is very significant when we remember how chapels themselves have been demolished.

When Wolverton began to develop as the new railway centre, the L.N.W. Railway directors as we have seen were very keen to raise the moral standards of the town, and whilst they did much for the Anglican church they were by no means averse to helping other denominations.

As early as 1839 Methodist services were held in local homes, with Mr Grills as the local preacher. In 1842 this group supported by a petition signed by ninety-five Wolvertonians persuaded the company to let them use rent free a large room near the canal for services and a Sunday school. The company went further and provided the pulpit. Anglicans and Wesleyan Methodists got on well together, for the Rev George Weight, whom we have previously mentioned, entertained the dissenting Sunday school teachers and the choir to supper at the vicarage from time to time.

But the Wolverton Wesleyan Methodists lacked a permanent pastor, and in 1864 we find the superintendent of the Newport Pagnell Circuit reporting that such a growing community was ill served by only having visiting preachers. The message was understood, and by 1870 Wolverton had its own Wesleyan chapel with 280 sittings and a regular pastor. They went from strength to strength, and indeed it could be said that they had more active members (ie, willing to work in and for the chapel) than any other chapel or church in north Bucks.

4 See Hyde and Markham's *History of Stony Stratford* for a précis of the legal documents covering the Wesleyan properties. John Wesley also preached at Little Brickhill in 1778 and 1784.

CONGREGATIONALISTS AND INDEPENDENTS

Meanwhile Independent or Congregational chapels had been built at Stony Stratford (which had a minister and a manse), Great Linford, Bow Brickhill (1810), Whaddon and other places.

Newport Pagnell has a history of dissent dating from 1659 when John Gibbs was ejected from the vicarage for refusing to admit the whole parish to communion, and founded the Independent Church.[5] Later on chapels were erected in Newport by the Particular Baptists, the Wesleyans, the Primitive Methodists and the Society of Friends which served a wider area than just the town.

In short almost every town and large village had a chapel or two. They were usually small often ugly, warehouse types of buildings with painted texts on the walls, a dominant pulpit, umbrella stands on the sides of pews and often a cold clammy atmosphere. Very few had permanent resident ministers. But whilst many of the Church of England's rectors and vicars enjoyed their good livings, their hunting and sometimes their pluralities, the underpaid preachers of the Nonconformist sects brought in more and more converts to their chapels especially from the under-privileged classes – excepting always the old ladies in church almshouses, or those who hoped for admission in the future.

HYMNS

All this was accompanied by much hymn singing. In fact one of the great trends of the period was the growing popularity of hymn singing with a recorder or an organ, as contrasted with the nasal intoning or singing of the Psalms. Almost everybody with a poetic quirk turned to hymnwriting. John Wesley published twenty-three collections of hymns between 1737 and 1786, and his brother Charles is reputed to have written over 6,000 hymns of which possibly 400 are still in use.

At Olney those superb friends, the gentle and melancholic William Cowper and the former slave trader John Newton, curate of Olney, produced the Olney hymns in 1771–72. No voice can tell, no pen can write the lasting appeal and comfort that came from the pen of the stricken poet, or of his adventurous friend.

---

5 T. P. Bull, *Rise of the Independent Church of Newport Pagnell.* By 1850 there were four resident Nonconformist ministers in Newport.

Hymns are light, duty-free baggage and any traveller on the eternal road could pick them up with ease. Only a year or two ago the Royal Scots Dragoon Guards played an instrumental version of John Newton's *Amazing Grace* which topped the record charts, and another recording with Judy Collins had a world-wide welcome.

Often the words of hymns had an authority that was only surpassed by the Holy Word, and when Mrs Alexander wrote in 1848 that ever popular *All things bright and beautiful*, the third verse:

> 'The rich man in his castle
> The poor man at his gate
> God made them high or lowly
> And ordered their estate.'

was not only accepted by the Duke of Buckingham with his palace at Stowe and thousands of acres, but also by the lowliest agricultural worker, as plain proof that things were as God meant them to be.

The Quakers sat and thought, the Catholics continued with the age long rituals, the Church of England had its set pieces in the Book of Common Prayer which included the Psalms and the lugubrious Litany, but the Dissenters discovered that praise to God could be congregationally vocal and congregationally enjoyable. But it was not until the Salvation Army established its first barracks in Fenny Stratford around 1880 that the jaunty joyful tunes really came in. They held four services on a Sunday and a prayer meeting with plenty of singing every evening, and their band with the unusual tambourines added a new joy on the way to salvation.

It is impossible to overrate the influence of hymns of all kinds on the people of north Bucks. Mothers sang them to their cradled offspring, men would sing them walking from Deanshanger to Wolverton works. But it was a later generation which took one of the saddest and most premonitory hymns, *Abide with me*, to be the preliminary quietener for the FA Cup final at Wembley.

But split and divided as the Nonconformists were, they found two points of unity. We have already mentioned the great hymns which were adopted by all sects except perhaps the Quakers, and in politics all chapels banded together often openly and aggressively to support the radical-liberal movement which had as its aims not only a new great reform act that would give them all the vote, but also the disestablishment of the Church of England.

It was from our great Nonconformist families like the Canhams and the Woollards in Stony Stratford, the Bulls in Newport Pagnell, the Linnells in Fenny Stratford, usually traders or merchants, and seldom the squirearchy, that some of the power came to return Liberal members like Sir Harry Verney to Parliament so often.

THE CHURCH OF ENGLAND

Every advance made by the Nonconformists was at the expense of the Church of England, and the Church was slow to counter this. But the Oxford Movement, 1840 onwards, helped to shrug off the langour and the lethargy to some degree, and urged the return to pre-Reformation beliefs, practices and ceremonial.

In 1845 the Evangelical Alliance was founded at Liverpool with the view of promoting unity among all Protestant denominations against 'Romanism and infidelity'. This 'low church' movement gained much ground locally, and as we have seen men like the Rev George Weight of Wolverton gave it practical force.

Later in the century the High Church movement with its tendency towards ritualism gained more ground locally. The creed still affirmed belief in the Holy Catholic Church, and the dividing line between Anglo-Catholic and Roman Catholic practices became blurred, but however indistinct it was, the Rev O. P. Henly, 'Perpetual Curate' of Wolverton St Mary's (Stony Stratford) stepped well beyond it in 1905–09. The Bishop of Oxford felt bound to act and in 1909 the Rev Henly was forcibly barred from his church and ejected from his vicarage. He later joined the Roman Catholics. All this was national news and a great shock to the locality.[6] But another shock came five years later (August 1914) when the Rev C. H. Stenson, curate of St Giles', Stony Stratford, became a Roman Catholic too. The little Catholic church of St Francis de Sales at Wolverton gained many recruits about this time and became a growing force in what had hitherto been a Protestant area.

Added to all this a community of teaching nuns purchased

6 For the full story of this see *The Nineteen Hundreds* pp59–63.

Thornton Hall in 1909 from the Harris family for a Girls College. Local Catholics trebled their numbers in a single generation.

These were not the only questions that troubled the Church of England, for in 1909 the newly appointed vicar of Stantonbury, the Rev Newman Guest, an Irishman with a keen sense of the dramatic, discovered that his church of St James had never been licensed for marriages. When the church was built by the L.N.W. Railway in 1860 it was simply assumed that it took over the parish responsibilities of the ancient parish church at Stanton Low a mile away, and by 1909 434 marriages had taken place at St James.

One Sunday evening in March, just after evening service, the Rev Newman Guest announced that about 800 of his parishioners were 'living in sin' and that their children were illegitimate. Local consternation can be imagined. Some of the 'sinners' were respected grandmothers over 60 years of age, and no one could be more upset than a grandmother when told by the vicar that she had been 'living in sin' all her married life.

Naturally something had to be done, and three months later the Home Secretary made a provisional order deeming all the marriages to be valid, and freeing past ministers and present churchwardens from the possibility of enormous penalties. Since then there have been few illegitimate children in New Bradwell.

Yet in spite of all the divisions in the Church of England, in spite of the even greater divisions among the chapels, religion was still the greatest force in England. Pastors were beloved by their flocks and church and chapel attendances were never greater. Then came the First World War and the spread of searching doubt, fostered by scientific enquiry. But there was also the effect of Sunday games and the 'desecration of the Sabbath'. The advent of the radio also helped. A more subtle cause was inflation that reduced the value of fixed stipends.

CHURCH LIVINGS
In volume I we have seen how as a result of the Enclosure Award the rector of Bletchley received about 500 acres in Bletchley and 100 acres in Fenny Stratford, which made it one of the richest livings in Bucks. In 1907 the living was estimated to be worth £460 a year plus the vicarage, fees and the Easter offering.

Passenham too had a net yearly value of £460. Wavendon was even richer, for although the glebe was only about 85 acres, the total income was about £495 plus the extras noted above.

On the other hand, such large parishes needed a curate and the rector or vicar paid him about £80 a year, possibly more. Here and there were pluralists, parsons holding two livings, but Hanslope and Castlethorpe combined only produced £180 a year plus extras, and the combination of Old Bradwell and Tattenhoe produced just over £140. Still poorer were parishes like Fenny Stratford, Old Wolverton and Willen, where the total income of the priest was rarely more than £120.

In short, before the First World War the average income of a rector or vicar was about £250 a year compared with the railwayman's average of £80 and the agricultural labourer's £50.

But by 1919 the artisan was up to £150 a year whilst stipends had not increased and the cost of living had gone up considerably. Only the parsons with private incomes could afford to live in the style of their predecessors. The tendency accelerated during the Second World War and particularly during the last decade. Today the skilled artisan has completely surpassed the parson in his standard of living, and some, get twice as much as an average Bishop.

As for Nonconformist parsons, the £80 to £100 of the 19th century only very slightly increased, and recruits to any sort of ministry became harder and harder to find. Yet as the emoluments decreased in value, so the standard of service seemed to rise, and our local records from 1888 on are full of references to ministers of the Gospel who gave so much devoted service not only to their parishes but also to local councils, hospital boards and so on. We were fortunate in having a succession of really good and able men who served God and the community with unfailing love and zeal.

It has been quite impossible to give the records of more than a few churches and chapels in our area since say 1840. There were so many forces at work, so many new churches and chapels created, and sadly quite a few historic old ones which decayed beyond repair or were sold to become warehouses or even cinemas, there were so very many changes of 'persona', that even in one generation a church could present three different faces to its congregation. Perhaps greatest of all the changes has been the decline of the great tensions between church and chapel and the successful beginning of the ecumenical movement. But all this I must leave to future historians for at the moment it is still the subject of debate and of intense active change.

9 Schools in the 19th century

EDUCATION in north Bucks in the 19th century might not appear to be a subject out of which great history might come for there was no local public school or grammar school with centuries of history, apart perhaps from the struggling Royal Latin School at Buckingham, and the creation of St Paul's College in Stony Stratford in 1863.

Yet it is this area which produces the enchanting story of 'Sister Dora' and the Doll's House, and which turned the Woolstones from unlettered villages to one of the most interesting educational areas in north Buckinghamshire. By contrast it was in Stony Stratford that Charles Dickens spotted a local dancing master and caricatured him in *Bleak House*.

As we have seen in Volume I, p233 *seq*, by 1750 there were schools (church, charity or endowed), at Milton Keynes, Stony Stratford, Beachampton, Wavendon, Broughton, Great Linford, Stoke Hammond, Soulbury and Bletchley, but by 1840 the value of the endowments, charities, or even church contributions had about halved in value. Schoolmasters and mistresses whose predecessors had been happy on £40 a year a century earlier, now found their position deteriorating slowly though a few became field surveyors or assessors to farmers. At Milton Keynes in 1850 the schoolmaster was also a sieve-maker, and had to endure the competition of another sieve-maker in the same village. Others were parish clerks, or organists – anything to make both ends meet.

In 1815 a National (Church of England) school was established in Fenny Stratford (see Volume I, p236), but the schoolmaster was supposed to live on a salary of 10s a week plus 6d per week for a few extra pupils if he could collect the fees. He couldn't. So the headmaster resigned and could not be replaced by anyone even meagrely qualified. Simpson had had a Board school since 1811, but this was scarcely flourishing.

There were no schools in many other villages, but by 1837

Great Brickhill had a Free school, in 1838 Newton Longville had a National school, and in 1840 Little Brickhill had a National school with about forty pupils.

Something had to be done even though many were of the same opinion as Lord Melbourne, Prime Minister, who in 1840 said bluntly to Queen Victoria, 'I don't know, Ma'am, why they make all this fuss about education; none of the Pagets can read or write, and they get on well enough.'[1] It was Philip Duncombe, lord of the manor of Great Brickhill, and the local parson, the Rev H. Foulis, who set things in motion by calling a public meeting in the National schoolroom in Fenny in October 1839 which resolved:

'That it is expedient to establish in this place a Day and Sunday School for the benefit of the Parishes of Fenny Stratford, Simpson, Bletchley, and Water Eaton, on the system of and in connection with the National Society.'

Duncombe and Foulis immediately promised an annual subscription of £10 each, the local clergy contributed their guineas, and soon £50 was gathered in, together with a donation from the Rev Foulis of £10 for a lending library. Very soon the revived National school was opened in the High Street at Fenny with about seventy boys and thirty girls as scholars. Another National school was opened at Bletchley with thirty scholars.

At Wolverton there was a sudden upsurge in educational facilities in 1839 when the London and Birmingham Railway decided that their new town just had to have schools, so they built a combined block of British, Endowed and Infants schools a stone's throw away from the great engine shed.[2] The master of the British school (sixty boys and sixty girls) received £100 a year plus coals and a house: the mistresses of the Girls and Infants received £40 and £30, again with coals and residence. These were superb rates of pay, and Wolverton was never short of teachers.

Soon after this National schools were established at Willen 1847) and Stoke Hammond (1844) with about twenty pupils each. By 1844 both Newport Pagnell and Stony Stratford had

1 It was Henry Paget, first Marquess of Anglesey, who established the Board of Education in 1833 and became a field marshal in 1846!

2 See chapter V and *Musson and Craven's Directory*, 1853. Later educational developments in Wolverton, including the Science and Art Institute, are referred to in the chapter on the expansion of Wolverton.

National and British schools with about 100 pupils each.

By 1850 there was a new National school at Great Brickhill (ninety-five pupils), and in 1856 Woughton had its own little school and Bow Brickhill followed in 1862. The Duncombe Estate Report of 1863 refers to the Great Brickhill school as having 'a neatly built school house: rent free', at the southern end of the village. Sheahan described it as 'a handsome structure consisting of two school rooms with a teacher's house in the centre erected by P. D. P. Duncombe'. There were then (1863) nearly 100 children attending. It ceased to be a school in 1960.

The creation of British, or Nonconformist schools, raised some awkward questions. In Volume I, pp119–20 and 196–98 we have recorded how many of our earliest schools were actually held in churches, and that others were founded by benefactions or charities from public spirited men and women, which were administered by the vestries with the parson usually taking a very active part. When the National (Church of England) school movement developed it was naturally assumed that the income from these charities should go to the new church schools.

But now the Nonconformists argued with some justice that these Tudor or later benefactions were for the whole town or village, and that the Church of England was quite wrong to limit its charitable grants only to church schools, and the apprenticeship grants only to church-going children. At Thornton it was clear that the Barton or Ingleton school, though operating in the chantry of the church was 'for the children of the said towne', and when its reduced income was transferred to Buckingham Royal Latin School it could well be argued that the same held good.

In Stony Stratford Michael Hipwell in 1609 had left quite a large estate and a couple of inns in trust, the income of which was to provide a free grammar school 'for scholars of the towne or of any of the next towns'. The income was never enough for this purpose, and the trustees in 1819 had decided to allocate the funds to the new National School Society as a grant towards the expenses of St Giles' School (now No 30 High Street), which was then erected. Soon after the British school was erected in 1844 there were vigorous expressions of dissatisfaction that none of the trust income was available for this Nonconformist school. In 1854 there was a public meeting of ratepayers which demanded:

'What have the Trustees of The Rose and Crown Charity done with the money since 1845?' According to the entries in the records of the *Select Vestry – St Giles, 1830–88* – they received the rude answer from the trustees 'that the Parish had nothing to do with it, and that they had been feeding the mind instead of the body'.

There was similar dissatisfaction with the administration of Stony Stratford's famous apprenticing charities, and in 1895 the clerk to the Stony Stratford parish councils felt compelled to write to the Charity Commissioners asking point blank whether the historic Whalley's apprenticing charity was an ecclesiastical charity. The answer was that it was a non-ecclesiastical charity with the exception of £4 a year paid to the vicar of Hartwell, and the practice of limiting grants to churchgoers 'did not appear to be warranted by the original trust'.[3]

The Nonconformists had won a battle, but not the campaign, and in 1897 they took up again the question of Michael Hipwell's school charity. The Baptist leader, Mr F. W. Woollard, roundly declared to the Charity Commissioners, that 'the Trustees of The Rose and Crown Charity have, in my judgement, for many years been travelling on the edge of illegality' in confining the charity to denominational purposes as opposed to a free school. The row echoed all over the area, but the trustees would produce no accounts nor take any notice of the parish council, and the Charity Commissioners deferred a decision. For a score of years this mulish behaviour continued – the one side kicking hard and the other refusing to budge.

Tension was probably at its worst early in the 20th century and indeed it was not until after the First World War that the various creeds began to work together for the common good. Later on the decline in purchasing power greatly reduced the values involved, and today the few pounds available from the ancient school charities would scarcely buy a couple of blackboards.

MR TURVEYDROP, ALIAS JOSEPH HAMBLING
Meanwhile in all our market towns there were private schools, mainly for girls and small boys, where dancing, deportment and sketching were more important than mathematics or domestic science.

3 *History of Stony Stratford* p184 *seq.*

At Stony Stratford, Joseph Hambling ran an academy from about 1840 to 1870 in a house at the corner of the Market Square and Mill Lane, and so engaging was his deportment that Charles Dickens took him as the very model for Mr Turveydrop in *Bleak House*. Here is Charles Dickens' description of this 'model of deportment':[4]

> 'He was a fat old gentleman with a false complexion and a wig. He had a fur collar, and a padded breast to his coat, which only wanted a star or a broad blue ribbon to be complete. He was pinched in and swelled out, and got up, and strapped down, as much as he could possibly bear. He had such a neckcloth on that his chin and even his ears sunk into it, that it seemed as though he must inevitably double up if it were cast loose. He had, under his arm, a hat of great size and weight, and in his hand a pair of white gloves, with which he flapped it, as he stood poised on one leg in a high shouldered, round elbowed state of elegance not to be surpassed. He had a cane, he had an eye glass, he had a snuff box, he had rings, he had wristbands, he had everything but any touch of nature; he was not like youth, he was not like age, he was not like anything in the world but a model of Deportment.'

Possibly Stony Stratford owed its good manners to this impressive dancing master, whose pupils came from far and wide, including Bedford. Dancing sessions were held in the *Cock Inn*, to the strains of a local fiddler and a pianist. The deportment lessons came when the musicians broke off for a drink: and then Mr Joseph Hambling was at his most superb.

'Sister Dora'

And now we come to the charming story of Sister Dora and the Doll's House. Alongside the river Ouzel, three miles south of Newport Pagnell, were two of our sleepiest villages, Great and Little Woolstone, with a total population of about 200 souls – only half a mile from each other; both had a church.[5] The two

---

4 *Bleak House*, 1853, chapter 14, p182. Hambling's house is clearly shown on the town maps of 1895. It was demolished shortly afterwards.
5 From 1831 to 1849 the Coptic scholar Dr Henry Tattam was the rector of Great Woolstone. He wrote *A Compendious Grammar of the Egyptian Language* in 1830 and *The Ancient Coptic Version of the Book of Job* in 1846. It may be imagined that his tremendous learning was little appreciated in the village.

villages had other likenesses. Both had a public house. At Great Woolstone the historic *Cross Keys* was also a shop, and the inn-keeper was also a pig dealer. At Little Woolstone *The Barge* was more recent, and catered for bargees as well as villagers, and there was a separate village shop run by the postmaster who was also a butcher. There was a smithy at Great Woolstone, but at Little Woolstone there was a carpenter, and a separate brick and tile maker, and of course the miller at the Mill. Half a dozen farmers and thirty farm labourers and their families made up the rest of the population.

It was to these two parishes that the Lord Chancellor appointed the Rev Edward Hill as vicar. This energetic newcomer from Wadham College, Oxford, decided that the villages deserved and required a school. In 1861 with the assistance of the National Society he erected, on a site given by William Smith, the largest landowner, a school in pure Victorian Gothic, bell-cote and all. To this was attached the little school-house with its gables and odd corners. There were of course many schools of this size and type being erected all over the country. We have such buildings still at Calverton, Bow Brickhill, Simpson, and so on, but not quite so charming.

The vicar then set about advertising for a schoolmistress. The advertisement was seen by a young lady in her 20s, Dorothy Pattison, daughter of the Rev Mark Pattison of Hauxwell Rectory, way up north. He was a large, overbearing, disappointed snob. In 1834 he suffered a mental breakdown, and soon was confined in an asylum for a few months, but the malady returned. He hated his wife and daughters. They were miserable for years.

Small wonder that the auburn-haired, hazel-eyed Dorothy wanted to get away – to be independent. She wanted to be a nurse – then a local curate, James Tate, wanted to marry her. There was an unofficial engagement, but the father forbad it. Had James Tate now urged an elopement she would have been delighted. He didn't – he was no Robert Browning. Still, every-body expected them to marry sometime.

Her mother died in 1860. Dorothy terminated the engage-ment. Everybody disapproved of her behaviour. 'I have made up my mind to leave Hauxwell and to work my own way' she wrote. She scanned every advertisement and finally came across

one for a lady teacher in an obscure Buckinghamshire village.
On 23 October 1861, she wrote to her brother Mark:

'I told you I was trying to get some situation . . . I seem to
have got the very thing, that of Lady Teacher in a village
school at Woolston. Work, stipend, a pretty house but . . .
The Trustees are desirous of a testimonial as to character and
fitness for the place . . . Mr. Hill (the Vicar of Woolston)
also wants to know if my Father approved of the course and
an undertaking that I go out into the world "with his
blessing". Now what must I answer to that – for it seems
to me impossible to make Mr. Hill understand our case . . .
Time is precious. They had 25 applications for the post and
there are many longing for it.'

Her application pleased the vicar, and her appearance still
more. She was appointed village schoolmistress at Little Woolstone at a salary of £26 a year. She wrote to her brother on 16
November:

'Today I heard that I am the successful candidate . . . How proud
I shall be when I first receive money of my own earning.'

She bought her railway ticket out of a small legacy her mother
had left her and was met at Bletchley station by the Rev Edward
Hill, who drove her to the new Great Woolstone Vicarage, where
she stopped until the paint in the little school cottage was dry.[6]

Dorothy was enchanted by her first sight of the school, with
its red-brick Gothic gables, diamond-paned windows, little bell-
cote and a good angular chimney. Adjacent was her cottage
reminding one of a doll's house. Behind lay a paved yard which
she scrubbed with vigour, a washhouse where she boiled her own
sheets in the copper, and a cellar where she shovelled her own
coals. The 'big boys' of her school, rising 11 years, helped to dig
and plant her vegetable patch. She was poor, and alone, but
happy. She was free.[7]

1861 was a bleak time in which to begin work as a teacher.
It was the first year for which we have a comprehensive survey
of English elementary education, that of a Royal Commission
under the Duke of Newcastle: Dorothy was well acquainted
with it. At that time only one in eight English children attended

6 It was designed by William Butterfield and built by James Rose, a brickmaker of
Newport Pagnell. It still stands.
7 *Sister Dora* by Jo Manton, Methuen and Company, 1971.

school. Only one in five stayed until 11 years of age. Education was not compulsory, as in France and Germany. In rural districts, as in the Woolstones, children were taken away from school to work at low wages on the land during harvest seasons. No schools were provided by the state. Buildings and funds were dependent half on private subscriptions and half on grants from religious bodies. Dissenters often sacrificed principles to get education for their children. In National schools teachers were subservient to the managers, the incumbent, and the church schools inspector. Schoolmistresses were usually drawn from poorer classes – a 'lady' lost caste becoming a teacher. As a clergyman's daughter, and sister of the rector of Lincoln College at Oxford, Dorothy Pattison was an anomaly.

She made friends with a daughter of George Finch, lord of the manor of Milton Keynes. A Woolstone couple wanted to adopt her: she refused, but accepted £10 per annum and then offended them by giving it away.

She loved the children; she loved the whole village, and the village loved her. Nothing like this had ever happened in the Woolstones before. All she was supposed to do was to get her thirty children aged 7 to 11 'able to read a paragraph, write a letter, make out a shop bill, learn the Catechism, and understand an ordinary sermon'. She did more. She created a choir, she began visiting the sick, and nursing them. All unpaid. In all this she had the support of the vicar and the affectionate co-operation of both villages.

And now three distracting things happened possibly of equal importance. First she had her silver teaspoons and teapot stolen one night when she was out sick nursing. Then she caught pleurisy, and weak from her illness convalesced at Redcar, and whilst she was still weak James Tate turned up, kind and gentle. Their oft broken engagement was renewed. James now wanted to marry quickly, and she was just preparing to do this when his parents objected, and the dutiful son called it off. He sighed like a lover, he obeyed as a son.

In 1862 Dorothy Pattison was 30. In looks, bearing and cheerfulness she seemed more like a girl of 20 – but she was now quite alone. She stayed another one and a half years in Woolstone, studying Florence Nightingale's *Notes on Nursing* and almost wanted to be a nun.

When she left the Woolstones she joined the newly established Sisterhood of the Good Samaritan at Coatham, near Redcar, as 'Sister Dora'. She became as the years went by a second Florence Nightingale. Her fame spread all over the north-east, and many articles and books were written about her.[8] She became an excellent surgical nurse and indefatigable in ministering to the sick and the unfortunate. She died in 1878 when in charge of a hospital at Walsall. The following year the *Daily Telegraph* wrote of her, 'What Florence Nightingale did for military hospitals, Dorothy Pattison accomplished in civil duty'.

Whatever her fame in the midlands and the north, it was only a little less in north Bucks. To say that she was remembered here with affection is a great understatement. Not until the youngest child she had taught died did the memory of her begin to fade. It is worth recalling her by preserving the little school, and the Doll's house that went with it, at Little Woolstone.

The main point of the story, however, is not only the character of Dorothy Pattison, but the fact that from about 1850 on, every village acquired a school, and the school a teacher. Later on the school became the cultural centre of the village, and the village schoolmistress was usually a personality in her own right. People remembered with real affection the teachers they knew in their childhood, and it was perhaps a sad time when after the Second World War so many of these village schools were closed down and the school bus whisked the children off to ever larger schools in ever growing towns.

ST PAUL'S COLLEGE

Whilst all this was going on a development occurred at Stony Stratford which might well have made it a really great educational centre. From about 1850 the need for something better than National or British school education had been met by a private 'Classical, Mathematical and Commercial School' situated at Belvedere House, Old Stratford. For 30 guineas a year it taught 'young gentlemen' Greek, Latin, French, geometry, mensuration, practical land surveying, stenography, plain and ornamental writing, bookkeeping, etc. It was conducted by Mr Thomas and his son with, as they said, experienced assistants.[9]

8 The latest is *Sister Dora*, 1971 quoted above. See illustration Plate 3.
9 See advertisement in *Musson and Craven's Directory* 1853.

In 1859 the wealthy Rev W. T. Sankey became the vicar of St Giles'. Within a year he had built a new and charming parish room, a new vicarage and a church infants' school. But Sankey's greatest effort was the creation of the new St Paul's School. The site was the several acres at the north end of Stony Stratford between Pudding Bag Lane and the Malletts, all once part of the Malletts estate; it included thirty or more slum dwellings and the ancient *Horseshoe Inn*. The slums in the lanes were pulled down, but one old house, with its sun-dial dated 1773, was retained, and the house is still an integral part of the buildings, though the sun-dial disappeared some years ago.

By 1863 Sankey had the satisfaction of seeing St Paul's College opened at a cost of £40,000, a tremendous sum in those days, and soon there were 200 pupils and a growing renown. During the next twenty years it produced many distinguished pupils, including several members of the Harmsworth family; George Grossmith, who was England's leading comic actor for thirty years; General Nixon, of Mesopotamian fame; and many others.

The college had a strict régime. Morning roll-call was at 5.45 am in summer, and 6.45 in winter, and work began immediately. After a break for breakfast, there was more tuition from 8.30 to 10.30, and from 11.30 to 1 pm.

The afternoon was devoted to games, and pupils were allowed to walk as far as the bridge or New Street; evening school was from 6 to 8.30 pm, and lights-out was at 9.15. The prefects had the power of 'fagging' younger boys, but they were told that 'Fagging must not be understood to refer to the performance of difficult menial offices'. The curriculum included a great deal of Latin and a little Greek, a little Science, Mathematics, History, Logic, English Literature, French and German, and on Sundays and saints' days there was an hour's religious instruction.

It was a great pity that such a fine school, which started so well, should have come into the hands of 'tyrants', for after Sankey's death it came, as Ratcliff says, 'into the hands of men who ruled as tyrants, and wielded the birch incessantly' – and the school declined. In 1882 there was a fresh management and new masters, but the bad name survived, and it closed down in 1895.

For a short time in 1896 it became a cigar factory, which failed dismally. The most strenuous efforts were made to interest

1 The first Duke of Buckingham and Chandos (wearing Garter Star) with the Marquess of Landsowne at the trial of Queen Charlotte. Painted by Sir George Hayton 1823. Courtesy of the National Portrait Gallery. See p8 seq.

2 The first Marquess of Chandos 1833. The original painting in the National Portrait Gallery was painted at the meeting of the first reformed Parliament. Succeeded as Duke of Buckingham 1839, bankrupt 1847, died 1861. Courtesy of the National Portrait Gallery. See p79.

3 Dorothy Pattison, school teacher at Little Woolstone 1861 who became famous as 'Sister Dora'. See p145 seq.

4 William Smith of Little Woolstone. A sketch from the 1893 issue of 'The Cable'. Smith was nationally famous for his system of steam cultivation. See pp163–64 and illustration No 10. Courtesy of Mr J. Day of Mursley.

F

5   The east end of Buckingham Church about 1862, showing the large armorial
window installed by the first Duke of Buckingham and Chandos around 1824. See p12.
The illustration is reproduced from J. T. Harrison's 'Historical Buckingham', 1909.

6   The Wolverton Mechanics' Soiree 1849. The building is the great Engine Shed
built about 1838 and now mainly the Brake shop. See pp71 and 84. Courtesy of the
Illustrated Newspapers Group.

7   A sketch of Denbigh Hall Bridge c.1850 showing a squadron of Hussars (probably
the Royal Bucks) proceeding under the bridge whilst the London train, drawn by a
Bury engine, rumbles overhead. The 'Denbigh Hall' Inn was on the far side of the
bridge. See pp67–68.

8   Great Brickhill Manor, the seat of the Duncombe family. Disraeli stayed here many
times whilst he was MP for the county (1847–76). After being a school for many
years it was demolished c.1938. See p111. Courtesy of Sir Philip Duncombe.

9 *Mr Turveydrop waiting at the famous portal of the 'Cock' Hotel at Stony Stratford. Drawing of the 'Cock' Hotel by C. W. Green, and that of Mr Turveydrop by 'Phiz' in 'Bleak House' by Charles Dickens. See p144 seq.*

10 *Smith's cultivator in action near Howards Works, Bedford, a sketch from 'British Agriculture' by Professor J. Donaldson, 1860. It cost 6s to 9s to plough an acre, and the team could do 6 acres a day. See p163.*

11 The Royal carriage: the day compartment. Built in 1869 at Wolverton and used by Queen Victoria, until her death, on her journeys to and from Scotland. In 1895 this compartment (then a separate vehicle) was joined to the bedroom compartment to make one carriage 60ft long and 8ft wide. The early royal trains were only four carriages, but in 1895 had grown to fourteen. Courtesy British Rail, Wolverton.

The photograph obviously cannot bring out the glorious blues and gold of the upholstery.

12 Rickett's steam car, made at Castle Foundry, Buckingham c.1850. Sketch lent by Mr G. Akister, Buckingham. See pp164–65.

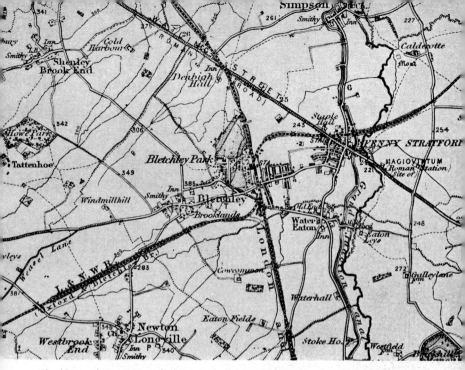

13 *Bletchley and Fenny Stratford in 1889, showing the importance of Bletchley as a railway junction. Reproduced from the 2nd Edition of the Ordnance Survey. Courtesy of the Director of the British Museum. Scale 1 in = 1 mile. See 'Records of Bucks' 1964.*

14 *One of the 'Bloomer' type of locomotives, designed by J. E. McConnell and built at Wolverton Works. This is the 'Osprey' finished in 1857. See p185.*

15 A traction engine hauling one of Hayes' boats from the works at London Road, Stony Stratford, to the canal at Old Stratford in November 1907. In the background is the Co-op, Stony Stratford. See pp160–62.

16 Another of Hayes' boats, the 'Suzette', being transported from London Road works to the canal at Old Stratford. See pp160–62.

other schools or institutions in the property, but not a single offer was made in four years. Then, in 1900, it came to the attention of that 'Knight Errant of the Gospel', Mr J. W. C. Fegan, a shrewd business man who had spent years in helping the homeless boys of London. Fegan was looking for a country home for his 'bold and pert and dirty London sparrows', and his biographer, Dr W. Y. Fullerton, tells us what then happened when Mr Fegan saw the college:

'Designed as a school for the sons of gentlemen, the buildings were almost luxurious, everything was of the highest quality, and the whole had cost £40,000. But the school was a failure, the insurance company to whom the property was mortgaged had foreclosed on the estate, and it was difficult to see what use could be made of such a property in such a neighbourhood. In a spirit of what in the event proved to be divine recklessness Fegan made an offer of £4,500, although there seemed scant hope of its acceptance. It was accepted immediately, for it was the only offer made, and a date was set for the completion of the purchase – June 25th, 1900 . . . It seemed impossible to get such a large sum in so short a time . . . but by prayer and picturesque personal letters Mr. Fegan obtained all but £9 by the set day. That night, at a Praise Meeting, the balance came from an old Christian man living in an almhouse.'

Within a short time 150 bright little 'London sparrows' from 8 to 11 years of age were brought to 'Fegan's Homes', and during the next sixty years something like 4,000 orphans found a real home in the buildings that Sankey intended for boys of quite other fortunes.

When 'Fegan's' or the orphanage closed down in 1962 it was soon taken over as a Roman Catholic school, but this too had only a short existence, and in 1972 the pleasant buildings, now pleasanter because the nearby gasworks had been closed down, were taken over by the *Société Générale*, an international finance company.

Meanwhile Bletchley had its own private 'St Martin's Grammar School', run by Mr and Mrs S. H. Still at a commodious house in Bletchley Road, which is now the Conservative Club and later at 'Elmers'. Its curriculum was very similar to that of St Paul's College, but typewriting also was included.

G

POPULAR EDUCATION

We must retrace our steps in order to cover what was happening with elementary education in north Bucks.

In 1868 as we have seen, the Reform Act gave the vote to every male over 21, and as Robert Lowe, Chancellor of the Exchequer 1868–73 grimly remarked, 'We must now educate our masters'. But as always education was a quarrelsome issue in which clergy of all denominations, schoolmasters and mistresses, theorists and trustees, all joined with a vehemence and often an intolerance which was hardly surprising since so many vested interests were involved.

In 1870 'Forster's' Elementary Education Bill was passed, and by 1876 every child had to go to school up to the age of 10. Religious instruction was allowed with the parents' consent, and the reading of the Bible without sectarian comment was permitted for other children.

This meant that as far as north Bucks was concerned the numbers of school children would be doubled, and somebody had to find the money for new buildings and new teachers. School boards were formed from 1871 on which could levy a rate for school purposes, though school fees were still collected from parents who could afford it. Sometimes two or three villages were combined in one board. In Bucks nearly 100 school boards were set up where school accommodation was insufficient. Where there were already schools built by a landowner or by the church the transfer was usually simple. The boards now advertised for teachers – usually for women at £50 a year, but found they were very scarce – and often a man was appointed at £80 a year.

Gradually quite a proportion of the population could read the popular daily papers, which with the abolition of stamp duty, became available at ½d a copy. The racing page became the most popular.

Primary education was free from 1891, and the numbers attending school rose rapidly, and still more so when in 1893 the school-leaving age was raised to 11, and to 12 in 1899. Not until 1914 was it raised to 14, though prior to this children could stay on an extra year or even two.

In 1902 another change took place as the County Council took over primary education from the school boards. Fenny Stratford and Woughton and Simpson boards were swept away like many others and in their place school management committees were set up with much more limited powers. In Fenny Stratford the result was regretted by everybody. The management committee had its first meeting in October 1903, and resented the fact that new appointments were being advertised by the county at £5 per annum less than the school board rates. By December a further dissatisfaction arose from the county's refusal to pay pupil teachers' fees for correspondence courses and finally at the same meeting came the last straw and it was recorded as follows:

'The Chairman proposed, and Mr. T. G. Kirby seconded, that we have heard with regret of the proposal of the Bucks Education Committee to deprive us of the services of our Clerk who has served the Education Authority here faithfully and well, and with conspicious ability for a number of years and who has our fullest confidence: that we protest against such a step being taken without our knowledge, and generally against the humiliating position in which we are placed and that we decline such position any longer.'

It was carried unanimously and for a year Fenny Stratford was without a committee. Even when the new committee was formed they wanted to appoint their own clerk, but without any success. In the matter of the caretaker however they were rather more fortunate. The County Council requested his dismissal following an adverse HMI's report. The managers delayed this for six months before advertising the post, and finally reappointed the original person out of the seven applicants, much to Aylesbury's annoyance. However, despite these small victories their powers were much smaller and within ten years they were reduced to discussing repairs to cupboards and gas meters.[10]

WOLVERTON COUNTY SECONDARY SCHOOL

The opportunities for secondary education in the 19th century were few and poor. In Buckinghamshire the six Grammar schools were badly equipped, their endowments extremely low and of course deteriorating, indeed the total income from endowments for purely secondary education in the entire county was under £900, and there were only thirty scholarships.

10 Information from Mr Edward Legg.

The County Council now proposed, 1901, to establish a new co-educational county school at Wolverton, but the Stratford and Wolverton Rural District Council gave it a dim reception, possibly due to the fact that so many possible pupils might come from outside the council's area. However, in January 1902 the 'Wolverton County Day School' held its first classes in the Science and Art Institute. There were thirty-two pupils in two forms.

In 1904 the County Council approved a grant of £2,000 for a new mixed Secondary school at Wolverton, and there were other grants of £1,750. But the cost of the new school and site was £6,000 – not the first or last time an estimate has been greatly exceeded. It was opened in September 1906. The new head-master was the bristling E. J. Boyce, at a salary of £300, who during the next thirty years created a school that was a credit to the county. In 1908 there were 175 pupils, both boys and girls aged 11 to 17, many from Bletchley, and the fees were £6 a year. The total yearly expenditure on the school in these early days was just over £1,000.

Nowadays we hardly realise what a new departure it was to have a mixed school. In all our previous history there were usually separate schools for boys, girls and infants, and both National and British schools, and Board schools following them thought it was imperative to separate the sexes from about the age of 5 years. And now, at Wolverton, boys and girls up to the age of 17 were educated together. There were many parents, teachers and reverend gentlemen who feared that to put teen-agers together so much would produce experimental immorality.

When the demure daughters and stalwart sons of farmers and shopkeepers did so meet there was the occasional Romeo-Juliet flare up, but no great harm was done.

Nowadays teenagers are perhaps wiser, and co-education has come to stay but seventy years ago it was an astonishing idea that teenage boys and girls should learn together in the same school.

It is worth recalling the extremely limited educational oppor-tunities in these pre-war years, for whilst every child was entitled to free elementary education up to the age of 14 years, there were practically few scholarships either to Secondary schools or to universities. The son of a working man was destined to be educationally handicapped for the rest of his life.

Between the years 1906–22 the Wolverton Secondary School won twenty-two university scholarships of £100 a year or less and this was considered to be very good, but as the catchment area of the school included almost the whole of north-east Bucks the manna was very thinly spread. There were many able youngsters in north Bucks who would have done most creditably at any university, but not until years later were the gates opened. Nowadays they are perhaps open too wide.

It was not only the universities that were closed shops in those pre-war days. Practically all the great professions – the law, diplomacy, the commissioned ranks of the Royal Navy and the Army, medicine, and even the higher ranks of the clergy – were closed to all who could not produce evidence of a 'good' education at a public school, or had served their long articles at their parents' expense. As we have seen, some of the denied young men found careers in business or even politics, and overcame the many frustrations.

For over forty years the 'Sec' continued to progress and among its governors, who equalled the students in loyalty and seriousness, were Lt-Col L. C. Hawkins, Canon W. L. Harnett, C. P. Woollard, J. M. Knapp, JP, Sir Harry Verney, DSO, Lady Leon, JP, the Rev D. J. Thomas, Lt-Col J. Williams, Albert Brown, JP, Ben Woodward and Frank Markham. The governorship of the last-named, 1928–31, was brief and undistinguished – except for the fact that he married the Head Girl!

In 1945 the school now under the headmastership of Donald Morgan was designated the Grammar School. In 1958 it was amalgamated with the Technical Secondary School and renamed the Radcliffe School, which in 1961 moved to new and ugly buildings in Aylesbury Street and became a Comprehensive school, with over 1,000 pupils, in 1968. It would have had hundreds more pupils, but for the fact that a Grammar school was built in Bletchley Park in 1956–57.

It would take an entire volume to relate the history of every school in our area since say, the great Education Act of 1944. Such great changes have occurred both in fundamental approaches, teaching methods and school design that we are in a brave new world; yet we still wonder if we have found all the answers.

10 Little Industries

As we have seen, it needed formidable Acts of Parliament to create a canal or a railway, but as far as any other industry was concerned there was almost complete freedom for anybody to set up anywhere and make anything he liked: it was an age of free competition and of few planning restrictions.

LACE MAKING

Some quite old industries were already on the wane. The home industry of lace making, which before 1820 utilised practically all the female labour in north Bucks was severely hit by the introduction of machine-made Nottingham lace, and both canals and railways helped to distribute it. In 1825 as Gibbs reports, the lace trade was stagnant. Those who used to earn up to 15s or more a week now got only 2 or 3 shillings. In 1830 even Stony Stratford petitioned Queen Adelaide asking her to wear more lace. She did, and it helped. But after 1840 the low railway tariffs helped the Nottingham machine lace makers even more. Yet in the 1860s there were still lace buyers and lace pattern-makers in the local towns. Amos Cowley 'lace manufacturer and tea dealer' of Wolverton Road, Stony Stratford had distinct rivals in James Marshall 'shopkeeper and lace dealer' of St Johns Street, Newport Pagnell, and in Wm Ayres, lace manufacturer, Tickford Cottage.

The hand-made Buckinghamshire lace had often a delicacy and quality that were unsurpassed, and it continued to be made inside and outside the cottages for yet another century. Almost every village can produce photographs taken just before the First World War or even later showing dear old ladies with their lace pillows and their bobbins, but it was no longer a great home industry.

THE STRAW PLAIT INDUSTRY

Another home industry that began to decline was that of straw plaiting by which local women and girls prepared the complicated plaits that were in such demand in the hat making centres such

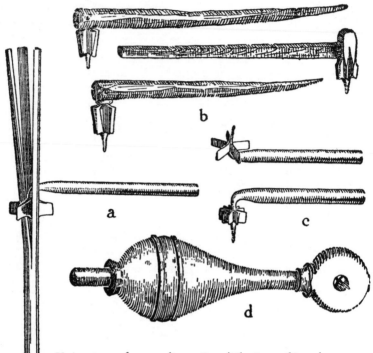

Various types of straw splitters. From 'The Story of Luton' p119.

as Luton and Dunstable. Around 1813 women were earning £1 per week in plaiting straw; and young people about 7s a week. Even in 1853 *Musson & Craven's Directory* could state that 'The making of straw plait is carried on in Buckingham and the neighbouring villages and is expected to increase'. Certainly all along the Bedfordshire border it seemed as if the formidable requirements of Luton and Dunstable would last for ever.

The trade had a certain elemental simplicity. Good straw prepared and cut into suitable lengths was bought from the straw dealer: it was then split by a clever little tool into four or more strands, which were then plaited so as to make strips about ½in wide. So far all that was needed was a good pliable straw, a straw splitter, a pair of scissors, nimble fingers, and plenty of spittle to moisten the straw if no water was available.[1] Twenty yards of

1 See illustrations in *Story of Luton* pp117 and 119. See also Gibbs' *Buckinghamshire Local Records, passim.*

plait made a score, for which the plait maker was paid from 10d to 1s 4d. A good plait maker could turn out 7½ score in a week and so earn about 8s, which was no mean addition to the family income when farm labourers were paid from 10s to 13s a week.

The home-made plait would be sold to dealers like George Roberts of Marsh End, Newport Pagnell, or more probably to the travelling buyers from Luton or Dunstable. Some would be sold to local straw bonnet makers. In 1853 Newport Pagnell had four; there was Esther Roberts, wife of the dealer, and then Elizabeth Pearce of Silver Street, Mary Ann Gilder of the Green, and Emma Allbright of St Johns Street. In Fenny Stratford there was Mary Ann Souster of London Road. One can almost picture their shop windows, with everything from the demure 'Little Bo-Peep' confections, to the sturdier and more popular types still associated with Salvation Army lasses. The straw sun bonnet was very popular, and the new bonnet at Easter with its trimmings and ribbons was a delight to all.

In 1851 nearly half the female population of north Bucks was either straw plaiting or lace making. Among the census returns we find that of the female straw plaiters a few were under 5 years of age, and 20 per cent under 9. The children mostly worked under supervision in 'plait schools' which were really workshops run by old women. We find the curate of Little Brickhill writing in 1857 'I feel obliged to start this (new) plaiting school as the children learn so much evil in the schools kept by the poor and

they are confined in small dirty rooms – never learn reading. I require their attendance at the National School for reading'.[2] The nimble fingers of little children were exploited not by hard faced Gradgrinds, but by their own mothers. They had to live.

The advent of the improved sewing machine around 1850 was undoubtedly a great boon for all women who could afford one, but it helped to kill the local straw plait industry. When the Luton manufacturers adapted it to replace the hand sewing of local milliners the home industry began to fade out. Competition increased. Around 1870 plait began to come from China – inferior plait at 3d a score. But by 1890 the quality had improved, and in 1891 much finer plaits began to arrive from Japan.

Plaiting as a home industry was ruined, but the straw hat industry prospered. Luton and Dunstable throve, but there were no more lace schools or straw plait schools, and only a few middle-aged or elderly ladies to continue to work in straw or cotton for the love of it. Yet as late as 1887 we find a straw plait dealer in Newton Longville, and three years later we find Ann James of 66 High Street, Newport Pagnell, advertising herself as a 'Straw Hat and Bonnet Manufacturer'.

LOCAL STEAM ENGINEERING: HAYES OF STONY STRATFORD

The success of steam power as the motive force for the railways naturally set the minds of many engineers pondering as to how best to use it for ships, for road transport, for farming, milling and a hundred other uses, and almost every town in the country had ingenious experimenters of one kind or another.

In 1840, only two years after the completion of the London and Birmingham Railway, Edward Hayes, a young engineer from London, decided to start up in business at Stony Stratford as an agricultural engineer, and in 1853 he is described as 'a consultant engineer and superintendent of College, London Road'. The 'College' was a bright name for the apprentices, who were very well taught, and of course added strength to the little firm. The firm prospered, and was, indeed, one of the foremost locally for creating and trying out new forms of machinery to assist the farmer, and in this Edward Hayes was greatly assisted by William

2 *Clergy Visitation Returns*, 1857, quoted by Pamela Horn in *Records of Bucks*, 1971, p42 *seq.*

Smith of Woolstone, to whom we refer later. Presently there were enquiries for mechanically driven boats, which led to the firm specialising in marine engines, and finally, towards the end of the century, the firm produced vessels ready to go under their own power to any part of the world, even though Stony Stratford was seventy or eighty miles from the nearest bit of coast. Absence of a broad waterway was no obstacle, for the young Edward Hayes, son of the founder, and the staff of eighty found ways and means of launching tugs, yachts or launches, up to 70ft long, sideways into the canal at Old Stratford, and of manoeuvring them through all the turns and locks until the Thames was reached. Larger vessels up to 90ft long would be shipped in pieces and assembled on the most modern pre-fabrication plans.

The reputation of the firm grew as it swept off a number of prizes in international yacht races, tug tests, and so on; and among those who came to Stony Stratford for tugs and launches were our own Admiralty, the Russian Government, the French Government, the Egyptian Government, and the leading port and dock authorities all over the world. At its zenith the firm could produce twin-screw steam launches 70ft in length, 13ft 8in wide, with a draught of 4ft, and capable of doing 14 knots: or stern wheelers 81ft in length, 14ft wide, with a draught of 1ft 9in. *Engineering* records that a 51-ft Hayes tug towed four Thames barges, totalling over 400 tons, loaded, against the tide.

Apprentices were well trained. One of these became Professor Osborne Reynolds, FRS, of Manchester, (died 1912), and another, B. J. Fisher, became chief engineer of the L. & S. W. Railway, and at least two became presidents of engineering institutions. The chairman of Harland and Wolff at the time of its greatest influence, Sir Frederick Rebbeck, KBE, was also a Hayes pupil in the 1890s. He helped to design the *Titanic* (1911). Edward Hayes, Junior, died in 1920, and five years later the firm closed down. Their last boat was a Thames tug named *Sparteolus* launched in 1925 which for years was engaged in the Pool of London. Shortly afterwards Hayes Watling Works became the London Road Garage.

Oddly enough it was the diesel engine which was partly responsible for the decline of Hayes Works, but undoubtedly the lack of brilliant successors to the Hayes' family was another reason. Nevertheless, during their prime this inland firm could produce sea-going craft that could challenge the tug-builders of the entire world and often beat them at their own game.

One of the interesting points about Hayes was how little they relied upon the railway to help get their products abroad. In fact they relied on traction engines and the canal. Nobody had yet solved the problem of producing rapid transport on the roads, but the traction engine did produce a solution to the problem of pulling heavy or awkward objects along them. Railway loads were determined by the size of tunnels, so that if any piece of machinery taller or broader than a tunnel had to be moved the railways were absolutely useless. Equally if great loads had to be moved even a couple of miles from say Stony Stratford to Old Stratford it was no use looking to the railways. They were inflexible, and Hayes of Stony Stratford had obviously to move launches or tugs up to 70ft from Watling Works to the Grand Junction Canal. For all this the railways were as useless as pack horses or donkeys.

The answer was found in the steam traction engine, which at its best had the pulling power of twenty-nine horses, and could climb gradients of up to 1 in 10, which again railways could never do. For loads of over $2\frac{1}{2}$ tons they were far cheaper to use than horse power. But of course they had their limitations – their speed was never more than 8mph and in spite of large driving wheels, up to 7ft 6in, and wide ribbed tyres up to 16in, they could sink into fields or even roads and be unable to work their way out without help.

Nobody knows who first used a steam traction engine in north Bucks, but by 1860 it was a common sight not only on the highways, but in the lanes and fields.

Few people liked these early traction engines, for they were smoky, dirty and noisy, and often men who drove them were rough types. The traction engine was soon linked up with threshing, and threshing contractors went from farm to farm with the engine, a threshing drum, a straw elevator and sometimes a chaff cutter. The crew consisted of the engine driver, a man to put corn sheaves into the drum, and a boy who did the cooking and odd jobs, and generally learnt enough to become an engine driver later on. Goodness knows what his cooking was like. The daily hire charge before the First World War was about £2 a day, but the farmer had to supply the coal and water and everybody took part in the rat massacre that followed.

SMITH OF LITTLE WOOLSTONE

Hayes had an exciting ally in the field of agricultural machinery, for at Little Woolstone there was an ingenious farmer named William Smith who had already earnt local renown by his keenness to introduce any sort of agricultural improvement.

The ancient Church Farm had been for two centuries the home of the Smith family, and here William Smith was born in 1814. He had his earliest schooling at Milton Keynes, and at 14 he was put in charge of a farm at nearby Woughton, which his father leased. When the lease expired in 1829, young William went to Linford Lodge Farm and assisted in running it until 1837 when, on the death of his father, he returned to Church Farm, and from then on began to experiment widely.[3] But first he arranged for 500 tons of manure to be brought from London to his own canal wharf every year, so that the soil was in good heart. He was much opposed to ploughing, which he said inverted the soil, and preferred 'cultivation' which meant a much lighter disturbance of the soil and produced a better tilth. It was a great disappointment to pioneers like William Smith that a traction engine could pull neither a cultivator nor a plough, for it was so heavy it got stuck, but as the steam engine was the only mobile engine available, they had to let it stand still and haul the implement with long wire ropes backwards and forwards. In 1855 he patented a 'combined double-breasted trench plough and subsoiler', the motive power of which was any steam engine of at least 7hp (nominal) with a separate windlass on wheels, anchors, cultivators, etc. It would take a long time to describe the entire operation. Suffice to say that he sold ten of these contrivances in Bucks and thirty to landowners in other counties within a few years, and had nearly 200 customers in 1862. William Smith gave demonstrations of his implements in many parts of the country, even as far away as Carlisle and Wales. In 1858 friends and neighbours presented him with a testimonial and cheque value 100 guineas 'for having brought steam cultivation to a successful issue'. In September 1861, together with Mr Hayes of the Watling Works, Stony Stratford, he staged an exhibition of steam power and farm implements there. A large number of agriculturalists and landowners were present, and the company later enjoyed refreshments at the Watling Works, which were brightly illuminated with gas made

3 See *Model Engineer*, December 1972, p1181, kindly lent by J. L. Day, Mursley.

in the works. Later Smith entered a competition organised by the Royal Society but was not satisfied with the judges' award and challenged it. Much correspondence between him and the Society ensued, but in the end he received nothing.

In 1863 Smith was boasting how much better crops were after steam tillage, and quoted interesting figures for the improved production. The local Parochial Assessment Committee read the figures with interest, and put up his assessment by 10s an acre. Enough to make any farmer swear!

An idea of Smith's capacity for organisation occurred in July 1868 when he and others harvested a field of wheat at Linford, thrashed it by steam-driven machinery on the spot, took it to be milled at Little Woolstone and made into bread at Newport Pagnell, all within twenty-four hours.[4]

In 1877 Joseph Arch, one of the earliest trade union leaders, came to Little Woolstone and addressed the workers, and persuaded several of them to join his newly formed National Labourers' Agricultural Union. So many difficulties followed that Smith resentfully stopped experimenting, sowed all his land to grass, and had the machinery stored and bricked up in a barn. There it remained until 1958, when the Bedfordshire Agricultural Show organisers opened the barn, restored the implements, and exhibited them at their show.[5]

CASTLE FOUNDRY, BUCKINGHAM

Possibly the most exciting local efforts to utilise steam power to propel carriages on the public roads were made by Goldsworthy Gurney of Aylesbury and Thomas Rickett of Buckingham. Gurney from 1827 to 1834 made steam road carriages that would travel up to 15mph and carry ten outside and seven inside passengers. But he was beaten by the hostility of ostlers and harness makers who stoned and destroyed a carriage at Melksham, and more so by the fact that turnpike trustees had put such enormous tolls on his carriages as to stop them. Some farmers too opposed him arguing that no more oats would be wanted, horses would be useless and land would be uncultivated if steam was used instead of horse power![6] He spent over £30,000 in his develop-

4 *Echoes of the Past*, Newman Cole and Warren Dawson, p62.
5 *Echoes of the Past*, Newman Cole and Warren Dawson, p59. See also illustration on p60.
6 Gibbs' *op cit* Vol III.

ments and lost most of it, but was knighted in 1863 for his services in lighting, heating and ventilating the House of Commons.

It therefore needed some courage for Mr Thomas Rickett of Castle Foundry, Buckingham to follow Gurney in the steam carriage business. In 1857 he set up his business to make harrows, ploughs, etc, but was soon theorising in other directions. After many experiments he produced in 1859 a compact locomotive steam engine, mounted on a substantial chassis but having only three wheels. In front, open to all winds was a bench which could seat three passengers, the centre one taking the tiller. Behind the engine was the stoker, again with no protection from the elements. With a full load of passengers, water and coal or coke, it weighed $2\frac{1}{2}$ tons.

It was a vastly different proposition propelling a carriage on the bumpy and hilly roads of the period, than pulling trains on smooth rails with gentle gradients, and the engineers of the time reckoned that it needed as much power to draw one ton on a road as fifteen to twenty tons on a railway. Nevertheless Ricketts' steam carriage worked. It ran at an average speed of 10mph and on good level roads could do 16mph – faster than any stage-coach.

Rickett sold his first road steam carriage to Mr Beard of Stowe. Another was ordered for Belgium. Then the Prince of Wales wanted to see it, and the sprightly Thomas Rickett drove it in January 1860, by the winding roads to Windsor where it was inspected by Queen Victoria and all the royal household. This of course was regarded as 'five-star' approval, and before long the Duke of Sutherland, the Earl of Caithness, the Marquess of Stafford and indeed many more had bought a Rickett's three-seater road locomotive. That built for the Marquess of Stafford was tested by several trial trips in 1859 between Buckingham and Wolverton, averaging 12mph.[7] Wolverton of course with its skilful mechanics and spare parts was the ideal place for adjustments before the return journey. The Earl of Caithness's machine was driven up to Scotland, and he proudly recorded that he travelled in it 150 miles in two days 'over some of the steepest roads in Scotland'. Some of these machines continued to give good service for a quarter of a century.

One of the disadvantages of any steam road carriage was that

7 Sheahan p232: also the *Illustrated London News*, 11 February 1860.

horses were so affrighted by the noisy, smoking, puffing monster that they either tried to leap across the nearest wayside ditch or promptly bolted. Men were used to railways and soon got used to steam roadsters. Horses never did.

In 1865 Ricketts built a road engine to haul a passenger carriage, but this was his last effort, for he died soon afterwards.

The famous Castle Foundry was closed in 1865, and the premises were converted into a Steam Corn and Cake Mill, and later (1892) used by the Condensed Peptonised Milk Company for several years.

FOUNDRIES

There were several other foundries around when Mr Rickett was making his interesting steam road carriages. Possibly the earliest local foundry was that of the Roberts family, at Deanshanger, two miles from Stony Stratford. When the canals were built the transport of iron and sand over quite long distances became an economic possibility which enabled almost anyone to set up a foundry provided it was near a canal wharf. When the Bucking-ham arm of the Grand Junction Canal was opened in 1801 it was inevitable that there should be a wharf for coal, slate, bricks, etc. It was alongside this that around 1821 Richard Roberts began the more exciting and exacting work of founding, by creating 'The Deanshanger Iron Works'. Very soon the family established a good name as the makers of ploughs, harrows and indeed many kinds of agricultural machines, as well as kitchen ranges. In 1847 the iron foundry was worked by a small steam engine outside the building and there was a detached blacksmith's shop. The quality of the workmanship and the boldness of the design gave the machines a ready market, and the firm of E. & H. Roberts Limited won over 3,700 medals mostly for their light economical ploughs. Some of their implements have been in use for a century.[8] The full story of the firm is given in Brown and Roberts' *Passenham*, 1973, pp135–39 and 220–23.

In 1890 the Works were employing eighty-five men, and around 1906 well over 100. The apprentices were as boisterous as one expects apprentices to be. My brother, Charles,[9] was an apprentice wheelwright with the firm from 1911 to 1914. He started

8 Examples of their machines, etc, can be seen in Stacey Hill Museum at Wolverton.
9 Later Mayor of Cheltenham and OBE.

at a penny (old pence) an hour, which was increased by a farthing an hour each year, but no wages were paid if an apprentice was absent from work, no matter what the reason. The hours were 57½ a week. When he was called up with the Territorials in 1914 his army pay was 1s a day and 'all found', and he felt much better off.

The firm received a severe blow in 1907 when the senior partner, Mr Edwin Roberts, died, and there was a disastrous fire in 1912, but an even more severe blow was the advent of the motor tractor a few years later. The firm somehow never managed to meet the new challenges, but struggled along for a generation until it closed down in 1927.

Renowned as E. and H. Roberts were in their day, they were closely challenged by Randalls of Bedford who in 1864 decided to set up a branch iron and brass foundry in Fenny Stratford at the corner of Victoria Road and Denmark Street with the aim of making castings for agricultural machinery. It was soon under the management of Charles Higgs Holdom. Within a few years additional premises were built in Simpson Road adjoining Fenny Lodge, and in 1881 the foundry was transferred to the corner of Queensway and Cambridge Street. The business remained in existence until the mid 1920s.

HERBERT AKROYD STUART (1864–1927)[10]

Meanwhile the old foundry in Denmark Street, called the Bletchley Ironworks, had been taken over by Charles Stuart who according to local report, spent too long in local hostelries on occasion, with the result that he was sometimes brought home in a wheelbarrow.[11] Fortunately he had help at work from his more notable son Herbert (or 'Bertie') who had been born in Halifax in 1864. He soon had a reputation for experimenting with petrol and paraffin heaters and engines, and the story goes that one day some hot slag fell on some oil in the foundry pit, and that Bertie was burnt in the ensuing small explosion. This made him think of using the explosive flash to drive an engine, and he developed this idea between 1886 and 1890, devising an oil engine which in several ways was more truly the ancestor of modern oil engines than were the early attempts of Dr Rudolf Diesel.

---

10 I am indebted to Dr Peter Jarvis for much of the information in this section, and it
   was he who carried out the interviews mentioned in other footnotes.
11 Information from Miss Mary Sinfield (1884–1973).

The basic idea behind Akroyd Stuart's invention is that whereas a petrol or gas engine is fired electrically from a spark plug, in an oil engine the heat of compression will vapourise fuel oil and cause the explosion, thus driving the piston in its cylinder. The early Akroyd engines had a bulb on the end of the cylinder which had to be heated to a dull red by a blow lamp. When this was done, the flywheel was spun and a jerk pump injected 'solid fuel' (ie, oil without air) into the hot bulb. The piston would compress the air from the cylinder into the bulb, and the resulting explosion would drive the piston down the cylinder again. The heat from this would keep the bulb hot enough for the engine to continue to fire by itself.

Eight engines are reputed to have been made at Bletchley, and four more were certainly made by George Wailes & Company of London during 1892. After tests, Herbert Akroyd Stuart sold his patent to Richard Hornsby and Sons of Grantham for £10,000[12] (about £100,000 at today's prices), and after this the engine was sold as the 'Hornsby-Akroyd'. Over 30,000 were built at Grantham alone over the next thirty years and were used all over the world. Several have survived locally. The original engine, No 101, was one of two supplied to Fenny Stratford Waterworks at Great Brickhill in 1892, worked until 1939 and was then placed in Ruston and Hornsby's museum. No 802 of 1895 is preserved in the Science Museum in London, No 3873 of 1899 (12½ brake horse power) is owned by Mr D. S. Johnson of Shenley Church End, and No 119754 of 1923 (84bhp)[13] known as 'Thumper' served for many years working a generator at the Post Office Repeater Station on the Watling Street at Fenny Stratford, and its last run was filmed by the Bletchley Archaeological & Historical Society in 1971. It is hoped that this engine too will be preserved; it is of a large type which was started not by heating the bulb, but by the use of compressed air.

Akroyd Stuart was a remarkable man, handicapped by poor health, poor materials, low standards of machining, and by his own stubborn opinions as to what engines should be like. Nevertheless he managed to make some astonishing advances, and his new combustion engine worked.

But over in Germany another keen mind, Dr Rudolf Diesel,

12 Information from Mr Rex Wailes, FSA, FIMECHE.
13 Information from Mr K. Peerless, Bletchley.

was more broadminded and more flexible. The diesel engine of today, whilst possibly originally thought up by Akroyd Stuart, is regarded by the world as a German invention. The diesel, or to give it its more accurate name, the 'compression ignition' engine, was patented by Dr Diesel in 1892, two years after Akroyd Stuart's patent. Krupps of Essen took up the idea. Diesel's original patent in 1892 was for an engine working on a fuel of coal dust and air, which proved unsuccessful, and only when considerable modifications were made was the M.A.N. diesel of 1895 practicable. The characteristic features of the modern diesel engine are the airless injection and the compression ignition, which were both used by Akryod Stuart. In 1898 the 'Diesel' engine was shown in an exhibition in Munich and soon became a commercial success. It proved ideal for ships and boats, heavy lorries and motor buses. Later powerful diesel engines displaced steam locomotives. For many grades of commercial vehicles, the diesel soon ousted the petrol engine, and today the farmers still left around Bletchley use diesel tractors which owe something of their origin to the man who worked at the Denmark Street foundry in Fenny Stratford.

What happened to Akroyd Stuart? He was in poor health, his patents were lapsing, and around 1910 he emigrated to Claremont, Western Australia, where his health improved and he continued his experiments at Akroyd Works, Perth. He died in 1927. In his will he directed that his business should be closed and all records destroyed. He left £500 to the University of Western Australia at Perth who still have an engine of his on display.[14]

North-east Bucks has had many distinguished engineers: Akroyd Stuart was the best of them all and it is pleasing to note that in 1964 the Bletchley Co-op and the Bletchley Archaeological and Historical Society placed a memorial plaque to him at the corner of Denmark Street, Fenny Stratford where he first began his exciting and often noisy experiments. He is the only man so honoured.

References
Engineering Heritage, Vol I, p157. Institution of Mechanical Engineers, London 1963.
Robinson, W. *Gas and Petroleum Engines* p695. E. and F. N. Spon. 1902.

14 Information from the Spalding family, Como, Western Australia.

Robinson, W. *Heavy Oil Engines of the Akroyd Stuart Type.*
Blackie & Son, 1931. This has a good photograph of Akroyd
Stuart as a frontispiece, which we reproduce elsewhere.
Hepworth H. S. *Bletchley District Gazette.* 15 March 1974.
The Science Museum has a fine model of the Akroyd Crude Oil
Engine, which we illustrate elsewhere.

TANNING

It will readily be understood from our previous chapters that the
great majority of people walked everywhere, and that only the
well-to-do could ride, whether on horseback or in light carriages.
Consequently there were boot and shoemakers in abundance,
stalwart and often quarrelsome individualists who had little
respect for those they shod. But every shoemaker needed leather,
and this was a team production – an industry whose origins
stretch back into deepest antiquity.

We know that there were tan pits at Stony Stratford hundreds
of years ago, indeed some of them still exist in the garden of
Stratford House near the Market Square. As the centuries rolled
on production and quality became more and more precise until
in the mid-19th century we find the firm of Sharp & Woollard,
curriers, well established along Church Street where the old
Bablake or poorhouses had been. They were a very go-ahead
firm, and the partners would ride out to the various villages,
and the towns like Buckingham and Newport, with samples and
prices, and also to collect accounts.

The firm of Sharp & Woollard, still in Church Street,
remains, with its long ancestry, the oldest established industry in
the town. It still has some of its early 19th century account books,
and in one at least of these are ancient recipes for leather dressing
which are most interesting and peculiar to modern ideas. There
was at that time no easy supply of ammonia, and the deficiency
was made up by having tubs for the use of the men in convenient
places, and utilising the product for the ammonia it contained.
In the recipes this ingredient is described as 'stale'. From all
accounts it certainly was.

When I joined the firm for a few months in 1914 the Sharp
family were represented by Mr Britton, and three very energetic
members of the Woollard family completed the directorate. Up

to 1914 they still rode out to the many villages, but with the war this pleasant activity ceased.

BREWING

Of equal antiquity to the tanning industry was the brewing industry. From the earliest times we have records of ale being brewed not only by local inns but also by local gentry, farmers and parsons. When Sir John Fortescue built his great mansion at Salden he took care to see that an efficient brewhouse was installed. Even parsons had their own brewhouse as we know from Cole's *Diary*, and every parson was a connoisseur. Naturally the quality of the beer varied immensely and we find Cole distinguishing carefully between the small ale he brewed for anybody, and the better brews intended for his friends.

Years later whenever an inn came up for sale the estate agents were careful to include full details of the convenient brewhouse and the adjacent cellars. When the *White Hart* (the UDC offices until 1974) at Stony Stratford was sold in 1840 the premises included 'a Valuable Malting with 6 Quarter Cistern and Garners etc. complete' and capital cellars.

Each of these inns were of course willing to sell beer to anybody, but gradually it was realised that by bulk production beer could be cheaper or more profitable and there grew up in most market towns a brewery or two that would sell to the pubs and the public at large.

In those days people drank twice as much beer as today, and it was about twice as strong, so that it is not surprising there were several recognised topers in every village. And if a man was not a toper everyone was willing to believe that he was a secret drinker. Off-licences flourished as much as the locals.

It took a long time for people to realise that a good brew would travel well by rail and brewers' drays; indeed it was not until 1851 that Fenny Stratford had a local brewery that could produce in bulk. The brewery was opened by Robert Holdom in 1851. It will be remembered that when the canal came to Fenny Stratford in 1800 a wharf and dock or basin was opened adjoining the Watling Street – a key position – by Mr Philip Constable, who soon erected a warehouse with a central crane for unloading the barges, and until his death in 1824 this wharf was profitable. But the coming of the railways, and the keen opposition from

Gregory Odell Clarke's wharf just the other (or north) side of the Watling Street greatly reduced its scope, and in 1851 the property was taken over by Robert Holdom who ran the *Bull and Butcher* in Aylesbury Street, and the *Wellington* in London Road. He was also a wine and spirit merchant, and had been a small brewer for years.

Holdom and his enterprising sons, George and Edward now began to build up a brewing business which supplied about fifty public houses, including the *Swan*, the *Bull and Butcher*, the *Wellington* and the *Foundry Arms* (1857) at Fenny Stratford, the *Park Hotel* (which was built by the Holdoms in 1869) and the *Eight Bells* in Bletchley, the *Crooked Billet* at Winslow, the *Rose and Crown* at Deanshanger and the *Fleur de Lis* at Hockliffe. They had difficulty in breaking into the Newport Pagnell area for not only were the Newport Brewery and the Cannon Brewery in the High Street, but two other brewers and maltsters as well.

Over the Northamptonshire border was a rival company, the Northampton Brewery Company, which supplied many pubs in north Bucks, and to the east was Wells of Bedford, who supplied many of the towns and villages along the Bucks-Beds border.

The Holdoms were pioneers in a thirsty field. By 1880 the firm was in such a thriving state that the two brothers bought for £1,050 the adjacent property in Fenny Stratford owned by Jesse Smith which included one of the most historic buildings in Fenny Stratford. In volume I, page 147, we related how the Fraternity of St Margaret and St Katherine had been founded in 1493, was dissolved by Henry VIII and the property leased to Lord Arthur Grey in 1569. We lose track of it until around 1911 Bradbrook had a good look at it and wrote:

'Between the Bull Inn and the Canal, there stands a very large barn, to which, at either end of it, have been made modern additions. This barn was part of the premises of the "guild" destroyed, temp. Edw. VI. It is of the 15th century, perhaps even of the 14th century. As it now stands, it is composed of timber frame on a stone foundation, the panes being of brick. Internally, it is about 75 feet in length, divided into five bays; the ground floor is about 12 feet in height; the upper floor is about seven feet up to the eaves, and about twenty feet up to the ridge of the gabled roof, which is now

Guildhall, hospital and chantry

Guild of St Margaret & St Katherine the Virgins

Fenny Stratford

|——————— 3m

Drawn by Peter Woodfield, Conservation Officer, MKDC, by courtesy of Valentin, Ord & Nagle Ltd, Fenny Stratford.

tiled, but was originally thatched. On the upper floor, the two bays at the northern end were formerly partitioned off and ceiled with plaster, which also covered the walls. This plaster was frescoed. At this date (1911), nearly all the frescoing has disappeared.'

but there was still a plaster frieze of the 17th century representing a cat and a fiddle, with birds and foliage around.

Into these mediaeval surroundings the brewery extended with its vats and pipes, steam and chemicals (even then) and it is surprising that so much remains even though it has been used for this purpose for well over a century.

In 1896 Edward Holdom who had bought his brother out ten years earlier sold the entire property as a going concern to Bletchley Breweries for £14,550. George Cave was the man behind Bletchley Breweries and we shall refer to him again very soon. Later the business was bought by the Aylesbury Brewery Company, who sold it in 1910.

The business was then acquired by the predecessors of Valentin Ord & Nagle, (who now own the whole of the property between the *Bull* and the canal) and from that day to this they have flourished as brewing sugar specialists with a growing national renown.[15]

Meanwhile there had been set up in the High Street, Fenny Stratford, Cave's Solid Beer Syndicate which had discovered the art or science or taking the water out of the beer and producing solid blocks (rather like slabs of chocolate) which when again hydrated produced beer of a quality that varied only with the amount of water added.[16]

When the Boer War broke out in 1899 and British troops by the thousands went to South Africa it was generally thought that the local breweries would be able to cope, but as the war dragged on and became more mobile the problem of getting beer to troops on long sweeping actions proved difficult. Cave's Solid Beer slabs helped provide an answer and Cave's prospered. But

15 I am grateful to the company for letting me see various legal documents and plans dating from 1833. Fortunately the old mediaeval barn is at present in good hands. For a photograph of part of the outside see volume I, plate 6. For a further description of the buildings as they were around 1912, see the *Royal Commission on Historical Monuments*, Buckinghamshire Vol II, p114, and also *Records of Bucks* XII p14 which portrays the cat and the fiddle fresco.

16 Information from Mr E. Legg. See his article 'The Inns and Ale Houses of Fenny Stratford', in the *Milton Keynes Journal* No 2, 1973.

there are sceptics who wonder whether the resulting brew had any alcoholic content at all. It looked like beer, it smelt like beer, but was it beer?

Cave's were still flourishing in 1907, but they seem to have folded up soon after. It was the last brewery run by townsmen. Today almost every pub is tied to a brewing chain.

And so in every village and town there are rival pubs no longer brewing their own ales, but tied in with a brewery company of growing dimensions. The arguments about the quality of the beer continue. Beers get lighter and lighter.

TAYLORS OF NEWPORT PAGNELL

One of our most surprising industries for well over a century has been that of T. & F. J. Taylor, mineral water and mustard manufacturers in Union Street, Newport Pagnell.

The first of the line, William Taylor, was a chemist, druggist, soda water manufacturer and oil and colourman, who set up business in 1834, and realised that his well produced water of unusual properties due to the deposits of great oolite limestone in the neighbourhood. We have other such wells in our neighbourhood, such as St Vincent's Well at Cosgrove, which was regarded as holy for centuries.[17] William Taylor never claimed holiness for his table water, but he made other claims and bottled it meticulously.

The mustard was then a side-line.

Mustard 'the least of all seeds' as the Bible says, has been for a thousand years one of the most important spices or condiments used in England. Our Anglo-Saxon forefathers used it. In Norman times it was mixed (very finely ground) with honey, wine and vinegar. Around the 17th century it became the great British spice, for whilst pepper, nutmeg, cinammon and saffron were more valuable, mustard was more available. 'Salt, mustard, vinegar, pepper' came into our nursery skipping rhymes long before the Victorian cruet became an essential feature of any dinner table. But unlike many spices, mustard could be grown anywhere, even on the clay soil of north Bucks. One early difficulty was the crushing of the tearful seed – for it had the same effect on human eyes as onions. Both the brown and white seeds

17 See *The Nineteen Hundreds* by S. F. Markham, p36.

have a yellow kernel which must be separated from the husk and ground into flour. But the mustard seed is very oily, so a little wheat flour was added, with turmeric for colouring, and that, with water added, is mustard.

At the start (in 1834) Taylors employed about a dozen people at about 11s a week, with overtime at 3d an hour with bread and cheese, and beer. The trade grew and by 1900 it was a thriving firm with a great reputation. Naturally there were competitors – fierce and hot competitors of whom the greatest was Colman's of Norwich. In the end Colmans won, for they bought up Taylors in 1950. But Taylor's Mustard Limited still goes on producing 'original Prepared English Mustard' with its 'Ingredients mustard flour, wheat flour, salt and turmeric'. 'Made at Newport Pagnell since the Reign of King William IV'. Few of our local firms have kept their name so long.

Local people looked on mustard not only as a spice, but almost as a certain cure for colds, chills and toothache. Mustard plasters would bring the blood to the surface and abolish sprains and strains in no time, and a mustard bath was reckoned to help cure rheumatism. It was a natural preservative which inhibited the growth of bacteria and fungi, great grandmother's antibiotic in a way.

THE PRINTING INDUSTRY

As has so often happened in north Bucks, when one industry dies, another seems to take its place. The decline in agriculture, lace making and straw plaiting was more than matched by the demands of the railway centres, and whilst these employed very few women, they produced an idea that helped.

It all began with the powerful Sir Richard Moon, chairman of the L. & N. W. Railway from 1861 to 1891, amongst whose friends were the McCorquodales of Newton-le-Willows. This famous printing firm had concentrated for many years on printing for the ever growing number of railway companies; consequently George McCorquodale and Richard Moon often met. In 1877 Richard Moon suggested that it would be a good idea to have a printing works at Wolverton to employ the daughters of the railway workmen there. The idea was taken up with zest. A plot of land was bought adjoining the railway works, and in 1878 George McCorquodale quietly opened a small one-storey factory of twenty employees – mostly girls. They were soon engaged on making registered envelopes for the GPO.

Success was immediate – almost spectacular, and in 1884 and 1889 three-storied buildings were added for general printing and binding. By now 120 girls and twenty men were employed. In 1890 a new dining room was opened by George McCorquodale – now a very old man – and this was his last visit to Wolverton.

The contract for registered envelopes has been retained by McCorquodale's ever since – nearly 100 years, but their Wolverton range has many other facets.[18]

McCorquodale's ceased to be a 'little' firm at Wolverton in 1890, and during the last eighty years has absorbed girls whose grandmothers had been lace-makers or straw plaiters. The change was a good one.

Fortunately we have some delightful photographs of some of these girls in 1890. The office girls wore what they liked, but the others wore not exactly a uniform but a steady fashion of a black blouse and skirt, over which a white apron with wide shoulder bands was worn when at work. It will be noticed that each girl has slightly different bands, etc. When they came to leave work they pinned on with large hatpins the trim Luton straw hats which again varied slightly with the girls' personal taste. The girls started work at 13 or 14 and were usually married before their 21st birthday. It was a happy firm.[19]

In 1905 the Envelope Department was built, and the whole of the Works re-organised and rearranged, and by 1907, 550 men and girls were in employment. It was a great development, but only the prelude to still greater successes. Up to this period, the hours like those on the railway, had been long, and it was McCorquodale's who first led the way to shorter hours. In the September of 1909 they changed the hours to begin at 8 am instead of 6.30 am and finish at 6 pm with a dinner-hour break at 12.30. On Saturdays they worked until 1 pm. The shorter hours produced better results and happier conditions. In addition to this, contributory pension funds, bonuses for years of service, minimum wage rates, holidays with pay, a mutual sick society and welfare officers were all introduced in later years, and, indeed,

18 See *The Nineteen Hundreds* by S. F. Markham, pp19–21, and the *Philatelic Bulletin* for November 1971, which has an interesting article on Wolverton by Mr George Boddington.

19 Information from Mr G. A. Boddington of Wolverton. See illustration, plate 13.

McCorquodale's could claim (though they seldom did) that they were not only the best printers and envelope makers in the country, but also among the best employers.

In 1910, the firm secured a further large Government contract for Postal Stamped Stationery, making necessary another large extension and the influx of a permanent Government staff to supervise and check production. It was no longer a little firm, but the second largest in north Bucks.

It is still pre-eminently a family firm and a family atmosphere is encouraged. Employees of three and four generations in succession are not exceptional, and different branches vie with one another in their boasts of service records.

THE PRESS

As can be imagined, McCorquodale's did very little local printing. This they wisely left to the established little printers, who were more numerous than might have been expected. First of all there were those who produced the local newspapers and did all sorts of general printing besides.

The earliest of these was William Nixon at Stony Stratford, who in 1854 produced *The Cottage Newspaper and the Stony Stratford and Wolverton Station General Advertiser*, which had a precarious existence and died with him in 1864. But he also produced school primers and short local histories which had a local success, and are now great rarities.

In 1870 another Stratford printer, Alfred Walford, produced the *North Bucks Advertiser* which lasted thirty years.

Meanwhile in 1859 *Croydons Weekly* was established at Newport Pagnell, and later changed its name to the *Bucks Standard*. It has thrived for well over a century. From 1867 when its circulation was only just over 1,100 copies a week it had to meet for many years the rivalry of *The Newport Pagnell Gazette, Wolverton Times and Olney Free Press*, but this ceased in 1915.

Fenny Stratford did not have its own local newspaper until 1879 when T. C. Warren and J. A. Warren started up the *Fenny Stratford Times* (later the *North Bucks Times*). It successfully coped with the challenge from 1886 to 1893 of the *Fenny Stratford Flying Post*. In those days most local newspapers had a definite political slant, and whilst the *Fenny Stratford Times* was Conservative, the *Flying Post* was supported by Liberal and temperance interests.

Possibly the lack of brewery and public house advertisements hastened its downfall. The *North Bucks Times* had plenty of them, but it finally merged with the *Bletchley Gazette* (founded in 1933) in 1972.

In 1901 at Wolverton, H. E. Barnard established the *Wolverton Express*, and it soon became one of the leading local busters in north Bucks. Then, as now, considerable space was given to the activities of the local authorities, including the various local parish councils. The local Volunteers took nearly a column in every issue, whilst in the camping season nearly half a page would be devoted to a description of their activities. Sermons too, would sometimes be printed at length, and bazaars, fêtes, processions, etc, reported almost minutely. Sporting news varied, sometimes there would be whole columns of it, and sometimes a mere paragraph. Oddly enough, although there were attempts to create a 'Births, Marriages and Deaths' column people seemed to be reluctant to publicise their family events.[20]

All of these were published at 1d a copy, and they were fortunate if they reached a circulation of 5,000 weekly. The *Buckingham Advertiser* never got near this figure – and struggled along on a circulation of 3,600 until after the First World War. It still survives, having defeated quite a serious rival in the *Buckingham Express*, which lasted from 1865 to about 1911.

By modern standards all of these were exceptionally dull papers with very few illustrations, and with repetitive items like the local railway timetable and the local directory, and syndicated news items from all over the world.

Most of these local printing firms ran a book shop and often a newspaper agency. They employed up to half a dozen persons. None of the editors ever made a fortune. They didn't expect to.

The youngest of our local newspapers and now the one with the largest circulation, is the *Bletchley Gazette*. It owed its origin in 1933 to the 20 year old Ron Staniford, a stationer's traveller (and a native of the town) and Harold Price, aged 35, who was running a one-man printing business. The new weekly was a hazardous enterprise that ran on hope and a very small budget. For years it rarely sold more than 1,500 copies, and the financial return to its founders could only be found with a microscope.

---

20 For a better description of the *Wolverton Express* see *The Nineteen Hundreds* pp31–34. The title was changed to the *Milton Keynes Express* in 1973.

From the start its slogan was a 'Bigger, Better, Brighter Bletchley'. After the Second World War Carl Moser joined the board of Bletchley Printers and took over the paper's editorial control. In 1951 it was sold to the present proprietors, and in 1972 absorbed the *North Bucks Times*, since when it has gone from strength to strength, with an editorial staff of twenty, and the new title of the *Milton Keynes Gazette*.

BRUSH MAKING IN FENNY STRATFORD

Nobody quite knows who started up the industry of brush making in the area. *Musson & Craven's Directory* of 1853 makes no mention of any such activity, but we do know that Samuel Hackney opened a brush factory in Tavistock Street in 1877. Six years later it became Root's Brush Factory. Shortly afterwards former employees, Henry and Mary Anne Cook, set up their own little industry nearby, and from this small beginning there emerged the Victoria Road factory.

In 1895 we find Root's in trouble with the new Fenny Stratford UDC who ordered their surveyor to make an enquiry into allegations of overcrowding and inadequate sanitary conditions. The next year the firm were ordered to put in a proper water supply. Three years later the firm submitted incomplete plans for an extension – and the UDC gladly approved.

Both Root's and Cook's continued to progress until the First World War, but they were soon to be surpassed by an old industry that became a big industry – that of brick making, which turned out to be so important that it deserves a chapter to itself.

Anyway by 1914 Bletchley was a well balanced area with no great ambitions and a general contentment, and the many little local industries added much to the variety of life.

However varied and interesting these local industries might be, they waxed and waned and often disappeared, or were swallowed up in amalgamations and take-overs. The great industry – the railways – went on: it seemed as if they were destined to go on for ever. For where a neglectful or drunken director could ruin a little firm, the railways would have a method of quickly replacing anyone who did not come up to high standards of efficiency and leadership.

Where the little industries only employed a few hundreds each at most, the railway employed thousands in north Bucks alone.

They were not only the largest employer of labour, they employed more than all the little firms put together. The history of north Bucks in the 19th century, and indeed for the first decade of the 20th century, was mainly the history of the railway with its great and still expanding works at Wolverton and with its growing engine sheds and junction at Bletchley. Inside these two focal centres there was now growing up a movement that was almost as powerful as the railway itself. Organised labour was now not only negotiating on equal terms with the great railway chiefs, it was also beginning to dominate the local councils and the local Liberal and Labour parties. In another chapter we shall see how it all began.

11 The Expansion of Wolverton and the Decline of the Villages, 1860–1914

WHEN we left Wolverton in 1860 it was a confident town suffering from growing pains which everyone hoped would disappear.

The L. & N. W. Railway like a wealthy generous grandfather had helped to provide houses, schools, churches, roads, piped water, a sewage system, and a great many other things that helped to make up the orderly progressive community. The Radcliffe Trustees were still the official lords of the manor, and assisted in many directions, though they were only doing what the Duncombes, the Knapps and other lords of manors had done for centuries without anyone much remarking on it or saying a thank you. One thing the L. & N. W. Railway board rarely provided was anything really beautiful in terms of architecture. The little streets both in Wolverton and New Bradwell lacked any glimmer of architectural inspiration. The churches and chapels and later on the Science and Art Institute were however fine exceptions to a general rule.

RAILWAY ARCHITECTURE

Where much of the canal architecture was accidentally beautiful – the humped back bridges and the winding lengths of water, towing paths and hedges creating landscapes of their own – the railways often begat ugliness in its straightest and most severe forms. A railway track may look beautiful to the railway enthusiast rejoicing in the best permanent way in the world, but few could describe the grim bridges, the equally grim platforms or the shunting yards and sheds as beautiful.

But there was one field in which some of the railway companies tried valiantly to get from their architects the most striking buildings of the Victorian age. The older generation will remember the stark impressiveness of the Doric arch at Euston, 'the gateway to the North', and the sweet proportions of the Stephenson Hall nearby both of which are gone. The modern Euston has an entirely different idiom. All over the country the great stations like Temple Meads at Bristol (Railway Gothic) with its great hammer-beam hall, or the neo-Gothic St Pancras terminal at London showed that neither ingenuity or skill had been spared.

To a certain degree this determination to make attractive stations up and down the country was a feature of the age. Our local stations show how far they succeeded. It must of course be remembered that one of the relatively new forms of architectural design was based on cast iron. The elegant iron bridge at Newport Pagnell, built in 1810 before the railways came, is a fine example of how flexible iron could become in the new foundries. But the railways unhappily did not often follow this example and the many railway bridges we still have in this locality, such as those at Wolverton, Skew Bridge, etc, were examples of ugliness. It was different with the actual stations: for here slender cast iron columns and struts supported railway station porticos with a grace and lightness that our church builders rarely produced in stone.

Given the fact that iron could be cast into almost any design, and support great weights, it is surprising that there was not more beauty in railway buildings.

When it came to the station façades the architects really varied, and up and down the country one can see everything from the long dullness of Bletchley to the cottage Tudor of Fenny Stratford only a mile away. Fenny Stratford Station is an 'L'-shaped gabled building with a high chimney, and all the platform side of it is criss-crossed half timbering in profusion.[1] From the opposite platform it looks something like a typical country pub – like the *Rosebery Arms* at Cheddington – and the smart white railings added to its attractiveness. Woburn Sands station also is a remarkably cosy structure with its half timbering and barge board gables. One or two stations such as these ought to be preserved.

In these early railway stations passengers wandered casually across the tracks just as they had wandered across the cobblestones of the local inn yard. It was not a healthy diversion.

1 For illustration of Fenny Stratford Station see *Railway Relics* by Bryan Morgan, 1969, plate 19.

EXPANSION AT WOLVERTON

We have seen in chapter 5, page 78 that in 1847 James Edward McConnell replaced Edward Bury as Locomotive Superintendent at Wolverton. He soon decided that the four-wheel Bury engines (which we illustrate on page 75) were antiquated and slow, and that, with board approval, he would replace them with mighty engines of his own design. His policy was to produce as large an engine as possible, limited only by the size of tunnels. In 1849 he built his first experimental engines at Wolverton, but these just happened to be a little wider than convenient, and some railway platforms and other lineside structures got shaved like a garage jamb. In 1851–52 he built his first express engines, which were quickly nicknamed 'Bloomers' after Mrs Amelia Bloomer, an exciting American lady who designed daring costumes for ladies which showed their legs. McConnell with his new express engines 'cleared away the decent skirting of an outside frame, and exhibited all the wheels to the traveller's gaze'.

Soon there were small Bloomers, large Bloomers and extra large Bloomers and, to judge from all reports, they were more efficient than anything Crewe was producing. These exceptionally powerful engines in their bright red livery picked out in white were a joyous sight wherever they went. We are fortunate in being allowed to reproduce Hamilton Ellis's painting of one of them under full steam. So Wolverton was now not just a repair and maintenance depot for engines, but a locomotive factory of great renown.[2] Over seventy Bloomers were built in all, and most of them at Wolverton. Their striking appearance with the tall red engines, the great unencumbered wheels and corniced brass domes tickled the public's fancy.

The Bloomers of course helped to quicken up time tables, and this in turn meant that there was less need for every train to stop at Wolverton to change engines or to give passengers a lavatory break. The famous Wolverton station refreshment rooms began to lose a little of their renown. It was only now that Bloomer engines were given individual names which varied from the breeds of dogs to castles, but whatever the name they behaved with pedigree perfection, and some continued in use for thirty years with some of the most famous trains of the day, including

---

2 See Hamilton Ellis' *Four Main Lines* pp28 and 44, Allen and Unwin.

the Irish Mail. Their production ceased soon after McConnell retired in 1862.[3]

Meanwhile McConnell persuaded the board that most of the area north of Stratford Road should be cleared of houses, and new houses and shops should be erected south of the Stratford Road. In 1858 more land was bought from the Radcliffe Trustees, and to the west new workshops were created (erection and boiler shop, smithy and carpenters' shops) whilst to the south, Church Street and Radcliffe Street were quickly built.

By 1860 Wolverton Works was employing about 2,000 men, including a well established signalling school. Signalling was then a matter of red, green and white flags. The white flags were to signal all clear. In March 1860 an article in the *Illustrated London News* was eloquent in its praise of the 'new railway colony of Wolverton'. It went on:

'The great expansion of Wolverton has rendered necessary the providing of further accommodation for the residents of the workmen and their families.

'About 150 cottages have been completed in New Bradwell. They are neat in appearance and are built in the most substantial manner, with every regard to the comfort and convenience of the residents.'

The article also describes the laying of a foundation stone by the Marquess of Chandos. It was almost his last public function as chairman of the L. & N. W. Railway, for a few months later he succeeded to the dukedom and left the company. There were rumours that his northern colleagues thought he paid too much attention to Wolverton and the southern part of the L. & N. W. Railway: others that there was a personal struggle for power between him and Richard Moon, who became the new chairman. We are unable to comment as the relevant Stowe papers are in the USA and the company minutes are of course discreet.

In 1864 the new Science and Art Institute was opened in Church Street. It was an attractive building of its period, and here for years the youth of Wolverton, Stony Stratford and Bradwell continued their education, producing a railway élite of no mean distinction.[4]

---

3 See *The Pre Grouping Railways*, Science Museum, 1972, illustration 10. There are some superb photographs of the 'Bloomers' at Wolverton Works.
4 In 1926 it housed a technical school, but in 1970 after being empty for a time it was burnt to the ground.

In 1865 our shortest local railway line, from Wolverton to Newport, first proposed in 1845, was opened, with its miniature stations *en route* at Bradwell and Great Linford. Newport celebrated, but the line was never unduly overcrowded with passengers.

But now there was another very important policy change. It was decided to transfer the responsibility for locomotives to Crewe, and to concentrate the scattered carriage and wagon departments of the entire L. & N. W. Railway into one huge works at Wolverton.

In 1864 and 1866 extra land was acquired from the Radcliffe Trustees to double the extent of the works. The expanded works included large carriage body and carriage repair shops, a carriage finishing shop, forges and a foundry, an axle shop, body and underframe shops, timber stores, a saw mill, several large paint shops and a dozen other specialised departments. These all had to be equipped with the best machinery available. Everything indeed had to be of the best. Even the wheelbarrows and trucks were built to last 100 years. Some have.

Before Wolverton Works could expand, more of it had to be scrubbed out. We have seen that as originally planned and built Wolverton consisted of the great engine shed immediately west of the old main line, and around the shed on three sides were 100 tightly packed little houses. Walker Street, Cooke Street and Garnet Street had already gone, now Gas Street and part of the important Bury Street with its dozen shops were demolished. They had only been up twenty-five years. Nothing like it had ever happened in Buckinghamshire before. When the lords of the manor in mediaeval times obliterated villages to make sheep farms there were great protests, but at Wolverton nobody even wanted to protest against the autocratic action of the railway directors, for they planned alternative accommodation not too far off, no jobs were at stake, and the destroyed houses were neither beautiful nor quiet.

Stratford Road and Church Street were the new shopping centres. In addition to this Wolverton had already acquired a market. This of course was not a cattle market, but a provisions and dry goods market in the new market hall where you could buy anything from a new book for 1d or a complete washstand set and chamber pot for about 2s. Wolverton was now a good shopping centre with a score of shops and the Friday market. One of the usual sights on a Friday was to see the women of Bradwell, with a child or maybe two in a pram, pushing their way up Station Hill to take advantage of the bargains offered at the market.

But these were not the only changes. Richard Moon decided around 1880 that Wolverton Works had to be by-passed, and in a short time a new permanent way with new and wider bridges was planned 1½ miles long from Bradwell Brook at the south to the Ouse at the north, linking up with the forty year old viaduct. It was elevated all the way and so required not only new bridges and a new station built on stilts, but the diversion of old roads. 'Moon's folly' as it was called went forward at speed. There were no local authorities to question planning details, for Parliament had given the L. & N. W. Railway autocratic powers which were firmly used by Richard Moon.[5] The old (or second) station had been famous in its day for every train stopped there, but now with corridor coaches and increased speeds there was no need for the great trains to stop at Wolverton, and the new station, opened in 1881, was rather dismal. Bletchley was now becoming more important and had a better train service.

The Works now began to extend eastwards right up to the new permanent way, whilst the low lying area between the canal, the old line, the new line and the old Wolverton Road was now earmarked for a sports park of considerable importance.

Unfortunately with all these developments the railway planners made a dreadful mistake, an aesthetic error of no mean dimensions – and that was to build an ugly, almost continuous brick wall about 10ft high for ¼ mile from the new Wolverton Station to the western end of the works. So for the next century this extended grim prison-like wall was the main thing visitors to Wolverton noticed all along the Stratford Road.

Brick walls need not be ugly, indeed many of our towns and villages have brick walls of great beauty. The arches of McCorquodales, the intricate work of some of the garden walls in York Road at Stony Stratford and Moon Street at Wolverton show what the brick-layer of the period could do when given a chance.

5 Moon continued as chairman until 1891, was made a baronet in 1887, and died in 1899.

But Wolverton's wall was ugly, and is still ugly in spite of a few recent gaps where little gardens grow.

In thirty years Wolverton had changed so much that a man who served his apprenticeship there in the 1840s and returned in the 1890s would recognise only the great engine shed, the *Royal Engineer*, and a couple of little streets left to remind him of his youth.

In this centre of modern industry, a lad served a seven-year apprenticeship before acquiring the status of a full tradesman. Here, where brains, skill and up-to-date equipment were assembled and ably directed, constant improvements were made in the technique of carriage construction. New designs, new safety devices, improved lighting systems, bogie wheels – all were thought out and applied in these works, changing the short carriage into the long saloon coach.

Everybody was learning his job. From the engineers, the plate-layers and the shunters to the newly appointed station staff, everybody was reaching out to his maximum potential to meet the ever-growing demands. Promotion was quick to those who found favour, except for engine cleaners who hoped to become firemen and then engine drivers. Often it would take ten years or more to go from one grade to another.

Wolverton was one of the think boxes of the nation: it was a safe and fortunate place to try out most of the new ideas. Even the porters were learning how not to refuse tips.

Working hours were long, discipline was strict; it needed to be, for the speed of some trains was frightening and caused many accidents. An ordinary train travelling at 30mph could not pull up within a mile and even Wolverton could not devise an adequate braking system.

The population of both Wolverton and Bradwell began to increase rapidly. Bradwell, which had a population of only 381 in 1851, jumped to 1,658 in 1861 and 2,409 in 1871. The two towns, separated by the railway line and the canal, added a thousand more to their joint population each decade and by 1901 they had over 9,200 souls: larger than Aylesbury or Buckingham (which had declined to 3,150). In all Buckinghamshire, only High Wycombe was larger.

Meanwhile the demand for houses grew. Wolverton began to extend southwards from the original nucleus which included

Young Street, Glyn Square, Creed Street and Ledsam Street.[6] Already the houses stretched along Church Street, Buckingham Street and Aylesbury Street, and criss-crossing these were Radcliffe Street and Cambridge Street.

Practically all the houses the railway built, both in Wolverton and Bradwell, were rented – many at 3s a week. But shops were let at 7s 6d a week and the 'villas' at £18 a year. The company now thought it was high time their workers should have a chance of owning their own houses. In 1859 they started selling building plots along the Stratford Road, with 40-44ft frontages for £62 or a little more.[7] But sales were slow, for neither the banks nor other money lenders were willing to advance hundreds of pounds on twenty or twenty-five year loans. In 1878 the company decided not to embark on the building of more houses in Wolverton.[8] A meeting was called at the Science and Art Institute and it was resolved there and then to form a Building Society. Richard Moon, the chairman of the company, gave the plan his support and promised to arrange for more land to be bought from the Radcliffe Trustees. A committee was elected to draw up the rules of the Society which should be submitted to the Registrar of Building Societies. These rules were approved, and in October 1878 the Wolverton Permanent Benefit Building Society was established. It proved to be a great boon to Wolverton and Bradwell people, and most of the houses built after 1878 were purchased through this society.

It was not inappropriate that one of the new streets should be called Moon Street. It went uphill.

As for New Bradwell, it was a town without a market and many other amenities that older towns enjoyed, but it had a spirit of its own.

STONY STRATFORD'S EXPANSION

Whilst Wolverton and New Bradwell were now expanding rapidly, the old market town of Stony Stratford was keeping pace with the new developments but also in a way of its own. Railway power ceased with the boundaries of St George's Parish, Wolverton and St James's Parish, New Bradwell, and the twin

6 These four streets were demolished in the 1960s.
7 Information from Mr R. Ayers.
8 F. E. Hyde's *Wolverton*, 1945.

parishes of Stony Stratford West (St Giles') and St Mary Magdalene continued their own quarrelsome way. The losses, and very
great losses too, due to the decline of stage-coach and wagon
trade, were quickly made good, for every widow opened her
house to lodgers and Stony Stratford became a dormitory suburb
of Wolverton – a nice one too, apart from the dreadful new houses
in the old inn yards which we have noticed earlier.

The new St Paul's School added dignity to the town and three
building parsons added much to the amenities and serenity of the
area, whilst Hayes' Engineering Works were just beginning to
expand.[9] But Wolverton Works was the dominant factor, and
from 1860 onwards there was such a steady development towards
Wolverton that a new parish of Wolverton St Mary was created
in 1870 to meet present and future needs.

The population of Stony Stratford which had been about 1,600
before the coming of the railway had doubled by 1891 and
another half a dozen streets were being built or planned.

THE DECLINE OF THE VILLAGES, 1851–1901
But whilst Wolverton, Bradwell and Stony Stratford were
expanding, there was a sad and lamentable decline in the population of our villages. Part of this was due to agricultural depression
with some very bad harvests in the 1870s, but part of it may have
been due to the fact that the railways helped to kill village
industries.

We have seen how the lace industry, which occupied so many
village women in the early part of the century, had dwindled
to about a couple of grandmothers in each village, whilst the
straw plait industry along the Bedfordshire border, just faded
away. And where other work was found for women, as for
example printing or brush making, it was in or near the existing
towns.

One cause of the long agricultural depression was that the
railways now brought cheap American wheat to areas where
only home-grown wheat had previously had a market. This
combination of bad harvests and low prices caused the ruin of
many local farmers, and of many others who were dependent
upon the farming community. Consequently there was now a

9 See *History of Stony Stratford* pp171–76

steadily growing stream of emigrants to the new railway centres, or overseas. Scarcely a week went by without a local family or individual leaving for the USA, or one of the colonies, all part of an adventurous stream which took hundreds of thousands of English men and women overseas and founded the greatness of one or other of the new English-speaking nations.

One of the earliest mentions of emigration from Stony Stratford occurs in the minute book of the Stony Stratford Baptist Church, which records that in 1847 'Brother Thomas Smith, our Sisters Elizabeth, Rebecca and Susan Smith, had left the country, the former for America, and the latter for Australia, and that letters of commendation had been supplied them'. Church and chapel documents record many such examples of voluntary emigration. There were others of a less willing nature, for example, in 1856–57 there were several sentences on local men for sheep-stealing, one of which, on George Meakins, was for transportation to Australia for fourteen years – a high price for a sheep!

Among those who emigrated to the United States a little later (1863) was a family from Stony Stratford by the name of Sutherland, who took with them their fifteen month old boy, Alexander George. Sixty years later, in 1922, he became a Justice of the Supreme Court of the United States, and in the following year visited his native town. In 1938 he was again invited to Stony Stratford, but failing health did not permit this visit, and he died in 1942.

During Queen Victoria's reign probably a thousand families left the area for permanent residence overseas. In every one of our agricultural villages houses tumbled into ruins, churches had smaller congregations, some, like Tattenhoe, Great Woolstone and Stanton Low by the end of the century had practically no congregations at all.

But however good the landlord, however industrious the farmers, two facts were obvious. The ever increasing amount of imported agricultural produce from the USA and the colonies (which then included Canada, Australia, South Africa and New Zealand) kept prices low – farmers were no longer gentlemen farmers, they were struggling for a bare existence and in addition the growing use of farm machinery made hands redundant. One result of all this was to reduce the population of nearly all our villages by a third of what it had been in the 1850s. Here are a few figures:

Comparison of population, 1851 to 1901		
Village	1851	1901
Beachampton	248	180
Bow Brickhill	591	448
Great Brickhill	730	491
Little Brickhill	555	278
Broughton	182	113
Drayton Parslow	490	369
Milton Keynes	317	219
Moulsoe	239	190
Mursley	553	367
Newton Longville	595	424
Shenley Brook End	283	186
Shenley Church End	210	166
Stoke Hammond	438	288
Swanbourne	646	405
Tattenhoe	55	16
Walton	100	84
Whaddon and Nash	987	584
The Woolstones	209	130
Woughton	337	202

Nearly every other village in the whole of north Bucks more than 2 miles from a railway centre, lost a third of its population during the same period. Some villages like Clifton Reynes, Newton Blossomville, North Crawley and Ravenstone lost half their population.

By contrast, the railway townships of Wolverton, Bradwell and Bletchley increased from 5,000 to 15,000 during the half century. This was due not only to the railways providing employment, but to the fact that new and expanding industries like McCorquodales at Wolverton, the brush industry at Bletchley, and the others we have mentioned in our chapter on 'Little Industries', were located near to railway centres.

Not all new railway workers came from Buckinghamshire villages; many came from south Northants: Deanshanger, Old Stratford, Potterspury, Cosgrove and Yardley Gobion all provided their contingents for Wolverton Works. The youth of the villages took the chance to escape from a dying agriculture before they were entrapped. The old folk could decay in their thatched cottages with roses round the door – the young folk moved to New Bradwell or Wolverton, into stolid, ugly, terrace houses which however were better than many village slums. They survived. They did well, and loved visiting the old folks.

Whilst the upsurge in the population of the railway towns was visible to anybody, with the new streets appearing almost yearly, and the new schools, chapels and so on, the decline in the villages was a little slower. The lads left home taking lodgings at Wolverton or nearby; they returned at weekends, but when the courting days ended at the altar they did not settle in the village of their birth, they took one of the tight little houses provided by the railway company. The old people died out, the worst of the old cottages were unlet: the little shops did less and less trade – but only gradually and over a generation. Church contributions began to dwindle, local pubs began to show diminishing returns. Burials were more frequent than baptisms.

In the legal documents of the period the word 'toft' occurs again and again – it meant a homestead plot where the house had fallen into ruin. The plot was no good for agriculture or anything else, since no one wanted to rebuild. They were as desolate as the often neglected churchyards.

THE DECLINE OF BUCKINGHAM

It was not only the villages that declined, the famous county town of Buckingham also entered a period of decay. We have seen that in the time of Browne Willis, Buckingham was the county town and indeed for another half century it flourished.

But in the 19th century a series of events took place which sapped its vitality. Its population declined from 4,054 in 1841 to 3,152 in 1901,* and this at a time when Aylesbury had almost doubled its numbers, and Bletchley and Wolverton had increased four-fold. There were several reasons for this. In the first place Aylesbury took over the dignity of being the county town early in the 19th century which meant that quite a number of functions and activities were transferred to it. In 1849 Buckingham lost its position as an assize town.

An equally important reason for the decline was that owing to

* and to 3,060 in 1921.

the early opposition of the Duke of Buckingham it was by-passed by the greatest railway in England. Not until 1850 did it achieve a station, by which time Wolverton and Bletchley were singled out for great advance. The fact that Buckingham was not on a main line hindered the establishment of industry.

Again, up to 1867 Buckingham had had two members of Parliament and was, with its surrounding parishes, eagerly courted by its MPs or candidates. By 1885 it was merged with the north of the county and although the poll was still counted at Buckingham it was no longer the political centre. Bletchley and Wolverton took over.

Then the agricultural depression of the 1870s hit Buckingham badly for its main business was that of a market town serving an almost solidly agricultural area. Less and less money was spent on market days.

Next we have seen that the great family of Grenville-Temple at Stowe had had its vicissitudes from 1847 until 1889 when the last Duke of Buckingham died. Possibly the Duke's greatest disappointment was that he had neither son nor nephews and when he died in 1889 many of his titles died with him, but the estates of Stowe and the Scottish barony of Kinloss went to his daughter, Mary. But even before this the importance of the family had diminished and there was a growing impoverishment. In 1890 Stowe was let to the Comte de Paris, the royalist claimant to the French throne. But as an exile he was not too wealthy. When he died in Buckingham in 1894, only part of Stowe was occupied by Lady Kinloss.

The next thirty years saw still greater financial embarrassments at Stowe and in 1921 the great palace that had cost nearly £3,000,000 to build and furnish, was sold for £40,000.

Unfortunately for England, at this great Stowe sale a million documents there were dispersed: most of them were bought by the American railway millionaire, Henry E. Huntington, and are now in the Huntington Library, San Marino, California. The library employs a full-time archivist to look after the Stowe papers alone. They consist of the papers of the Temple, Grenville, Brydges, Chandos and Nugent families and are continuous from about 1564 to 1920.[10] Some of the papers however remained in

10 Information from Lady Kinloss, and from the Huntington Library. The third Duke's railway correspondence alone comprises fifteen boxes.

the hands of solicitors or estate agents, and most of these are now in the Bucks County Record Office at Aylesbury. Unfortunately the successive Dukes never learnt to destroy uninteresting letters.

The last of the Grenvilles, Lady Jemima Temple-Nugent-Brydges-Chandos-Grenville, died in 1946, by which time Stowe had been a public school for over twenty years. All these factors put together, the loss of political importance, the impoverishment of its greatest family, the decay of the villages all around (Stowe itself lost half its population), resulted in a stagnation that lasted half a century.

Meanwhile both at Wolverton and at Bletchley – and at New Bradwell, the streets were rollicking with children. All the schools were under pressure, new shops, new chapels, new churches and new pubs sprang into being. Along the Wolverton Road at Stony Stratford no less than four new pubs came into being within the eight years 1867–75 – all this within a quarter of a mile – and all flourished.

One of the interesting features of the period of which we write is that whilst prices generally and wages, were gently rising, the value of land was going down. In those days a cottage in a village could be bought for £30, but naturally this would have no modern amenities and would in all probability be a thatched picture with two rooms up and two down. The better type of cottage, as for example in Bletchley or Stony Stratford, was around 1900 being sold for about £100, or was let for 5s per week. A slightly better type of house in Wolverton and parts of Bletchley was let at 6s per week, sold for £160–£200. Both in Wolverton and Bletchley it was the engine drivers and foremen who first bought the new houses. Tradesmen of course had had theirs for years.

From 1891 on Wolverton entered upon a long period of prosperity and expansion and its history from then until 1914 has already been covered in *The Nineteen Hundreds*, but since that book was published new light has been shed on the influence of Wolverton overseas.

OVERSEAS TEAMS, 1903

Wolverton Works, like those at Swindon and Doncaster, had had for years demands from countries all over the globe that were building railways, for technicians of all kinds. British capital

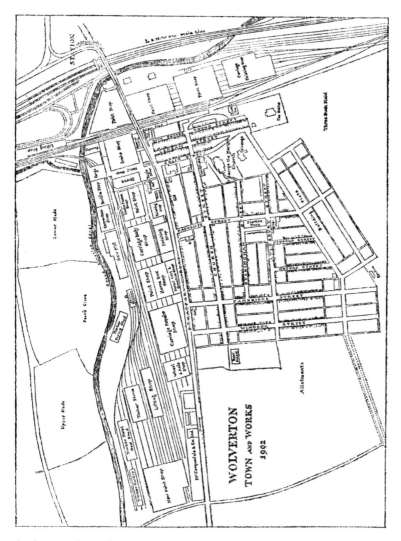

had started up lines in Canada, India, Egypt, Australia, South Africa, the Argentine and a dozen other countries, and it was only natural that men with the know-how should be asked to go out not only to create the railways, but also to run the railway workshops that kept the wheels rolling.

As early as 1880 teams of men left Wolverton for this purpose – mostly on short term contracts – but our best documented example comes from 1903. Early that year the notice boards in the works advertised the fact that the Government of Cape Colony needed railway fitters, coach body makers, track maintenance men, and so on. Harry Scrivener, Joe Henderson, Arthur J. Wesley (Stantonbury) and several others volunteered and in May 1903 they signed agreements to serve for one year at 11s a day (eight hours) to begin with (half rate during the voyage out) and then 12s a day. They went to Salt River Works, served their year, and expected to be retained. But official retrenchment was in the air, and they came back, some feeling that they had just been used to train 'blacks' in jobs that merited a full apprenticeship in England.

Harry Scrivener went on to the Argentine, and Joe Henderson to India, but Arthur Wesley found a girl who refused to set foot on board ship, so he stayed in Wolverton and lived locally ever after.[11]

One of the most interesting opinions on the Wolverton L. & N. W. Railway works about this period comes from an American journalist who visited the works early in 1908, and thus recorded his impressions in the *New York Herald* in May. He was of course impressed by the royal train, and by the general efficiency; then he asked Mr C. A. Park: 'You have no labour troubles, have you?' 'None', he answered, 'Why should we? The men live here in their homes and do not want to go away. Strikes are out of the question with us. We pay everybody for what he does. The better men get the better pay, the less efficient the poorer pay. Everything is piecework. They are contented, happy, well paid, and prosperous.' Park may have been aware of the growing force of trade unionism in Wolverton: it was to explode into a bitter strike three years later as we shall see in a later chapter, but Park was sacked in 1910 after twenty-four years as superintendent.

At this period the works were working the 54-hour week which had been introduced in 1872. For most people in Wolverton the morning began with 'the first hooter', which went at 5.20 am and was a signal for the general uprising of most of the male population. Work commenced at 6 am, with a break at 8.15 for breakfast. Work was resumed at 9 am and continued until 1 pm and again from 2 pm to 5.30. On Saturdays the hours were

11 I am indebted to Mrs Adams of Stony Stratford for lending me various documents dealing with this matter.

6 am to 12 noon, with the usual breakfast interval. Often there was 'short time' which meant missing the Saturday morning's work, and the first 'quarter' on Monday.

For those who came from Wicken, Potterspury or Yardley Gobion, the day began before 5 am, for whether one cycled or came by the 'Old Mail' it took nearly an hour to get to Wolverton. The 'Old Mail' was a wagonette or brake which rumbled its way daily back and forth with its load of working men, and often still carried the mail. Sometimes the men in a village clubbed together to provide their own horse and brake. At Nash for example, £40 was subscribed in this way and the men paid 1s 6d per week to be driven backwards and forwards to Wolverton daily. It cost 1s 6d per week to stable the horse at the *Royal Engineer*, Wolverton, and about 4s per week for stabling and grooming at Nash. The resultant profits paid off the capital.

At Beachampton a Working Men's Van Company was thus formed, and it was run so successfully that they could hold an annual dinner out of the profits.

From Castlethorpe, Bletchley and Newport Pagnell the men came in by special workmen's trains, and from Stony Stratford or Deanshanger by the historic tram.

THE OLD TRAM

In all this age of steam there were very few tramways until in 1870 an Act of Parliament permitted 'street railways', but even by 1877 only 363 miles had been authorised and only 213 miles were actually being operated in the UK. It was therefore perhaps surprising when in 1882 a group of men, mostly Stony Stratford tradesmen, got together to consider very seriously the prospects of running a steam tram from Wolverton to Stony Stratford. Keen observers had noticed that every day hundreds of men walked from Stony Stratford to Wolverton Works, and walked home again in the evening. In addition McCorquodales had opened a printing works at Wolverton in 1878, which now employed scores of women, many of whom lived in Stony Stratford and the adjacent villages. There was a sort of transport for those who could afford it, for as early as 1850 Mary Chapman, landlady of the *Cock Inn*, had established a bus service from there to Wolverton Station with a fare of 6d. But both she and her successor, Fanny Clarke, only ran the bus when there were sufficient travellers. Their average takings were only £2 to £3 a week, and there was little profit.

The first formal step was in 1882 when the churchwardens of St Giles' called a special meeting of all ratepayers to consider a proposal to apply to the Board of Trade for an Order to sanction the new tramway. The ratepayers approved the line coming along the Wolverton Road, subject to a track not exceeding 6ft in width except at the Stony Stratford end and outside Wolverton Works where shunting loops were allowed.

In November a company called 'The Wolverton and Stony Stratford Tramways Company' was formed with Abraham Culverhouse as its chairman, and John Field as its secretary. Within a year it went smash, but phoenix like rose again under the guidance of Frederick Charles Winby, a civil engineer and contractor, and he soon obtained in 1883 a new Tramways Order from the Board of Trade authorising a single line of 4ft gauge from Wolverton Station to the *Barley Mow Inn*, Stony Stratford. This he sold to a new tramways company which had a nominal capital of £30,000 in £1 shares. He contracted to build the line and take part of the price in shares. But only thirty-four shares were sold – Stony Stratford tradesmen for some reason now being very suspicious of the whole proposal. The company was dormant until 1886.

And now a new face comes into the picture, that of Charles Herbert Wilkinson, a local contractor who had tried to get the Newport–Olney branch railway line going, but without any success. Wilkinson, in August 1886, entered into a contract with the company to build the line for £13,325, of which £2,000 was to be in shares. The name of the company was now changed to the Wolverton, Stony Stratford & District Light Railway Company. Shares were again offered for sale, this time with more success, and the work went ahead. The new line, just over 2 miles long, was built to a 3ft 6in gauge. On 27 May 1887 the line was opened.

We have pointed out that there were few tramways in England at this period, but it was something of a surprise to the locality when they realised that the two engines were German, made by Krauss of Munich. Later ones, built by Thomas Green & Son of Leeds, were much more suitable.

The original rolling stock, in addition to the German engines, consisted of two workmen's cars carrying 120 passengers each (100 seated), one upholstered coach seating eighty passengers, a smaller one seating twenty passengers, and four wagons. Two of the wagons or trucks were made with convertible wheels, in order that, when the *Cock Hotel* was reached they could be pulled off the lines and around the town by horses.

The tram was a great success. Passenger takings topped £45 a week, mainly from workmen's weekly tickets at 1s a week entitling the passenger to four journeys a day. It was a wonderful bargain, for whilst 1s a week was a fair bite into a wage of about 25s a week, the men shrewdly calculated how much it saved them in shoe leather, for boots were as much as 7s a pair. Nearly 700 passengers a day were carried.

But a few years later a formidable challenge arose in the form of the 'safety' bicycle.

CYCLING

For many years the hazardous 'penny farthing' bicycle, with a front wheel of up to 58in diameter, and a rear wheel of sometimes less than 17in diameter, with its solid tyres and elementary brakes, had been used by acrobatic youths with hard bottoms. Now there came a series of improvements; cranks and chains produced the low 'safety' bicycle. The pneumatic and detachable tyre, and better braking, made cycling not only silent and swift, but also economical and safe. It was the cheapest method of getting from place to place along any reasonably level surface that man had ever devised. It still is.

Coventry, Birmingham and Amersham now produced them by thousands which sold locally at prices from £5 each. Soon there were bicycle and tricycle agents and repairers in every town and large village. Probably the first around here was Harry S. Roberts of the Condor Cycle Works, Deanshanger (no apparent connection with E. & H. Roberts) who supplied them to the eager youth of Stony Stratford and district as early as 1889. Within a decade there were three such agents and repairers at Newport Pagnell (including Salmons), three at Stony Stratford, four at Fenny Stratford, three at Wolverton, and one at Shenley Church End.

Practically every family had a 'bike' by 1895 and the Cyclists Touring Union became a power in the land. In 1897 the Fenny

Stratford Urban District Council records the receipt of a letter from the CTU 'calling attention to the damage done to pneumatic tyres of cycles by thorns left upon the Highway by parties responsible for the upkeep and trimming of adjoining hedges'. Since most of the councillors were cyclists it was unanimously agreed that the council's highways should be kept free from thorns and hedge clippings.

Cycle clubs sprouted up: gymkhanas and races were held all over the area. The most famous was the Whitsun Festival held at Wolverton Park (provided by the L. & N. W. Railway in 1885) which attracted competitors from all over the country. To add to the jollity the company cleared a large workshop for use as a ballroom for the evening's enjoyment. It excited far more interest than the keenest of football or cricket matches. Whitsun week at Wolverton was a wonder.

The old cumbersome penny-farthings however continued to circulate for a generation. Indeed, as late as 1910 one of the sights of the town was the almost solid mass of workmen cycling to or from work, the younger men on the new 'racing' bikes in the van, the middle-aged on 'safety's' in the middle, and the older ones on the penny-farthings bringing up the rear. The cyclist could always beat the tram, he had a flying start.

In 1888 the tramway was extended to Deanshanger where E. & H. Roberts' Britannia Ironworks was still expanding, but this line was never a success and the extension was soon abandoned. The company was now in financial difficulties, and in 1891 was taken over by a syndicate headed by H. S. Leon (afterwards Sir Herbert) of Bletchley Park. Gradually he acquired a controlling interest, with the Field family still holding a good minority interest, and Arthur Long Field being managing director and secretary.

The local manager was now Mr Louis Clovis, who resided at Old Stratford, and whose full name, as it was disclosed just before his death, was Louis Clovis Bonaparte. His successor, Mr Edwin Braggins, was the last man in Stony Stratford to wear a top hat daily, for he regarded himself as not inferior to a stationmaster, and a top hat was still part of a stationmaster's uniform, even as late as 1908.

Many stories are told of the tram, and of its staff, which later included the redoubtable 'Little Billy', who was a conductor for thirty years. It had its difficulties, but by and large it provided a most satisfactory service between the two towns for thirty years.

When I joined the company in January 1913, as a junior clerk, it was still thriving. I remember Sir Herbert Leon of Bletchley making an inspection visit on 18 August 1913. Already the buses were starting up a competition that was to become unbearable. Soon after the peace in 1918 the bus competition was stepped up. The old tram could only do 8 or 9 miles an hour: the buses did 30. In 1919 the tram company went into liquidation, the Wolverton UDC declined to take over the line, and finally that year the L. & N. W. Railway bought the undertaking, the main reason being that it was essential to get men to Wolverton Works from Stony Stratford. At that time there were 550 persons who bought weekly tickets, most of whom were railwaymen, but barely a hundred other passengers each week. During these last years its total takings were only about £30 a week, which was barely enough to pay for a staff of eight, to keep the engines and track in repair, and to buy coal and other necessaries.

When the General Strike came in 1926 the old tram stopped never to run again.

Everybody loved the old tram – but they used the buses. Picture postcards of it were sold by the thousand, and are still treasured in many local homes.[12]

Before we move on to Bletchley it is worth recalling that in the period between say 1900 and 1914 Wolverton Works enjoyed its greatest days. In 1910 it employed about 5,000 men, most of them skilled craftsmen with a pride in their jobs, with pleasant homes. There were better facilities for sports of all kinds than almost any other town in Buckinghamshire, a low death rate, and such a moral and law abiding population that the churches flourished and expanded, whilst the police seldom had anything more serious to deal with than petty pilfering from the Works.

Wolverton was the home of the royal train, and in 1903 new saloons were made for their Majesties' convenience. A few years later a new system of electric lighting was developed that was ultimately adopted by railways all over the country. Wolverton was 'walking tall', but it was Bletchley that provided the engine drivers, and these were still envied and admired by all.

12 For technical details of the engines, etc, see Charles E. Lee's article in *The Railway Magazine* for August 1952.

THE LONDON, MIDLAND & SCOTTISH AMALGAMATION

We have seen that duing the war of 1914–18 the railways had been stretched to their limits and their efficiency had been greatly improved by war-time measures which scrapped all the finicky differences there were between 200 different railway companies and blended them into one coherent service. It was essential that the best of these wartime development should be preserved, and in 1921 Parliament approved the creation of four great amalgamations of which the London, Midland & Scottish was probably the greatest, for it combined the former Midland, the London & North Western and twenty-seven other companies. It was the largest private railway in the world.

It was an attempt to eliminate competition and duplication of resources and to standardise fares and charges. As far as the L. M. & S. Railway went, Derby, the former Midland head-quarters became the new power centre, and Wolverton Carriage Works became subordinate to the Carriage Department at Derby. This was a great blow to Wolverton's pride, for Wolverton men had long asserted that Derby could not build wheelbarrows let alone carriages. Derby kept the cream of construction for itself – the diners, the restaurant cars, the sleepers, etc, whereas Wolverton had to be satisfied with ordinary passenger stock, refrigerator vans, banana vans, etc. Worse still in some eyes was the change in the livery. Crimson lake was the new colour for carriages and for the engines.

At this time the railway traffic was at its peak. More passengers were carried in 1920 than at any other time in the history of the railways, and in 1924 freights reached their peace-time peak, and whilst Wolverton though still employing about 4,500 men was now reduced to second place as a carriage building centre, the men felt secure. It looked as if railways would be needed for ever. But no further expansion was planned for Wolverton, and no more residential development took place until 1928.

For another twenty years Wolverton Works continued to employ about 4,500 men, for whilst some other L. M. & S. railway centres were closed down, many of the redundant skilled men were transferred to Wolverton, and by 1937 there was a waiting list of over 300 for council houses. But we are running ahead too fast, and must go back to see what was happening at Bletchley and Fenny Stratford.

12 *The Parish Pump*

THE RECORD OF THE FENNY STRATFORD UDC 1895–1911

MANY people think of history as a succession of battles, disasters and great inventions, and indeed in volume I much has been said about the soldierly Grey family in Elizabethan times, and the sorrows and afflictions of the Civil War. But there is a gentler side to history, the history of industrious men coming together fortified by democratic election, who patiently month after month face up to the problems of ensuring good water supplies, sanitary sewage arrangements, paved roads and street lighting. It is the history of the parish pump, of the district sludge cart.

But it is not a dull history. Here in miniature we can see how the nation became healthier, more vigorous and happy, and one tells the story with pride and sometimes with a quiet laugh at lost tempers, poaching scavengers, and reversible decisions.

We have seen how in 1832, 1867 and 1884–85 the great reform movement had created a democracy in which every man had a parliamentary vote. The electorate controlled the nation at its peak, but in the parishes and the manors the man in the street had practically no say at all unless he was a churchwarden, an overseer, a member of a Board of Guardians or of a Burial Board. There were generally 'vestries' or meetings of the inhabitants in every parish for the election of parish officers (including petty constables) and for the settlement of parish affairs, but we come across few references to such public meetings in our local records. Burial Boards had been set up around 1858 since more and more churchyards were full up and new cemeteries were needed, often to serve two or three parishes at once. More powerful were the Boards of Guardians who had to look after the living who could not look after themselves. Under the Boards of Guardians were set up Sanitary Committees who were responsible for water supplies and sewerage.

So, in small ways democratic local government had taken over some of the powers of the vestry and the lords of the manor.

And now Parliament decided that the time was right for Tom, Dick and Harry, or their elected representatives, to take control of local affairs.

It might be observed that the early democratic advances were not due so much to great reforming zeal, but rather to the fact that where neither church nor squire wanted to carry out certain unpleasant and costly duties, a local democratic body was set up with power to impose a rate.

But the new reforms had more idealism behind them, so that when County Councils were set up in 1888 they were not only the agents of the government for their particular county, the government paying most of the bills, but they could also criticise, discourage, enthuse, or just not move at all if a certain government directive was unpopular or unworkable. From the first the County Councils have attracted the finest types: willing volunteers of experience who would have made any system work.

COUNCILLORS

In January 1889 the first elections showed that both the old and the new nobility, clergymen of all denominations, and successful yeomen, were prepared to fight for a seat on the new body. Local representatives on the new Bucks County Council included: H. S. Leon, Bletchley; F. W. Woollard, Stony Stratford; Robert Wylie, New Bradwell; Thomas Taylor, Newport Pagnell; Lt-Col Alex Finlay, Little Brickhill, and T. F. Fremantle of Swanbourne, all of whom served for over twenty years. On the Northants County Council Earl Spencer, KG, was the chairman, and the Duke of Grafton, KG, and the Marquess of Northampton, KG, were councillors. Three KGs on one County Council! The aristocracy were determined that democracy should succeed.

One of the really remarkable facts about England from about 1888 onwards was, and possibly still is, the devoted voluntary service given by so many who served on local councils. A second fact is that up to quite recently there was practically no reward other than an inner conviction that the individual concerned was doing his best for his locality or his country. Such local honours which did come were more for political than for council services. There were many who served for twenty-five years or more such as H. P. Dimmock, JP, of Bletchley, (thirty-nine years), Michael

Farrer of Cold Brayfield, and Ray Bellchambers of Bradwell, and indeed there are many others.

Often these grand records ran in families. The Woollard family of Stony Stratford has served for at least four generations if one begins only with F. W. Woollard's election to the County Council in 1888, but the record probably begins earlier than this. Equally the Holdom family of Bletchley and Little Brickhill has produced half a dozen local councillors beginning with Robert Holdom around 1850, and continuing through sons, grandsons and great-grandson till today. If there was any reward at all, it was to become a JP – but this in turn meant still more voluntary work.

It will be remembered that at this time Britain was the greatest power in the world. The great Victorian epoch was at its most powerful and splendid peak. But behind the tremendous fleet, the expanding overseas trade, the imperial complacency, there was a background of small towns and villages with appalling sanitary conditions, a high death rate, questionable water supplies and the still unsolved problems of how to make decent conditions for the people at the heart of the great British Empire.

THE PARISHES

Up to about 1844 our parish boundaries were much as they were under Alfred the Great around AD 890, but over the centuries some had become densely packed towns, whilst other parishes like Stantonbury and Tattenhoe had less than forty souls each.

In 1844 and in 1856 and 1869 powers were given to divide parishes. By the Act of 1894 Parish Councils were appointed for rural parishes of 300 inhabitants or upwards, to consist of five to fifteen members (women were eligible) to be elected annually. Alongside the 1,400 English ecclesiastical parishes there were now 7,142 civil parishes, which occasionally coincided with the ecclesiastical parish.

And now with the County Council set up, and the parishes rearranged, there came the grouping into District Councils, which could be of two kinds, Rural (RDC) or Urban (UDC). Broadly speaking parishes were first grouped into RDCs and then allowed to opt out into a UDC if their population merited it.

So by 1894 all north Bucks was divided into civil parishes, each with a Parish Council: a score or more would be combined into a Rural District Council.

In north Bucks, Rural District Councils were thus set up at Newport Pagnell, Wing, Winslow and Buckingham. Buckingham had been made a municipal borough in 1835 and retained its status, whilst the new RDC encircled the old town. But any two or more adjacent parishes (if they were Urban) could hive off and form their own District Council. The town of Newport promptly became a UDC in 1897, whilst the towns of Stony Stratford and Wolverton,[1] combined to form a Rural District Council, and Fenny Stratford and Simpson joined to form a UDC in 1895.

To the south-west of the Newport RDC lay the Winslow RDC including that town and villages like Shenley Brook End, Whaddon and Drayton Parslow, whilst on the eastern edge of the county was the Wing RDC, which included Stoke Hammond and Soulbury and almost surrounded the Linslade UDC.

Of these District Councils we have chosen Fenny Stratford UDC for a closer study, but any one of the others would present very much the same picture, with of course local idiosyncrasies that still distinguish communities only a few miles apart.[2]

The parishes had little power: then as now they were concerned with footpaths, lighting and a few similar subjects of no great concern. But the District Councils were entrusted with water supplies, sanitation, nuisances, housing, planning, and so on. It needed a constitutional expert to decide just where the division of power, or even of territory, was between one local authority and another.

Some absurd and almost idiotic groupings eventually resulted, and within a few years there were two local government offices in Newport, two in Buckingham and others at Fenny Stratford and Stony Stratford.

It could have been chaos all over England, but the English seem to be able to work either with order or with chaos.

Each of the new districts now had elections for a dozen or more councillors. These were not only unpaid, but often spent their

1 The history of the Wolverton UDC has already been related in the *History of Stony Stratford*, and in *The Nineteen Hundreds*.
2 For an interesting record of the Newport Pagnell Rural District Council see its *History* by Councillors R. G. Bellchambers and A. Eley published in 1974 by the RDC, and also A. W. Eley's *The Passing of Rural Independence*, published in 1974 by the Bradwell Abbey Field Centre.

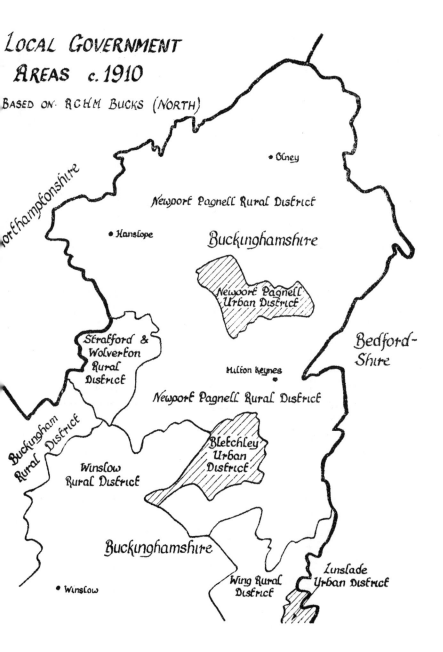

LOCAL GOVERNMENT
AREAS c. 1910
BASED ON RCHM BUCKS (NORTH)

Northamptonshire

• Olney

Newport Pagnell Rural District

• Hanslope

Buckinghamshire

Newport Pagnell Urban District

Stratford & Wolverton Rural District

Bedford-Shire

Milton Keynes

Newport Pagnell Rural District

Buckingham Rural District

Bletchley Urban District

Winslow Rural District

Buckinghamshire

• Winslow

Wing Rural District

Linslade Urban District

own money to help the town. They did not ask for expenses, nor for privileges. Their reward was the incomparable glow of knowing that in their own small way they could help to make their district a cleaner and more civilised place.

FENNY STRATFORD, 1862

What was Fenny Stratford like when the UDC took over? Fortunately we have a description of the town as Sheahan saw it in 1862:

'The two principal streets of which the town is composed are built at right angles, the one skirting the main road (the Watling St.), the other the cross road leading to Aylesbury. They are macadamised, partly paved, and present a neat and clean appearance. The houses are for the most part of red brick and tiled. The town is supplied by water from wells, and was first lighted with gas on 31 December 1857.'

Sheahan's account omits several points of possible interest, but it is clear that there was no piped water supply anywhere and consequently no scientific or hygienic disposal of sewage.

As we have seen, the great change from road to rail transport almost smashed the stage-coach posting activities in Fenny Stratford, but there were still a dozen public houses or off-licences, and it still remained the shopping centre not only for Bletchley and Water Eaton, but for half a dozen villages around. Aylesbury Street and the adjoining High Street was the shopping centre. Around 1860 it had eleven shoemakers, seven seamstresses or milliners, five tailors, six drapers, six butchers, four grocers and three bakers. Heavier crafts were represented by three wheelwrights and three blacksmiths. Shops and sheds and houses alternated along Fenny's market centre.

Nearly everybody walked into Fenny to do their shopping and carried their parcels home. There were however other ways of getting supplies home. Often a baker would have a bread round, a butcher likewise would have a van which visited the villages, and even more interesting were the hucksters, peddlers or badgers coming from nowhere but calling at house after house with a portable display of ribbons, cottons, needles and so on. Neither the shopkeepers nor the local JPs liked these 'vagrants', and a somewhat harsh system of licensing dating back to 1603 was still officially in force.

In 1864 Bletchley had only three shops, a grocer, a tailor, and a general store. Woughton, Woolstone and Milton Keynes had no shops at all: Fenny Stratford therefore was a market town with a cattle market, and it even had luxury shops such as a jeweller and a watch and clock maker. There was also a reposeful undertaker, and a local printer who later produced the *Fenny Stratford Times* (1879).

As for 'sodden Simpson', it had seven pubs and a dozen shops, most of which were along the Watling Street and were reckoned by most as part of Fenny.

The area changed very little during twenty years or so. It was around 1885 that the Newport Board of Guardians set up a Fenny Stratford Sanitary Committee with big responsibilities. One of the first jobs of the committee was naturally to survey the scene, and in 1886 they entrusted Henry F. Armitt with the job of drawing up a 50 inches to the mile map of Fenny Stratford. The map 7ft × 5ft, is a lovely production in colour. Every house between Belvedere Farm and the *George Inn* along the Buckingham Road is clearly shown. Between St Martin's Vicarage and the newly built *Park Hotel* there was only one house – *Halfway House*, an inn now known as the *Bletchley Arms*. The limited sewerage system of the day is shown and apparently it terminated either in local brooks or in the canal near the Watling Street bridge.[3] Within a few years, in November 1890, the Fenny Stratford Water Works in Great Brickhill parish were opened at a cost of £10,000. This had been achieved by the Fenny Stratford Sanitary Committee of the Board of Guardians. The yield was estimated at 80,000 gallons a day. The controlling authority was still the Board of Guardians. Thus, when the new UDC came into existence a certain amount of valuable work had already been done, but the problems ahead were enormous.

To read the minutes of this first really democratic assembly that Fenny Stratford had ever had is like entering another world. For the first time in a thousand years the powers of the lord of the manor of Fenny Stratford had been genuinely abrogated. Henceforward he no longer controlled the town as Browne Willis and a score of predecessors had done. The lord of the manor might still be the largest landowner, but had no more say now in his

---

3 The map was carefully preserved by the Bletchley UDC to whom my warm thanks are rendered.

parish than any other ratepayer unless he was an elected councillor.

The new men of power were a mixed lot. Many were unused to power except in the minor position of churchwarden, overseer or guardian. They were unskilled in debate. They knew no standing orders. They just knew that the will of the majority of the twelve members would prevail. The twelve elected to the new Fenny Stratford UDC were:

W. Alderman	J. Baisley	A. Bramley
J. Garner	T. G. Kirby	G. Mead
C. Merry	G. Sear	J. Sipthorpe
J. Tregenza	A. Whitney	S. Wootton

Their first job on 1 August 1895 was to elect a chairman. Kirby and Baisley, both of Fenny Stratford, were proposed and seconded. The voting was four each, the remainder not voting. Deadlock! After much discussion a second vote gave a similar result: another deadlock in a situation for which there was no precedent and apparently no way out unless one or the other of our stubborn councillors changed sides. There was of course no chairman to give a casting vote: there were as yet no officials to use the full weight of their influence. It was a unique situation.

'Ultimately', as the minutes say, and this guarded word possibly indicates that hours had gone by and everybody was exhausted, 'Ultimately, on being appealed to, Mr. C. Merry gave his vote for Mr. Baisley', so James Baisley, a hay and corn dealer, became the first chairman on a delayed minority vote.

Two years later there was another 'situation'. Let us quote the minutes:

'The Annual Meeting was called at the offices for April 21st 1897 at 7 o'clock. There were present Mr. James Baisley and Mr. John Sipthorpe at twenty minutes past seven. The Clerk stated that the meeting had been called for the purpose of electing a Chairman and Vice Chairman for the ensuing year. As there were not enough Members present to form a quorum he had no alternative but to adjourn the business. Later Messrs. A. Bramley, J. Garner, G. Sear, G. Mead, C. Merry, A. Whitney, S. Wootton and W. Alderman entered the Board Room and Messrs. Baisley and Sipthorpe having returned, the Clerk said they could now proceed with the Meeting.'

Once again the chairmanship was contested, but Baisley was re-elected by five votes to four against T. G. Kirby.

A similar situation occurred in April 1899. This time James Baisley and Albert Bramley both received five votes for chairman, but Baisley was in the chair, and 'upon the advice of the Clerk' gave his casting vote for himself. He continued in office until a year later he was replaced by Albert Bramley.

It is possible that these divisions which continued for years may have been due to the fact that some members of the Council, including Bramley, Garner and Kirby were ardent teetotallers, whilst others, including Baisley and Sear, were all for drinks. Since teetotallers were usually Nonconformists and liberals, and others were Church of England and conservatives, the fissure was deep and wide.

Among the dozen first elected members of the UDC was a platelayer, George Sear, the first trade unionist member of any of our local district councils, and for the next twenty-seven years (with a short interval) he was a steady attender. His election marked the beginning of the increasing power of the railway unions both in the Bletchley and the Wolverton councils. Others who served for over twenty years were James Baisley and Albert Bramley. Bramley was a coal and lime merchant of Simpson, but did much of his trade at Railway Yard. T. G. Kirby also served for over twenty years. These were the real fathers of the council.

At their second meeting the UDC decided to advertise for a clerk and rate collector combined, 'Applicants to state salary requirements'. Francis Bassett, Esq, was asked to act as treasurer. The 'Esq.' here is indicative of the fact that Bassett was a professional man, a banker, and so had a definite status!

On 20 August Thomas Best was appointed clerk and rate collector at £20 a year, subject to his providing a bond for £300. Dr M. Hailey was appointed MOH: he had asked for a salary of £25 a year: he was offered £20, and accepted. The UDC now advertised for a surveyor and inspector of nuisances at £150 per annum. At a later meeting, out of sixty-two applicants, Mr John Chadwick of Petersfield was appointed. It was a fortunate appointment for during the many years to come he was a most far sighted and persuasive surveyor.

Chadwick liked to describe himself occasionally as an architect or civil engineer, and enjoyed seeing after his name the letters

FGS, MSA, and MRSanInst. Fellowship of the Geological Society cost a guinea a year, and few qualifications were required, but it probably gave everybody a feeling that he was the right man to be surveyor and inspector of nuisances. He certainly was, and as we shall see he helped to change the area from a muddy, smelly, unsavoury and insanitary conglomeration with a high mortality rate, to an area with reasonable water supplies, good sewage disposal arrangements, and much improved mortality figures.

At that time the greater part of the sewage was discharged in its crude original and unpurified state into the Ouzel, into Cottenham Brook, Water Eaton brook, or into the Grand Junction Canal near the Watling Street bridge – the canal authorities actually welcoming it because it helped to keep up the water level. Cottenham Brook in fact took the sewage from both Bletchley and Fenny Stratford and from where it crossed the Water Eaton Road until it reached the Ouzel it was black and evil smelling. The polluted water flowed north to the bathing place!

The Wells

Again at that time many people drew their drinking and washing water from wells, with or without pumps, in their back yards, or from town pumps in the middle of the street.

From time immemorial almost the only way of getting a water supply in any of our villages was by sinking wells, and indeed on the everlasting clay it was only necessary to go down ten feet or so to ensure a continual supply. Most wells were open, topped with a windlass, bucket and rope, but the parish well and inn wells were enclosed and a pump installed which certainly lightened the labour of drawing water. The parish pump was one to which all could go, and as in Biblical days, was often a point where women would dally to gossip, and a dusty traveller like Jacob might ask Rachel for water and receive kindness as well.

The early Ordnance maps show every pump known to the surveyors – marked with a 'P' for pump, and it was from these that the Fire Brigade could on occasion get uncertain supplies. In Stony Stratford the town pumps were at the crossroads and another in the Market Square, in Fenny Stratford it was in the middle of Aylesbury Street next to the cattle market. All the inn pumps were near lavatories.

17 The sheep market in Aylesbury Street, Fenny Stratford c.1912. The cattle market was in the cul-de-sac adjoining and the town pump just to the right. Courtesy of Mrs Pacey, Woburn Sands. See pp205 and 210.

18 Aylesbury Street, Fenny Stratford c.1890. Courtesy of Mrs Pacey, Woburn Sands. See pp205 and 210.

J

19 One of the earliest 'Diesel' engines. The Hornsey–Akroyd engine No 802 now in the Science Museum. See p167 seq. Courtesy of the Science Museum, London.

20 Model of the Akroyd Crude Oil Engine patented in 1890. The lower plaque reads: 'Invented by Herbert Akroyd Stuart, MIME, Bletchley Ironworks, England. Inventor's present address: Akroyd Works, Perth, Australia'. Courtesy of the Science Museum, London, where the model is now stored. See pp167–69. Crown copyright.

21 The first tram in 1888. The engine was of German origin, having been made at Munich: it continued in use until 1926. The figure in the foreground is possibly Sir Herbert Leon, who became chairman of the company in 1891. See pp199–201.

22 The old Stony Stratford–Wolverton tram off the lines at Wolverton. Note the 12ft high wall that separates the works from the rest of the town. See pp199–201.

23 The first chairman of the Fenny
Stratford UDC 1895, James Baisley. See
p212 seq. Courtesy Bletchley UDC.

24 Sir Herbert Leon, MP for the
Buckingham Division 1891–95 and a
most prominent figure in Bletchley for half
a century. See p271. Courtesy Bletchley
UDC.

25 Herbert Akroyd Stuart, inventor of
the diesel engine. One of Bletchley's
greatest sons. Reproduced from W. Robinson's 'Heavy Oil Engines of the Akroyd
Stuart type'. Blackie and Son 1931.
Courtesy Science Museum. See pp167–69.

26 McCorquodales, Wolverton, in 1900. The Printing room. Contrary to appearance the female operators are in their late teens and early twenties. An interesting 'period piece'. See pp176–78. Courtesy of Mr George Boddington.

27 Originally built in 1906 as the Wolverton County Secondary Day School this interesting Edwardian building has been in educational use ever since, and is now the principal block of Bushfield Middle School. See p154 seq.

nty School, Wolverton

28 One of the first motor cars ever seen in Stony Stratford. The date, 1898 and the occasion is the wedding of Annie Franklin to Richard Ashley and the location is Vicarage Road. See p245.

Original photograph loaned by W. J. Franklin, 23 Wolverton Road, Stony Stratford.

29 Stony Stratford Market Square c.1890. In front of the church can be seen a group of Tudor cottages, one of which, Jeffs House, was demolished in 1906 and the others nearer the church in 1973. Beside the lamp post is the drinking fountain much used on market days.

30   *A fine specimen of a traction engine in service for years with Holland and Sons, Vicarage Road, Stony Stratford. Courtesy of Mr R. Ayers, whose grandfather is at the controls. See p235.*

31   *The greatest attraction of the Stony Stratford fairs before 1914 – 'Taylor's Bioscope' with its intricate calliope. It also visited Hives Field off Tickford Street, Newport Pagnell on many occasions. Courtesy of Mr Dick Earl, Tickford Street, Newport Pagnell. See pp234–35.*

32 Salmons and Sons Works at Newport Pagnell, 1924 showing the production line of the NP cars. Courtesy of Miss Margaret Salmons. See p251 seq.

33 The Newton Longville smithy, on the right, was demolished in the 1960s. For centuries this was one of the social centres of the village. See pp237–38.

The Old Blacksmiths Shop. Newton Longville.

Typhoid

Under such circumstances typhoid was inevitable. People heard the word with horror – it was something invisible – swirling through the town causing ghastly pain and suffering. They treated it with respect and fear which today we accord to cancer. It was the stealthy killer with no known cure once the vomiting started. It was, however, general knowledge then that the commonest mode of transmitting typhoid was by contaminated drinking water. Cesspools and bad sewers formed hotbeds for the preservation of the typhoid germ. At that time even milk cans were washed in polluted water, for the sewage and the germs leaked easily into wells.

Typhoid was in fact endemic over our whole area. In the 1890s at Stony Stratford several members of the Woollard family who had their own well in Church Street were struck down. At the same time, some members of the family of Mr Wood, the Old Wolverton miller, were afflicted. Mr Wood promptly claimed expenses and damages from the council, and got them! Up to this period very few of the local houses had piped water or an inside privy. 'The necessary house' as the lawyers still called it, was still built separately from the house, often alongside the coal shed and the well, and the visit to one or the other in the cold winter mornings was anything but a pleasure. Then there was the weekly or monthly task of emptying the 'sanitary bucket' into a hole dug in the garden, with the inevitable enrichment of the soil, but also with the inevitable smells. For those who had no gardens a 'night soil cart', rather like the ancient tumbril, made its not infrequent rounds.

At Fenny Stratford there was now, under the new UDC, a definite campaign, and in the next few years wells were ordered to be closed at:

Denbigh Hall Road
Cambridge Street
Aylesbury Street, including the Ivinghoe Brewery and the International Tea Company.
Cottages near Canal
High Street, including those at the *Foundry Arms* and the *Chequers Inn*
Victoria Road

Many in Simpson, including the pump known as the Parish
Pump or Matthews Pump, and the one at School House,
Simpson.

The UDC closed forty wells in a few years, and compelled the
owners to use the piped supplies.

The typhoid scare was indeed real. In August 1897 the surveyor
reported several cases of typhoid in the district. The next month
scarlet fever once again added to the troubles of local doctors.
In December of the next year there was another outbreak of
typhoid – this was unusual, as typhoid was usually associated with
hot summers.

Gradually the menace was diminished, and within ten years
the average number of typhoid cases was reduced to a sixth of
what it was in the early 1890s. It took longer to master tuberculosis and diphtheria. In July 1901 the surveyor reported nine cases
of diphtheria, and the MOH was ordered to look into them.
By August there were thirty-one cases. The schools were now
closed and the council gave instructions that the earth closets
at the Bletchley schools should be 'regularly cleansed', and that
the Fenny schools should be thoroughly disinfected. Tuberculosis,
however, was still almost untreatable, and it took years before the
same combination of science, medical persistence and local
authority action all helped to free the area of a killing scourge.

WATER SUPPLIES AND BLETCHLEY

The two most constantly recurring questions before the Fenny
UDC were those of the water supply and of union with Bletchley,
and the two were indissolubly mixed. Fenny Stratford and Simpson, with the closing of the wells, were needing more and more
water, and Bletchley, which had now begun to expand, was
equally thirsty. Bletchley, as part of the Newport Pagnell RDC,
drew its water with their permission from the same pumping
station as Fenny. Fenny wanted control.

Indeed of all the questions that perplexed the Fenny Stratford
UDC the most intractable was the problem of an adequate and
good water supply. It has caused a good many sleepless nights to
engineers, surveyors and even councillors.

One might have thought that north Bucks, with its average
British rainfall and the Ouse and Ouzel rivers would have had
enough natural sources to meet the demands of a relatively small

population, but the Ouse was a sluggish, highly polluted river, and the mills, still using water power, demanded that river levels be not unduly lowered. There was no local lake of any size, and when the railway company began to develop Wolverton and New Bradwell and Bletchley too they found the greatest difficulty in getting adequate water supplies.

Something more and something purer was necessary, and the new surveyors went far afield to find a reliable water supply. Fenny found that the Great Brickhill supply, where pumps and a reservoir were erected about 1892 – was now in fact barely sufficient. Added to this the controlling authority was the Newport Pagnell Board of Guardians which joyously extended mains to parishes and villages. Fenny too was growing, and when our Mr Chadwick decided that most of the wells were anything but clean and wholesome, the need for more water became imperative.

In December 1896 Fenny suggested a joint water committee with the Newport RDC in which Fenny should have five members out of six. The next month it was suggested that Fenny should purchase the Bletchley rights, and now the Newport RDC suggested that Bletchley should be transferred to the Fenny UDC and its water rights too. A week later (26 January 1897) a Bletchley parish meeting was held which unanimously resolved that the Bucks County Council should transfer the parish to the Urban Council. A year later the Fenny surveyor reported that even by pumping two shifts they could only expect 100,000 gallons in a day, and present consumption was rising to 60,000 gallons. But his council thought the margin was sufficient and 'did not see their way to incur further expense in an endeavour to augment the present water supply'.

Just at this time (1897) the Peptonised Milk Company asked if in the event of a milk factory being erected the council would undertake to supply 50,000 gallons of water daily. The council replied that they were willing to supply the company with water, but could not see their way to giving a guarantee. Fenny lost its chance of a new industry. It will be remembered that there was already a Condensed Peptonised Milk Company at Buckingham, founded in 1892.

Meanwhile the surveyor was hunting around for more water supplies, for even the few wells left at places like Denbigh Hall and the adjacent cottages were often without water. The Aylesbury Brewery Company, which owned the historic inn were told they could have piped water if the company would pay two-thirds of the cost. Piped water was installed in 1898.

In June 1899 water was so short that it had to be turned off at night, and three months later the council 'journeyed by horse "break" to Great Brickhill for the purpose of inspecting certain springs with a view to obtaining an additional supply of water'. In the result they asked the Duncombe Trustees to sell a further half an acre of land 'at the bottom of the Spinney south-west of the existing works and next to a road'.

Chadwick and his colleagues searched the area almost field by field. Every gravel or sand pit was explored and tested. From Shenley and Stockgrove to Linslade the search went on. There was indeed water at Linslade and at Leighton Buzzard, but too far away to be economical. In 1907 better prospects seemed to be available at Birchmoor Farm, Woburn, and at Sand House along the A5 in the parish of Heath and Reach, where under the clay was a deep layer of greensand which acted like an underground reservoir.

Sand House was chosen and soon a well 9ft diameter and 95ft deep was sunk and the water came trickling in through the sand. To keep the sand out fine screens were necessary. To keep the screens clear suction pipes were necessary. But in spite of all this, vicious minute particles of sand got into the machinery and gave unending trouble. They still do.

ENCROACHMENTS

There was one other point that Chadwick impressed upon the council, that they must get back for the public the encroachments that had been made by powerful local landowners – some of them going back fifty or sixty years. The council's powers in this respect were shadowy to say the least of it, and the Duncombe family and other encroachers were well liked and well respected.

Chadwick had seen and studied the Bletchley Enclosure Award of 1813 (which is described in pages 291–94 of our first volume), and realised that whilst this laid down that certain public roads were to be 40ft wide including the Buckingham Road, Victoria Road, Winslow Road, Leighton Road, Bletchley and Water Eaton Roads, and the Stoke Hammond Road, and the Watling

Street and three major roads in Simpson were supposed to be 60ft, he had not these widths to play with. Also he realised that the adjacent fields, had somehow or other expanded their acreages if one compared the Enclosure Award with the newer Ordnance Surveys.

It did not follow that these landowners were a lot of land thieves, for the Enclosure Awards gave the grass growing on road verges to adjoining proprietors, and local landowners thought they had some legal right to fence the verges. Now (1896) the UDC tried to interest the County Council so that the full force of the law could be exerted, but the county unwisely acted on their own, and there was a clash. The County Council apologised and left the UDC with a free hand – adding that if the county were to interest itself in this matter 'it would involve them in an endless task over large areas'.

Perhaps the most prominent case of encroachment or absorption that deserved the attention of the County Council was at Bradwell. We have seen in volume I how the Enclosure Award of 1789 decreed that a public road 40ft wide from Bradwell and Great Linford to Great Woolstone should be made up. By 1895 all but a hundred yards of it had been completely absorbed by neighbouring farms.

Finally the UDC instructed Chadwick to remove the fences bounding the encroachments on the Denbigh Hall and Water Eaton roads. Chadwick was delighted to do so. And all were pleased when in January 1898 the County Council decided to make up and metal the roadside waste recently regained from the Duncombe Trustees in the Bletchley road.

Bathing Behaviour

Another question the UDC had to contend with was nudity and obscenity combined. A bathing place had been established on the banks of the Ouzel near the Watling Street. The councillors were rightly horrified when continuing reports came in that the lads went bathing stark naked and used the most horrible language. Nothing like it had been heard since the navvies dug the canal. But these striplings of Fenny had an Anglo-Saxon vocabulary that surprised even ex-Army veterans who had become policemen. All this was too much for the city fathers who ordered drawers to be worn and the police to listen. 'Every person', they ordered in 1897, 'using the Bath must be provided with bathing drawers'.

Bletchley was not alone in this. All over north Bucks there were natural bathing pools sanctioned by age-long use long before UDCs were thought of, and at these there was the same libidinous behaviour that must have delighted some of the ancient Greek gods. It was a good job there was no wine to go with it. Gradually the nudity and the obscenity were minimised, but it took many years to render the air less blue.

And now we must let the minutes speak for themselves on a few other topics.

Page 68, Tuesday 28 April 1896
 Chequers Inn:
 The Surveyor presented his report from which it appeared that application had been made for the registration of The Chequers Inn, Fenny Stratford, as a common Lodging House. The Surveyor recommended that the occupier be required to have the rooms lime-washed and provide for the separation of the sexes. Agreed.

Page 110, Tuesday 27 October 1896
 Estimate:
 The Finance Committee presented their Estimate for the current Half Year which was unanimously approved and it was agreed that a General District Rate be prepared at 1s 6d in the £ in the Lighting area and 1s 3d in the £ outside the same.

Page 174, Tuesday 8 June 1897
 Nuisance – Rectory farm, Simpson:
 A letter was read from Mr. Frederick Badley calling attention to a nuisance at Simpson Village caused by decomposing carcases of sheep thrown into the brook from the Rectory farm. Ordered that notice to abate the nuisance be served on The Rev. William Rice and that in the event of the same not being complied with the Clerk and Surveyor take the necessary steps to enforce the same.

Page 237, Tuesday 22 February 1898
 Deed of Gift by Herbert Samuel Leon, Esquire, of land for Recreation Ground:

A letter was read from Mr. Henry P. Cobb, Solicitor to Herbert Samuel Leon Esquire of Bletchley Park, enclosing Deed of Gift of a piece of land forming until recently part of the Glebe of the Rectory and Parish Church of Bletchley, situate in the Parish of Fenny Stratford, containing by admeasurements Nine Acres two roods and twenty three perches or thereabouts, together with a pathway leading thereto from the Bletchley Road, for the purposes of a Public Recreation Ground.

The Chairman proposed and Mr. Thomas G. Kirby seconded that the best thanks of the Council be given Herbert Samuel Leon Esquire for his munificent gift. Carried unanimously.[4]

Page 208, Tuesday 9 November 1897

Flooding of road:

A letter was read from the Clerk to the Bucks County Council dated 5th Novr. 1897 respecting the flooding of road between Simpson and Walton, complained of by this Council. The County Council proposed erecting raised foot-planks as a temporary palliative.

Page 345, Tuesday 14 February 1899

Wages of Roadmen:

On behalf of the General Purposes Committee Mr. A. Bramley proposed that the rate of wages of the present Roadmen be reduced from 14s to 12s per week. He explained that the reason of the movement made in this matter by the Committee was that the present men were all old men and were therefore unable to do a fair day's work. . . . Proposition carried.

This is one of the last items in this particular volume of *The Minutes of the Fenny Stratford Urban District Council.*

Later on we learn that the weekly hours of work were 54 in the summer and 51 in the winter. In cases of illness the man was paid in full for the broken week, but no more.

The second volume of *The Minutes of the Fenny Stratford Urban District Council* takes us from 1899 to 1902. In 1900 James Baisley

---

4 Herbert Leon had been the Liberal MP for the area from 1891 to 1895. See chapter 16.

was at last defeated in his efforts to retain the chair, and the habitual teetotaller, Albert Bramley, was elected by seven votes to three.

The teetotal influence on the council was now strong, and time and time again they refused to allow any event to be held in the Leon Recreation Ground if strong drink was provided. The August Holiday Athletic meeting of 1900 for example was a dry affair. In July 1900 the Rev H. F. Oliver, who wanted the Recreation Ground for a peace demonstration (the South African War was now going badly), objected strongly to the teetotal restrictions, and this and other public events such as the actual celebrations for peace in South Africa, and the coronation festivities of 1902, were held elsewhere.

These were however trivialities compared with the final decisions authorising the new sewerage system.

In September 1901 the council approved contracts for the laying of sewers (£6,300), erection of sewage outfall works (£6,114) and air compressors and engines etc (£3,399) – all to different contractors. At last the sewage scheme was on the way. One imagines that the council must have been awed by the amount of public money they were spending, for even the clerk took up his finest quill and wrote the amounts in beautiful copperplate half an inch high. And now came a subject which was to bedevil the council for a decade.

In January 1898 the council agreed that, subject to the sanction of the Bucks County Council the name of the district be changed from the Fenny Stratford Urban District to the Bletchley Urban District. Within two months the Local Government Board had agreed to the formal transfer of Bletchley Parish to the UDC, and in May 1898 the council decided to go ahead with the change of name, but the Bucks County Council now suggested there should be a meeting of 'the Inhabitants and Parochial Electors' to consider the matter. The meeting was called on 28 September, and after considerable discussion it agreed to the proposed change. But two months later (November 1898) the County Council 'declined to accede', and it was not until 1911 that the change was made after a unanimous vote of the Fenny UDC.

In May 1911 the Fenny UDC was renamed the Bletchley UDC, and a new and invigorating chapter in local government opened up. Bletchley then had a population of 800, Fenny Stratford 4,000 and Simpson 500. There were at that time twelve councillors, six for Fenny and three each for Simpson and Bletchley. Elections for one-third of the members were held yearly.

These returns bring out that Fenny Stratford was very much the senior partner, and that Bletchley and Simpson were still villages. It will be seen that Fenny Stratford was grossly under-represented. There was thus some justification for the title of the council remaining unaltered, but Bletchley it became and Bletchley UDC it remained until 1974.

One of the new members for Bletchley was Hon-Surgeon-Colonel Giles, who lived at Holne Chase. He was already a CC and a JP, was to become Sheriff in 1907, was soon joined by Herbert Samuel Leon, also a CC and a JP, and former MP for the area. He too was to become Sheriff in 1909. Giles was a sturdy Tory whose tactlessness did not always endear him to his opponents, who nicknamed him 'the Fire Eater'. Certainly Giles and Leon were men of top county standing, and their influence on the council must have been great. In May 1911 the formal step was taken, and Bletchley UDC (to which was added in 1934 Water Eaton) began its sixty-three year long career.

In its sixteen years of existence the old Fenny Stratford UDC had a record of clean, careful government that will bear comparison with any other area in England. It had carried out the functions delegated to it by Parliament with a modest staff which no one could say was overpaid. It had laid the plans for a much needed sewerage system that would no longer use Cottenham Brook as the main outlet. It had closed forty or fifty dubious wells. It had tidied up highways and byways. It had patiently gone into the question of encroachment by landowners of great or lesser degree on the verges of the Water Eaton road and the Watling Street. Street lighting was improved, and they had made efforts to minimise bad language in the streets and at the bathing place.

The Bletchley UDC which took over had an equally good record over the next sixty years.

During this epoch Bletchley became one of the healthiest areas in the whole of England. The infantile mortality dropped to a sixth of its 1895 figure (from 15 per cent to 2 per cent); the death rate was almost halved, and these figures were all much lower than the averages for England and Wales.[5] Typhoid, diphtheria and tuberculosis had almost disappeared. The expectation of life had increased so that if anybody died in Bletchley under the age of 70 except through wars or accidents there were unspoken wonders as to what sort of life he had led.

It was the supersession of the parish pump by piped water, hot and cold, by the creations of bathrooms in many houses, by the installation of effective sewerage and the closing of open sewers and infected wells that had helped to work this slow miracle. And the administrative force was the local UDC. They are worthy of a historic 'Thank you'.

Let us repeat that we have gone into some detail with the Fenny UDC. We might have gone into equal detail with the other district councils in north Bucks – but that would fill another volume, and the activities of the Stony Stratford District Council have been adequately recorded in *The Nineteen Hundreds* pages 91–94. In each of these there was the same public spirit, the same feeling that all councillors then had that one must be just as careful in spending the ratepayers' money as with one's own. It is a unique story, for in no other country have voluntary, untrained men been entrusted with so much power and exercised it out so honestly and so successfully. I have searched diligently for a rogue amongst them, and have been gratifyingly disappointed.

This is not the last we shall write or hear about the local District Councils for with the County Councils they had the power and the money to influence all our destinies. Where in the early Victorian times the dukes and the earls and the squires held autocratic power and used it autocratically, most of their power was now wielded by democratically elected councillors guided by skilled officials, and as their powers widened by successive Acts of Parliament so the numbers of officials grew until great palaces called county halls were needed to house some of them.

Democracy could sack any councillor it did not like. It never had, and probably never will have, the power to sack speedily an unpopular or even incompetent official.

---

5 In the 1960s the death rate for England and Wales was 11.5, for Buckinghamshire 9.7 and for Bletchley 7.6. Maternal mortality in Bletchley was practically nil.

13 Pastimes

IN these days when everybody has leisure, and enormous sums are spent yearly on everything from professional football to subsidised marinas, when County Councils and District Councils spend hundreds of thousands of pounds every year on picnic sites, leisure centres and even literature advertising all these activities, it is difficult to realise that a century ago leisure was a commodity so rare that only the wealthy or the unemployed had enough of it. There was little of the modern weariness in trying to be amused.

True it was, of course, that Saturday afternoon was free and Sunday was a day of rest, but for the dairy farmer, the housewife with a brood of children or the labourer with his garden or allotment, there was very little change from the weekday round. Working hours and the time spent in getting to work were over sixty per week, and if these hours were shorter in winter it was only because there was no adequate artificial light with which to carry on work after sunset or before dawn.

Not until the Factory Act of 1874 were working hours restricted to fifty-six a week, ten hours daily from Monday to Friday, and six hours on Saturday morning. In fact it could be said that there was little real leisure in life, only holidays. And by holidays one does not mean a month off with full pay! One means the occasional bank holiday, and very rarely a special event such as a coronation or a first-class royal wedding.

The greatest holiday of the year was Christmas, with Boxing Day as a bank holiday, and from the time of Queen Victoria's wedding in 1841 onwards this season took on a new Germanic flavour with Christmas trees and holly, such as Charles Dickens described with so much gusto. Other bank holidays were Easter Monday, Whit Monday and the first Monday in August. Wolverton had its own special holiday in addition – Whit Tuesday.

It was on these rare bank holidays or Saturday afternoons that there took place those sports which have disappeared with the years, such as prize fighting with bare fists and no limit to the number of rounds,[1] cudgel playing, bull baiting, cock fighting, and other quaint and innocent frolics that were often not so innocent. Another ancient pastime that our changing weather seems to have seriously curtailed was that of skating. From about 1850 to 1917 there were apparently much sharper winter frosts than nowadays. In December 1870 for example there was safe skating on the canal all the way from Stony Stratford to Bucking-ham, and year after year the flooded frozen meadows along the Ouse or the Ouzel were the scenes of much graceful activity. Even tents were erected on the ice, for refreshments and skate fitting.

Some of the equally ancient sports such as fox hunting and horse racing still remained, and we might have a quick glance at them before we turn to the team sports of football, cricket, etc.

FIELD SPORTS

We have already referred to fox hunting in chapter 2, and it only needs to be added that both the Whaddon Chase and the Grafton continued to kill foxes. Members of both hunts were quite convinced that by hunting they were rendering great services to the nation; it encouraged the breeding of good horses, which as everyone knew were a great national asset; but perhaps the limit that could be said in praise of hunting was reached in December 1908 when at the Fat Stock Show Dinner at the *Cock Hotel*, Stony Stratford, a local MFH stated that 'unemployment would increase by sixty to seventy per cent if hunting were done away with'.

The Hunt Ball was usually held at Buckingham, and the local wits would jest that 'Everybody there was either a Selby-Lowndes or wanted to be a Selby-Lowndes', but Lord Dalmeny did not, and immediately after the First World War new excite-ment was added to the hunt. The excitement reached its climax in the 1920s when the hunt split into two quarrelsome factions and argued as much as they chased. A temporary period of peace, however, was achieved in 1921, under the mastership of the Earl of Orkney, when both the Prince of Wales and the Duke of York (later King George VI) joined the hunt at a meet at Great Hor-

1 Prize fighting has been referred to at some length in chapter 5.

wood and had a good day. But in 1923 Lord Dalmeny took over the mastership and held it for seventeen years. Every year since then has seen the area of the Whaddon Chase diminish, and now with the development of the city of Milton Keynes it has lost another 10,000 acres of good fox hunting country. Now there is nowhere for a fox to lay his head between Calverton and Wavendon. The cunning old fox knows perhaps that only in hunting country is he safe from extinction.

OTTER HUNTING
Another blood sport that has suffered by local industrial development is that of otter hunting. The Uthwatts, lords of the manor of Great Linford, were its great patrons, and from 1869 onwards the Bucks otterhounds hunted the otter along the Ouse and the Ouzel, and other streams miles away, in picturesque blue uniforms with red caps, and caught and killed more otters than the Whaddon Chase killed foxes. In fact they averaged twenty-one otters killed each season.[2] It seems a pity so much craft and energy was devoted to these ends, but they had the full support of all the angling associations which were growing fast in popularity. Mr W. Uthwatt always maintained that a couple of swans would do more harm to fish than twenty otters, but no angling association ever wanted to shoot swans. Otter hunting died out only recently when the Milton Keynes Development Corporation acquired the Uthwatt estates, and although the Development Corporation has avowed its determination to encourage local sports it is unlikely they will subsidise otterhounds or provide kennels for them.

NEWPORT RACES
As for one of the most ancient sports of all, horse racing, it was Newport Pagnell which provided the site and the organisation for them for well over a century. The site was Bury Field – one of the last great areas of common land in Buckinghamshire, and here from the times of George II to 1836 races were organised which attracted competitors and spectators from three counties.

Gibbs, the Aylesbury historian, records that races were held here in 1820, 1823 and 1828 and that good sport was enjoyed by

2 *VCH* I 162 *seq.*

the gentry from many miles around. Osborne, the railway historian, writes (in 1840) that annual races were established in Newport in 1827 and were regularly held every August until his day at least.

In 1836 the races began to show distinct signs of decay. Only one horse 'Ruinous' was entered for the Gold Plate, and walked over, while only seven horses (including 'Ruinous') ran in the other two races, which completed the card for the day. Even the bookies were discontented.

The Newport Races were not revived until 1868, when a steeplechase meeting, with one five furlong race on the flat was held.

Years later they became 'Pony and Galloway races' and in the *Bucks Standard* for 19 April 1890, for example, we find an advertisement inviting licensed victuallers and others to tender for booths or stalls adjacent to the race-course on Bury Field. All this was 'by permission of M. G. S. Knapp and the ladies of the Manor'.[3] The races seem to have died out before the First World War. Someday a full history of Newport Pagnell will be written and we shall learn how these races started, what sort of rumpus and excitement they produced in the town, and why they died out.

FOOTBALL AND CRICKET

The origin of football is lost in antiquity and obscurity. It is sufficient to say that our Plantagenet kings forbad it since it interfered with archery, and that for centuries the ban was never repealed. But somewhere around 1850 the rules of the game were established and the entirely mystical figure of eleven men a side established. There was tacit agreement that it should be played in a field and not in the streets, but it took years before the Fenny Stratford council could stop street playing.

The history of cricket is much more definitely established with the formation of the early clubs at Hambledon and Marylebone around 1730. Once again the uneven figure of eleven a side was established and the game became popular all over north Bucks. Cole, the great Bletchley diarist, records that on 30 October 1766 Tom, his footman cum farm-foreman, and Mrs Willis's servants

---

3 The Knapps were lords of the manors of Little Linford. There has always been much controversy over proprietory and manorial rights in Bury Field. The Knapps did not buy Newport manor until 1905.

and others all went off to a cricket match at Fenny Stratford. But whether they played or watched is not clear. An interesting point is that the date – the end of October – shows that cricket was not then restricted to the summer months.

A few years later cricket had become the predominant summer sport of the whole area, and almost every village had a cricket club and pitch of sorts. At Deanshanger the traditional pitch was the village green, and when the local landowner John Clarke tried to enclose it in 1815 local people pulled down the rails, and accompanied by Lord Charles Fitzroy deliberately played both cricket and football on the Green, whilst a couple of solicitors rode around on their horses. In 1836 Clarke tried a new move; he prosecuted half a dozen Deanshanger men at the Stony Stratford Petty Sessions for 'malicious destruction of the herbage of (Deanshanger) Green by playing at cricket'. The magistrates including the sport-loving Rev Loraine-Smith of Passenham, dismissed the case, and 'seventy people played games on the Green that night'. Cricket on the Green at Deanshanger continued for many years.

On such pitches centuries were rare indeed and most matches were determined within an afternoon, and attendances were high. In July 1876 we learn from Gibbs that 4,000 people attended a cricket match at Buckingham, and attendances of over 1,000 people were not uncommon at Newport, Stony Stratford and Bletchley. From 1886 onwards Wolverton had a fine cricket ground at the Park and the games there often attracted large crowds.

In 1904 the Bletchley Station Cricket Club was formed and in 1907 won the Railway Challenge Cup. They played on the ground adjoining the Park Hotel, as did also the Fenny Stratford Cricket Club. Bletchley Park, one of the prettiest and best cricket grounds in the county had its own team, but the ground was often used for minor-counties matches. Great Linford, with few such advantages, produced some excellent cricket teams, and for years was at the head of the North Bucks Cricket League.

FOOTBALL

Both football and cricket demanded a fair sized, level pitch with good, short grass, and this requirement was not easily met, for most of our local fields still had ridge and furrow, and there were only a few lawnmowers – drawn by a pony or pushed by hand. When Herbert Leon presented the Recreation Ground to the Fenny Stratford UDC in 1898, the first thing the Council did with it was to get it levelled. From then on the 'Rec' was in constant use for both cricket and football. On 13 September 1898 we find the following entry in the Council Minutes:

'Football: It was reported that arrangements had been made for the Bletchley Football Club and the Fenny Stratford Albion Football Club to play football in the Recreation Ground, subject to rules to be framed by the Council, during the coming season at a nominal charge of One Pound (£1) each.'

We do not know how long the Fenny Stratford Albion Club lasted, but it seems to have been followed around 1905 by Fenny Rovers who soon had a programme of fixtures with other clubs in the newly formed Buckingham League. These matches produced great crowds, intense excitement and much rough play. Perhaps the medal for roughness (or rather the blackest of black marks) should go to a match played in the Buckingham League at Woad Farm by the river Ouse at Newport Pagnell in April 1907, between Newport Pagnell and Fenny Stratford Rovers. After twenty minutes of play, F. Kilsby, one of the Fenny forwards, ran through and shot at goal, but the ball was caught by the Newport goalie. Kilsby charged him, and had the surprise of his life when the Newport goalie kicked his backside. The referee, Mr R. Williams, of Wolverton, promptly ordered the goalie off the field. The rest of the game was vociferous in the extreme. Fenny won 2–1 against the depleted Newport side, and as the final whistle went the crowd made a dash, not for the referee, which would have been in keeping with local tradition, but for the Fenny forwards, and two of them, Kilsby and F. Vince, were caught, and pushed into the river. The crowd then made its way to the *Ram Inn*, where the Fenny team were changing, and when, after an interval, the Rovers came out and tried to go home in their brake, they were met with a shower of stones, rotten eggs, fish, and garbage. Two cycles were smashed in the mêlée, and the driver of the brake and several players were injured.

Meanwhile the police had arrived, restored order, and took the names of the leading culprits. The brake then left for Fenny.

But the crowd were by no means satisfied, for they took a short cut and caught up with the brake along Caldecote Street, near Cowley's Parchment Works, where the river came out into a shallow bend often used for the washing down of carriages. A determined effort was made to upset the brake into the water, but the Fenny team gave as good as they got, and finally arrived home with several casualties.

Such behaviour called for action. The first repercussion was at the Newport Petty Sessions the next Wednesday, when the three Newport ringleaders were each fined 2s 6d and costs, or seven days. It was, of course, said that if they had been tried at Fenny they would have been jailed for months.

The next repercussion was more serious. The League officials held an enquiry; Newport Town Football Club received a stern admonition and was heavily fined. The club could not, or would not, pay; consequently it disappeared, and for several years Newport Town was not on the football map. Fortunately such incidents became rare, and local football was no longer a substitute for tribal warfare.

Fenny Rovers went on to win the Bucks League Cup, and the next year Frank Kilsby was absorbed into the Northampton Town Football Club and signed on as a professional.

Hockey and rugger came late on the scene, neither was as popular as soccer or cricket, but both had a panache and a quality of membership that was a cut above the average, and every member knew it. But whatever the sport, the local papers tried to cover it with some knowledge, and if they failed sometimes to describe a thrilling hockey or rugger match it was out of sheer ignorance.

QUOITS AND BOWLS

Up to about 1914 one of the most popular pub games was quoits – the really old fashioned kind where a heavy steel ring was pitched at a target embedded in a solid square of the clayiest clay the area could provide. As steel clashed on steel it gave out a metallic ring that could be heard quite a long way. It was of course a messy game, and after a game the players' hands were worse than a ploughman's, and there was only ever an outside tap with neither soap nor towel for ablutions.

Quoits was replaced by bowls, a game which after having

been illegal for centuries, gradually infiltrated into the district from about 1890 onwards. It is interesting to recall that for centuries every apprentice in the area on taking up his apprenticeship had to sign an indenture on which he faithfully promised not to frequent taverns or ale houses, nor to play at 'Dice, Cards, Tables (skittles), Bowls, or other unlawful games'. It was not until about 1845 that these stringent regulations were relaxed.

The first bowling greens in the neighbourhood appear to have been at Wolverton Park and Newport Pagnell, which from 1890 onwards had greens and teams of great merit. Stony Stratford apparently had no public bowls green until 1923, when the bowls section of the sports club was started. Meanwhile, a few pubs and most clubs had a bowling green, and great was the enjoyment thereof.[4]

After the turn of the century, with its slightly increased leisure time, other sports came into our area and these included lawn tennis, croquet and golf. It seems surprising that as early as 1906 Bletchley had a nine-hole golf course which extended over land at Brooklands, Holne Chase and what were then Bletchley glebe lands (Council Minutes). Soon after this another nine-hole course was established in Bury Field, Newport Pagnell. But far more popular than golf was lawn tennis, for every house of the gentry, and almost every vicarage now had its adjacent tennis court where a delightful kind of pat ball tennis was played by both sexes. After the First World War some of the successful farmers added a tennis court to their amenities. The game began to assume a fiercer aspect when Wolverton Secondary School took it up as a recognised sport around that time, and coaching began.

CYCLING

It is difficult to say which was the most popular sport before the First World War, but it is possible that it was cycling, and in another chapter we have referred to the advent of the safety cycle and the transport revolution it created. Even before then there were cycling clubs, as at Buckingham, where proud owners of the 'penny-farthing' bicycle would meet, compete and eat. Around 1885 cycling became a great national sport, and no one can mention English cycling without referring to Wolverton

4 The development and success of local social clubs is described in *The Nineteen Hundreds* pages 114-17.

Park and its renowned Amateur Athletic Association.

In 1885 the L. & N. W. Railway company provided 7 acres of land for a permanent sports ground known as Wolverton Park and here, on the site which once included the disreputable 'Hell's Kitchen', they provided a cycle track, a running track, a football pitch and bowls and tennis courts. It was unique in the entire area, and Wolverton railwaymen soon made it famous throughout England for its Whitsuntide sports. The cycle track was considered to be excellent, and attracted English champions.

For half a century these sports were regarded in Wolverton and the entire district not only as the apex of the sporting year, but as the time for family reunions and jollifications.

For many years cycling had been one of the favourite pastimes of the youth of Wolverton, and the development of cycling clubs was encouraged by the churches or local political bodies. The Mazeppa, founded in 1892 had over 150 members, and its yearly activities included several paperchases, a hill-climbing competition, free-wheeling competition, parades, cricket matches and an annual dinner. The Reform Cycling Club, founded in 1900, was a Liberal organisation and had as its second function propaganda work for that party. The Constitutional Club was the Conservative reply. The smallest club was the Onyx. These clubs organised an annual cycle parade ending up at Bradwell Recreation Ground which collected a great deal for local charities.

Wolverton Amateur Athletic Club possibly reached its zenith in the 1920s. In those years the cycling section included Jimmy Knight who rode for England, whilst on the athletics side Mr Matthews was a fine high jumper, and both he and Fred Baxter, who excelled in the 100 and 200 yards sprints, represented England. For many years on and off the club won the Bucks Amateur Athletic shield – High Wycombe usually proving their sternest opponents.

The club still continues today, but the cycling section has faded away, and the track is barely suitable for even slow pram races.

FAIRS
Whilst Wolverton enjoyed itself at Whitsuntide with its athletics and family reunions, other towns enjoyed themselves on their own feast days with the accompanying two or three-day fairs held on the days dedicated to the patron saint of the local church.

Stony Stratford for example, since it had two churches, had 'statute' fairs in honour of St Giles and St Mary Magdalene.

For 700 years these annual 'statute' fairs had been occasions not only for the selling of horses, cattle, sheep and pigs, but for horse play, and they continued throughout the 19th century. They were much more important than the weekly or fortnightly cattle markets which took place at Stony Stratford, Buckingham, Newport Pagnell, Fenny Stratford (re-established in 1878), Winslow, Olney and so on, which were business occasions, for the Statute fairs were celebrations with all the fun of the fair from swings and roundabouts to rifle ranges and brandy snap stalls. Everybody welcomed the occasion with a gay boisterousness.

Fairs were a primitive tonic sanctioned by age-old custom. They were occasions when girls could be moderately impudent without reproach, and were sometimes clasped by unchaste hands and lustily embraced. Possibly if the lads had known what the girls thought they would have been even bolder! The 'Statty' fairs gave much innocent pleasure – but the Devil, in whom nearly everybody believed, had his opportunities.

At Stony Stratford the annual Statute fair was always held in August, in those days it stretched from the Market Square, along Silver Street, and around the Green. It was now the scene of the first 'animated pictures' to be seen in the neighbourhood. Every year from about 1902 Taylor's 'Bioscope' with its monster multi-coloured organ and blazing electric lights vied with Billings' roundabouts and Thurston's switchbacks for the public fancy, but these were only the centre pieces of the fair, for all around were not only the traditional coconut shies and rifle ranges but also stalls where they sold tubes of water for squibbing down girls' necks (a peculiar way of showing one's interest or affection, but always greeted with laughing shrieks).

It was at these fairs soon after 1890 that the highly elaborate and colourful showman's traction engine, with its polished and gleaming copper and brass fittings was first seen, and from then on the traction engines of the showmen added increased gaiety to fair and circuses at Stony Stratford, Newport and Fenny Stratford. These great engines had a dual purpose, not only did they haul the great trucks loaded with switchbacks, roundabouts, swings and so on, often four in a sequence, but they also served as a power station to run the various mechanical shows and provide electric light for them all. And when Taylor's came along with their 'Bioscope' the traction engine provided electricity for hundreds of coloured electric bulbs and powered the calliope which was an absolute marvel.

The smaller stalls selling brandy snaps or rock were lit by naphtha flares which had a pungent, persistent and unforgettable smell.

Up to 1903 the speed of all traction engines was limited to 2mph through villages and towns, and 4mph on the open highway, and even in 1903 this was only increased to 5mph. But this was enough to encourage the use of traction engines with huge containers behind them, for household removals, and around 1910 Samuel Holland and his son of Vicarage Road, Stony Stratford invested in a superb specimen which we illustrate elsewhere.

Wolverton probably showed the first indoor animated pictures in our locality for from about 1901 onwards Jury and Co's Bioscope was a feature of the annual entertainment given by the Working Men's Club to the children of the town. In 1906, over 600 children were invited, and on leaving were presented with three pennies (wealth indeed in those days, when a farthing would buy a sugar mouse, or a bag of sweets), two oranges, and a bar of chocolate. The Bioscope was received rapturously, and the programme in 1907 included no less than nine different short films.

These, of course, were the days of the silent screen, but lack of talkie apparatus was often made up for by other means. At Taylor's Bioscope a man sat behind the screen, and whenever he could sing the appropriate song, or make the appropriate noise he did so.

From time to time these fairs were supplemented by circuses or by the travelling 'penny gaffs', or theatres, which usually presented a programme of lurid melodrama in which the villain really was a villain, and the heroine usually in tears over her 'chee-ild'. In April 1907, for example, the Victoria Theatre set up in the Newport Road, Stantonbury, and its plays varied from *The Sacred Trust* to *Wine and Women*. It is interesting to note that the advertisements claimed that the theatre was 'free from vulgarity'. These gaffs and the circuses were all well attended and were talked about for weeks.

In 1911, the cinema (as distinct from the travelling Bioscope) reached the area. It was at Wolverton that the first cinema theatre was built, and for many years it was known as Barber's Electric Picture Palace. The cheapest seats were then 3d and the dearest 9d. Films were advertised according to the number of feet they contained, and there was quite a local sensation when, in one of the early programmes there was included the film *Zigomar* of 3,200 feet. It was the same Mr Barber who bought the old Wesleyan-Methodist Chapel in Fenny High Street which later became the County Cinema.

Shortly after this the Electric Picture Palace was opened in Newport Pagnell, and here as at Wolverton, Stony Stratford and Fenny Stratford, most of the films were of American origin. North Bucks began to be Americanised in no uncertain fashion. Okay!

JUBILEES AND CORONATIONS

However much Wolverton enjoyed its Whitsun sports, and Newport and Stratford and other towns enjoyed their annual fairs, there were throughout the century half a dozen occasions when everybody rejoiced at once, and these were the jubilees or coronations that came along with delightful irregularity.

Somebody had a good idea when in 1887 it was resolved to celebrate Queen Victoria's fiftieth anniversary of her accession. The little widow of Windsor, since the Prince Consort's death in December 1861 had literally gone on strike against public functions, and everybody was glad to celebrate her emergence, if only for a few days, from her unpopular retirement, for her Golden Jubilee.

When in 1897 she had reigned sixty years, her Diamond Jubilee was celebrated with much greater festivities. We can single out over the next half century half a dozen comparable occasions:

Queen Victoria's Diamond Jubilee,	21 June 1897
Coronation of Edward VII,	9 August 1902
Coronation of George V,	22 June 1911
Jubilee of George V,	7 May 1935
Coronation of George VI,	12 May 1937

THE DIAMOND JUBILEE

It is difficult in these days to imagine the outburst of loyalty –

the patriotic fervour – which characterised the Diamond Jubilee of Queen Victoria. To have reigned for sixty years was in itself an achievement, and when such a reign had been accompanied by a growing strength and prosperity for the whole nation there was a genuine reason for jubilation. But there was something more than this, a real feeling of affection for the little grey-haired Queen at Windsor. At Wolverton many had seen her in person, for in the old days Wolverton had been a compulsory refreshment stop for all the more important trains, and many times had the Queen stepped out of the Royal train and enjoyed the hospitality of the station. For many years Wolverton has maintained the Royal train and provided most of its personnel.

Throughout the whole of this area every possible preparation was made to celebrate the Diamond Jubilee royally – and looking back they had an astonishing variety of things with which to celebrate. There were, of course, the local bands, the bellringers, the usual number of people who could sing or recite, or run and jump, and a few with a capacity for making large noises by firing anvils. To fire the anvil the smiths carried out the anvil from the adjacent smithy, charged the square hole in the upper face of it with gunpowder, and then exploded it with a red hot rod. The resulting roar was very satisfactory to many.

At Stony Stratford a committee was formed of all the Parish Councillors (the East and the West were then separate parishes) and soon the plans were ready, but not until there had been a fierce debate as to whether it was better to give the children and old persons a treat or to have an illuminated town clock. The children won the day.

The actual anniversary was on Sunday 20 June, which was of course an impossible day except for church services. The moment midnight passed however the bells crashed out merrily. Early in the morning finishing touches were put to the dozen or so streamers across the High Street or to the many patriotic decorations of shops or private houses. Chinese lanterns and fairy lights were all in readiness. On the Monday morning there was a church parade at St Giles', with the Stony Stratford company of the 1st Bucks Volunteers, and the separate contingent of the Medical Staff Corps. The Fire Brigade were there too. Then, after church, came the procession all around the town.

On Tuesday the fun reached its maximum. In the morning

some enthusiasts 'fired the anvils' in a royal salute on the Green – a noisy proceeding of some danger to all concerned. Then the Band, accompanied by cyclists in fancy dress, paraded the town, and the church bells rang again. In the afternoon 1,000 people gathered in the Market Square; the children were there, all being marshalled for the procession, the Friendly Societies were there with banners and sashes, and what with the Fire Brigade and everybody else, the procession was nearly half a mile in length. Finally off they went by Silver Street to the Green, up and down the Wolverton Road and down the High Street to St Paul's College where they arrived in time for tea. In the quadrangle of the College 850 children managed to find seats, the 120 old people had their meat tea in the dining hall, and the remaining 1,000 inhabitants of the old town either helped serve or distributed the commemoration jubilee mugs or beakers, oranges and buns.

In the many sports that followed the Parish Councils were supposed to provide tug-of-war teams from their councillors, but the civic fathers, perhaps on account of the tea or the sun, felt quite unable to line up. Games and dancing followed, and scrambles for nuts and sweets for the children. At 10 pm all had to go home.

Although the town did not get its illuminated clock as a memorial to the Queen, it gained by another memorial, a drinking fountain (for horses and people) by the Congregational Church. The drinking fountain only lasted thirty years, when it was ruthlessly dumped on the scrap heap by a Council which had forgotten both Queen Victoria and the horses.

The villages celebrated with equal enthusiasm according to their population and means. Wherever the churches had bells they were rung. On every village green there were sports and teas, and at Newton Longville, where the historic smithy had been functioning for centuries and was the social centre of the village, the smiths, by the name of Green carried the anvils out on to the Green, and then exploded the gunpowder to the general joy of the children. The anvils were also fired on 5 November – Guy Fawkes' Day.

THE FENNY POPPERS

It will have been observed that there were many occasions when the Fenny Stratford Council was very divided. Queen Victoria's

Diamond Jubilee provided another occasion, for when the Amal-gamated Society of Railway Servants invited the Council to join a public procession and attend a service at the Baptist Chapel, five members voted for it, whilst the other five present abstained. Whether they had religious scruples about attending a chapel service, or whether they thought the young trade union branch a bit presumptuous we do not know. Otherwise Bletchley and Fenny Stratford's celebrations were very similar to those of Stony Stratford plus the 'Poppers'.

At all these occasions noise was an essential, for it is the oldest way of celebrating, and the biggest noises could be obtained either by 'firing the anvil' as at Stony Stratford and Newton Longville or by blasting off the 'Fenny Poppers' at Fenny Stratford.

It was not every parish which owned a miniature battery of artillery. Fenny Stratford has had a battery of six guns, probably since 1770, and these guns are known to fame and the neighbour-hood as the 'poppers'. It is noticeable that neither Browne Willis nor the Rev William Cole make any mention of them in their respective manuscripts, though Cole does relate that on 22 Nov-ember 1766 a friend of his had been to Fenny Stratford where they had 'a great Bonfire and Guns firing for their Dedication'.

The original 'poppers' becoming worn and unsafe were scrapped in 1859. Dr Bradbrook records that the last time they were fired in 1856 one of them burst: the firing took place in the close or paddock at the back of the *Bull Inn*, and a fragment was blown on to the roof of the *Bull and Butcher* and partially destroyed it. After this catastrophe a new battery was ordered, and one of the old 'poppers' was sent to the foundry as a pattern. The present six 'poppers' therefore were all made of gun metal in 1859; they were forged (not cast) and then bored by the Eagle Foundry, Northampton.

In appearance the 'guns' resemble quart tankards. Each one weighs 19 or 20 lb, and they are 7in high, 3¼in in diameter at muzzle. The bore is 6in long and of 1½in calibre. The charge is 4oz of 'shilling powder', the discharge is effected by the applica-tion of a red hot rod to the touch-hole, and the result is a satis-factory bang. During most of the year the battery reposes in Fenny Stratford church tower, emerging on St Martin's Day (11 November) and at such times as it is desirable to make a joyful noise, or even a mournful one as on the occasion of the funeral of Queen Victoria in 1901, when they were discharged eighty-one times (to mark the years of her age), and Bradbrook says they were heard as far off as Olney, twelve miles away.

The Coronation of 1902

The new King's coronation was fixed for 26 June 1902. All of a sudden he got appendicitis, and careful plans based on the Diamond Jubilee pattern had to be postponed until 9 August.

At Wolverton the Fire Brigade, the band, the children and all processed around the town, and a tea for the children followed. The most unusual event was the roasting of an entire ox at the corner of Windsor Street and Stratford Road, then a vacant lot, but on which now stands the *Craufurd Arms*. After several hours of roasting and basting everybody who brought a plate with them was allowed to have a slice. The stern condition that a plate should be brought was a precaution which effectively prevented stray revellers from Bradwell or Stratford profiting from Wolverton's celebration.

At Stony Stratford there was a similar free tea and treat for the children, but no roasted ox. But among the amusements which Stratford favoured was the competition of 'Climbing the Greasy Pole', which has been fully described in *The Nineteen Hundreds*, page 13.

For the coronation of 1911 the Bletchley UDC appointed a special coronation committee to make the celebration even more noteworthy. It was suggested that a most excellent and lasting memorial of the joyous occasion would be by the erection of two public conveniences, one at each end of the town. It is not quite clear why they thought lavatories were really suitable reminders of a coronation, but anyway no shopkeeper or resident in Fenny or Bletchley wanted a lavatory near his premises, and the proposal was dropped.

Other coronations followed, and the precedents were followed, out came the bands, the banners, the 'poppers' and the decorations and everybody rejoiced.

Music in the Air: Bells

From Biblical times onwards music has been the recognised accompaniment of rejoicing or other public emotional occasions, and music of course includes bell ringing, which is a well recorded local form of celebration. A mere glance through the *Royal Commission on Historic Monuments* (North Bucks 1913) shows that almost every one of our local churches had a ring of bells, some of great historic interest, and bellringers held a respected place in the affections of townsmen and villagers alike. We have seen in earlier chapters how the bells were clamorously rung for national victories, and even for the smaller celebrations such as the opening of the canal, or indeed any occasion when a Duke of Buckingham or the Marquess of Chandos came in state to Wolverton to lay the foundation stone of new workshops or even a market hall.

The bells in fact were the voices of the people, and from funerals to weddings, from coronations to even daily calls to service they called to prayer or rejoicing as the occasion demanded. Occasionally they would be rung for the sheer joy of the thing, and many of our church belfries have finely painted plaques or peal boards describing how such and such a group of bellringers at such and such a time rang a 'Grandsire Triples' which took three hours of timing and pints of beer and sweat. Bletchley is a good example.

The bells are still one of our most valued forms of music, and when a church like St Peter and St Paul at Newport Pagnell had its carillon installed the melodies had a nostalgic quality that could never be forgotten. *Robin Adair* was and is a great favourite.

When they were silenced in the Second World War because it was thought they might be useful as tocsins in the event of invasion, it was a great deprivation.

ORGANS

Nearly every church too had its merry organ. Cromwell's order to destroy all organs may have been carried out, but certainly with the Restoration organs began to appear in more and more churches. Willen has a small late 17th century organ case which is one of the most beautiful in the county.

An organ required, as an essential, a choir to go with it. Organists and choirmasters between them (both often being the masters at the local Church of England school) managed to teach music and train the voices of many who otherwise would only have picked up much more rackety refrains at the local pub on Saturday evenings.

Sometimes the love of music thus engendered in church or chapel led to secular orchestral or vocal societies being formed, such as the Fenny Stratford Musical Society (1890 on), which gave three oratorios or classical concerts a year. It existed for nearly half a century, and was probably at its zenith prior to the First World War under Lt-Col W. J. Levi. Their sopranos could augment the grief of any funeral and their glees delight the hearts of any octogenarians who could hear them.

BANDS

However popular church bells or church music was, there was from about 1830 onwards the allure of the brass band.

Nobody knows when the first brass band appeared in one of our local towns or village street. We do know that whenever a Marquess or a Duchess came around to open a canal or a railway extension there was always a band there, but this was probably a yeomanry or volunteer band from Buckingham. Deanshanger had greeted Queen Victoria with a 'rustic' band in 1845, but possibly Fenny Stratford led the way. In fact in 1888 the Town Brass Band (later the Fenny Stratford Town Prize Band with silver instruments) could already boast of nearly half a century of music, and it had a keen local rival for years in the Bletchley Shed Brass Band, but this faded away about 1880. People heard the martial music through their feet. In those days music had to be robust, otherwise it would never have touched the heart of a Buckinghamshire bumpkin. Consequently its music always sounded better than it was.

In 1901 a Bletchley Station Band was formed, and led a very active existence especially during the railway strikes.

When in 1898 Sir Herbert Leon gave the town the Recreation Ground, one of the first public requests was that a bandstand should be erected, and here every week one or the other bands gave a concert that was much appreciated until the radio took over after the First World War. When other local bands wanted to play in these attractive surroundings the UDC usually refused permission. New Bradwell could boast a comparable bandstand a little later on and Wolverton Park had one too. The Stony Stratford Band usually played on the Market Square, and Fegan's Orphanage Cadet Band usually played marching.

There were of course some who did not like bands, and their

chief objection to the playing of wind instruments was that doctors said it definitely prolonged the life of the player.

HOME MUSIC

From the collective music of bells, bands, choirs and societies, we turn to the personal or private musical activities. It will be appreciated that the great number of agricultural workers could afford nothing more than a hand-whittled pipe. But in the houses of railwaymen and farmers there now began to appear the piano. It was in fact a status symbol like colour television today, but whereas one can just flick on colour television a piano needed a pianist' and many professed to be tutors of the keyboard. Young ladies especially, were taught to play and young men occasionally to sing. The result, with the moony ballads of the period such as the *Indian Love Lyrics* was of course anticipated by all.

Probably the most revolting form of music was the new phonograph. Edison had marketed this dreadful instrument of torture in 1888, and by 1895 the early models were to be found in a few public houses locally and a few years later almost everywhere. Whatever the theme the record always began in a nasal voice with *Edison Bell Record* and finished with the same twanging sign-off. Most of the records too, seem to have been made by untrained singers from Kansas or Chicago, and since the instrument itself was far from being mechanically perfect the resultant raucous din was enough to frighten any child or dog.

It was followed by the gramophone which was certainly an improvement.

As one looks back over the list of the many things our grandparents enjoyed when they were young – two things stand out uppermost – first, how much they looked forward to and enjoyed their leisure. They had a genuine zest for it. Secondly, how little they needed in the way of expensive grand stands and booking offices to be able to enjoy themselves. Leisure was fun in its own right and they did not need elaborate equipment to enjoy it. They loved life as it came, without frills, complexities or drugs.

Leisure nowadays is no laughing matter; it is a very serious business.

14   The Motor Car

NOBODY knows when the first motor car came chugging along the Watling Street, but it came to be generally accepted with some strong protests in our area in 1898, for in June of that year a pretty young Stony Stratford bride decided to go to her wedding in a Daimler Phaeton or a Daimler Benz with bodywork by Salmons of Newport Pagnell.

She was not the first local girl to ride in a motor car, but she was the first to entrust herself to the new fangled contraption on the most important day of her life. The bride was Annie Franklin of Stony Stratford, a local builder's daughter, who lived at 26 Wolverton Road, and whose grandfather lived in Vicarage Road. The bridegroom was Mr Dick Ashley who was then employed by the Swansea Transport Company. It was of course quite an event. One of our illustrations shows the daring young couple surrounded by admiring relatives and friends.

Probably the two earliest motorists in this neighbourhood were the Rev G. M. Capell, of Passenham Manor, and Mr 'Puffer' Atkinson, of Cosgrove Priory. The Rev Capell, who was rector of Passenham for forty-four years – from 1870 to 1915 – was a charming man with a torpedo beard and an inventive mind. He had been responsible for many successful inventions, principally relating to extraction fans for mines,[1] the prototypes of which were made up by Mr Roberts, the Deanshanger blacksmith. As can be imagined Capell's chuffing, tiller model, De Dion, was his pride and joy. Mr John Atkinson's car was a Benz, tuned up by Mr Hamilton, who subsequently set up an important garage at the Old Stratford crossroads. But whether tuned up or not, all observers agreed that the cars were extremely noisy, and created dreadful clouds of dust whenever they came honk-honking along the highway. And joy was high when one or the other of these cars broke down, and faithful old Dobbin was hitched in front to tow it ingloriously home or to the nearest blacksmiths.

1 See Brown & Roberts, *Passenham*, 1973, p156.

Perhaps an even keener motor enthusiast was Walter Carlile of Gayhurst, who was MP for north Bucks. In 1898 he and Dr E. H. Hailey of Newport Pagnell, in conjunction with the firm of Salmons, and Charles Lawman, the confectioner, started up a motor bus service between Newport Pagnell and Olney.

Our enterprising band bought a very remarkable vehicle, a two cylinder 4½hp motor bus. It was, according to E. S. Shrapnell-Smith, probably the first rural bus service in England. The bus could carry twelve passengers at most, so that income was relatively small, whereas maintenance costs with these early buses were very high. Unfortunately this particular vehicle had neither a reliable engine nor reliable brakes. To overcome the latter defect a 'sprag' was fitted, a kind of iron spike, which, when the vehicle came to a stop on Cross Albans hill, was let down by the conductor in the hope that it would dig into the road and so arrest the progress of the vehicle. Often on such stops the passengers would have to get out and push to get the engine started again. Unfortunately the bus had a habit of 'jumping the sprag' and proceeding regardless down hill backwards. As can be imagined ladies were not at all impressed by the device, and this, combined with the unreliability of the engine, caused the whole concern to be a financial loss.

Walter Carlile also had a succession of cars for his own use, and around 1900 had a Daimler Phaeton with a body built for him by Salmons. The car was a dead ringer of the car used by the Franklin family for the wedding of 1898 with the tiller steering, gig candle lamps, solid tyres, wooden spokes and a chain drive.

Another keen local enthusiast was the teenaged Sir Everard Duncombe of Great Brickhill. When he came of age in 1906 his birthday presents included 'A motor speed indicator, a silver mounted motor drive record, and a fur motor rug'.

In 1904 there is recorded the first motor fatality in the district, when a small boy was killed at Shenley. This, as the *Wolverton Express* said:

'will cause many who have an inveterate hatred for motor cars to condemn the new method of travel more vehemently than ever. But motor cars are necessary evils now-a-days, and serious accidents from them are few and far between in this neighbourhood'. The motorist was completely exonerated, but the Coroner, Mr E. T. Worley, in summing up, went on to say: 'For my part, I wonder there are not more accidents, considering the legislature has allowed what are practically railway engines to run along the highway.'

THE ROADS

One persistent feature of this period was the shocking state of the roads. One would have thought with slow moving horse traffic, and less motor traffic there would be so little wear and tear on the roads that once made good they would last for a decade or more. But the very opposite was the case, and even in the towns themselves the streets and roads were full of puddles and mud, whilst in dry weather the dust nuisance was abominable. In May 1904 the surveyor to the Stony Stratford and Wolverton District Council, published his fifth annual report, and in it there occurs this paragraph:

'Probably no road in the county has more mechanically propelled traffic than the Watling Street, and when, as in the case of the High Street at Stony Stratford, it becomes the main street of the town, with many business premises on either side, it is very necessary that every effort should be made to keep down the dust. At frequent intervals during the day motor cars can be seen passing, the course of each being marked by a cloud of dust, which hangs in the air for a considerable time afterwards, and in any normal season regular and plentiful sprinkling of the High Street will be necessary.'

In April 1906 the local councils thought they ought to do something more and the Newport Pagnell RDC wrote to adjacent councils asking them for support in an approach to the County Council to limit the speed of these vehicles 'for they create such great clouds of dust as render the sight of other vehicles almost impossible and they have no time to get out of the way'. They suggested a limit of 6mph through towns and villages. Fenny Stratford UDC were sympathetic but could not agree as to whether 5 or 6 or 10mph was the most practical. Three years later the Fenny Stratford UDC asked the County Council for a definite limit of 5mph each way from the Aylesbury Street-High Street crossroads. The county agreed to a 5mph limit, but only for 50 yards along each crossroad.

This went a little way only to minimising dust, but other

methods were being tried out. There was of course the water cart which every market town and large village had used for a decade, but a more durable method was the tarring of roads. Nobody knows who first had the idea of using what was almost a waste product of the gas works for this purpose, and indeed it was not until about 1905 that supplies of tar were available in anything like the quantities required.

In 1907 the whole of the High Street at Stony Stratford was tarred, and in the following year the Stratford Road at Wolverton. Even these measures had their opponents for there were those who said with truth that the tarring made roads slippery for horses, and others who said the cost of 1d per square yard was far too expensive. In 1909 the County Council decided to pay for the tarring of the central ten feet of all main roads through towns, and the next year somebody thought up the bright idea of sanding the roads after tarring.

But the by-ways were still untarred, and villages like Shenley and Broughton still suffered from a Saharan dust storm whenever a motor car rushed through on a dry day.

Dust was not the only trouble, there was also the mud. The pounded gravel of most roads, plus a liberal admixture of horse manure and clay from local fields or paths, produced, whenever it rained, a swashy glutinous substance that made progress dirty and difficult. And of course the potholes in the local streets produced puddles of uncertain depth. The local remedy for this at the time was the sludge cart, the whole idea of which was that the mud should be scraped or pushed into sloppy heaps and then shovelled into the large rectangular tank which formed the main part of the sludge cart. Complaints to local councils that the sludge cart had not been around were frequent, and they came not only from villages like Milton Keynes, where the mud was sometimes 9 or 10in deep, but also from most of the streets in Wolverton and Bletchley from time to time. Foot scrapers were necessary for every house. 'Wellingtons' had not been invented and leggings were an essential part of the outfits of everyone from farmers to postmen. Ladies wore high laced boots or stayed at home.

In 1910 it was estimated that traffic passing through Stony Stratford High Street every week included 1,800 horsed vehicles, 500 motor cars, and 41 traction engines. Yet in spite of this increase, local inns made few attempts to cater for the automobile.

Very rarely did an inn instal a petrol pump or stock a few cans of oil. All this was left to a new development, and the French word 'garage' was added to the English language, but nobody liked calling the attendant a 'garagist'. There was something not quite nice about the word.

Possibly the first 'garage' in the district was set up in 1902 in the High Street of Stony Stratford by Mr A. J. Negus, who was very happy to be able to sell petrol to all and sundry at the then ruling price of 5d per gallon.[2] It was Mr Negus who first advertised 'two 15 h.p. cars for hire'. The new garages flourished, and so brought an added prosperity to the towns along the highways.

How slow the local hotels were to welcome the motor trade is evident from the advertisements for the *Bull Hotel* in Stony Stratford in 1909, when motor traffic was becoming considerable. It advertised:

'BRAKES, WAGONETTES AND DOG CARTS
LANDAUS AND BROUGHAMS
HEARSE AND CARRIAGES'

and underneath, in small type follows:
'Every accommodation for motors and cyclists'
Equally the *George Inn* at Bletchley advertised flys and wagonettes, but never mentioned motorists.

Nearly all the inns and hotels kept some form of transport and a horse or two. The larger hotels, like the *Bull* or the *Swan* at Fenny, still had quite a selection. They would mostly have a brougham, a 'fly' or cab, and a 'gig' or dog-cart. The brougham and a pair of greys was the favourite for weddings, the Victoria or landau for a gentle drive on a sunny day; the fly was used mainly for taking people and luggage to the railway station, whilst the gig or dog-cart seemed to be the favourite for shopping or business calls. Over and apart from all these were the wagonettes, which seated three in the front and eight at the back, and the larger brakes, which were largely used for 'outings' by clubs and organisations from the football teams to branches of the local political associations.

One of the features of the transport of this period, which has

---

2 This looks cheap, but actually when we consider the devaluation of money it was expensive, for it would be equal to 65p a gallon today (1975) or even more. Motoring was a rich man's pastime.

now almost completely disappeared, was that of the local 'carrier'. He was usually a very respectable person, owning a horse and van, or a donkey and truck, who at regular intervals made a journey usually from his given centre to two or more villages. At Stony Stratford, for example, there were in 1907 no less than six who thus served the town and the surrounding villages. The full list is given in *The Nineteen Hundreds*, page 53.

Mr Robert Mabbut of Stony Stratford was, perhaps, the last of the great carriers who earned their living by carrying parcels, letters, and even small boys, from the market towns or stations to the rural villages. Nothing was too much trouble for him, and whether his particular care was a barrel of oil, or a dog, he looked after it, and charged according to a reasonable reckoning of his own. But no carrier ever made a fortune.

In 1913 as we shall relate, the army manoeuvres were held in this district, and whilst the horse was overwhelmingly in evidence not only for cavalry, but for transport, everybody noted that the 'top brass' rode about in splendid open cars and despatch riders used motor cycles, but there were only about a hundred motor cars and 180 lorries compared with 3,000 carts or wagons. From now on every top executive and every wealthy man in north Bucks had his own car, and one or two of the more go-ahead firms were trying out lorries. The doctors were far more reluctant to change, and the farmers couldn't afford to.

In another chapter we have described the invention of the 'Diesel' engine by Akroyd Stuart of Bletchley, and later we refer to the contribution that Salmons of Newport made to the passenger motor car industry. The local contribution was great, but not as successful as it deserved to be.

What was not realised then (1914) was that the motor car and the diesel tractor between them would bring something like near disaster to the great railways of England. For almost a century they had been the predominant movers of people and goods. Coastal shipping, canals, traction engines and so on were all slower and less efficient. But now there were rivals not tied down to hard lines, that could take people and goods from door to door, and soon even more speedily than the railways, except on the longest runs.

Neither Bletchley nor Wolverton could imagine that the need for railwaymen and new coaches would minimise, and that a future Labour Chancellor of the Exchequer would describe the whole railway system as 'a collection of old iron'.

SALMONS AND SONS OF NEWPORT PAGNELL

One of our local firms which helped this trend was the old established firm of Salmons of Newport Pagnell. This was originally established round 1820 by Joseph Salmons as a coach bodybuilding business which originally employed a dozen men. It produced elaborate carriages or sturdy carts that far outlasted the horses that pulled them. He was succeeded by three sons, Joseph Junior, William and Thomas, and the business grew and prospered.

We have seen in an earlier chapter that when the Rev William Cole of Bletchley wanted a new chaise in 1767 he had to go to London for it: now the local gentry could find superb products locally, and the prices were really competitive. Cole paid £60 for his London chaise: Salmons could produce 'a more genteel and better made' one for 50 guineas! A one-horse cart was £30, which was too dear for the local council who bought one from Dundee for £27 (1899).

By 1860 Salmons were employing twenty-six men and four boys. Most of the coach-makers were unmarried journeymen from all over the country who found good lodgings with local widows.[3] But this was only the beginning; the two sons of Joseph Salmons, Jnr, George and Lucas, were among the pioneers of 'horseless carriages' as the early motor cars were known.

Even before the First World War Salmons had become one of the most enterprising motor car firms in England. By 1914 there were 350 employees working at the Tickford Street Carriage Works, and some cycled miles to work from one or the other of the neighbouring villages.

At the beginning of the First World War electricity was introduced into the factory, and a power plant installed. During that time too, a large number of ambulance bodies for Russia were built. The fact that it was fully geared up electrically led the army to take over a part of the works known as Olympia for a telegraphy school run by the Royal Engineers. Bury Field provided their camping ground, but they found a rare welcome in Newport Pagnell homes.

3 Information from Mr A. Fleming.

After the war there was a radical change of mood with the growing motoring public – customers were no longer content to ride in their horseless carriages open to the elements, and Salmons – under the leadership of George and Lucas, and their sons, Allan and Fred, developed an all-weather body that, for many years, was nationally known as the Tickford Body.

It was during the 1920s that Salmons produced their own car called, appropriately, the 'N.P.', after Newport Pagnell. Components were assembled in Newport Pagnell, and a specially designed radiator was used. They were but one of the many firms making their own brand of motor car, and although the 'N.P.' did not rival the renown of the Morris, Austin or Vauxhall cars, it had its enthusiastic devotees.

The firm's advertisements in 1924 described the 'N.P.' car as

'14/22 H.P. 13.9 RAC rating
Chassis price £300
Front wheel brakes £20 extra'

The body was created to personal choice, and this was the most profitable part of the business.

By the year 1938 the company had reached a new peak with a weekly output of between thirty and forty Tickford car bodies. There were now between 400 and 500 employees on the payroll, and Ian Boswell was chairman and managing director. In February 1943, the name Tickford Limited, was adopted – 123 years after the foundation of the family firm!

Salmons will always be remembered in the motor car history as the makers of the Tickford Body, whose elegant lines were to be seen on many of the motor cars owned by the well-to-do and well-known of the 1920s and 1930s. Salmons, or Tickfords, might have became a great industry, like British Leyland, but something was lacking. Possibly the 'N.P.' car failed because design and detail were continuously altered. The Tickford Body became less and less marketable when the saloon car became standard and the open car the exception.[4]

It was in 1955 that David Brown bought the business as a logical step to consolidating Aston Martin and Lagonda cars, all the bodies having been made by Tickfords since 1953. The firm is now known as Aston Martin Lagonda Limited.

4 Information from Miss M. Salmons of Newport Pagnell, who has a fine collection of photographs of Salmons and their products.

The Aeroplane

It was in the year 1910 that north Bucks saw its first aeroplane. In the April of that year the *Daily Mail* offered a prize of £10,000 to the first person to fly from London to Manchester in a heavier-than-air machine. There were a score of entrants, among them the unknown M. Paulhan from France, and the English Mr Grahame-White.

The day set for the event was 27 April, but it opened with windy weather, and since in those days a strong puff of wind was likely to blow an aeroplane clean over, all the competitors showed considerable discretion about leaving the starting point.

But at Fenny Stratford and Stony Stratford this was unknown, and from dawn onwards crowds of watchers eagerly scanned the skies from vantage points along the Watling Street or adjacent hills. Everybody who had a moment to spare gazed steadily southeastwards, but hours went by without anything larger than a crow being seen. Round about 6 pm the rumour came through that the Frenchman had actually started, and by now everybody was on the look out. About 6.45 pm a small speck could be seen coming from the direction of London. Gradually the speck increased, and soon a curious structure of canvas, wood, and wire was seen. As the rickety Farman bi-plane came over the Brickhills the pilot could be clearly distinguished, for in those days the pilot sat in the middle of the plane without even a windscreen to protect him. It was the Frenchman! Within eight or ten minutes the plane had disappeared from view.

Then came the rumour that Grahame-White had left and was hot in pursuit of the Frenchman. Sure enough, three-quarters of an hour later, in the failing light, his plane was spotted, and like Paulhan he came directly over Bletchley following the railway. Then, a few minutes later, he came down at Roade! Somehow or other the fact became known locally in another few minutes, and almost everybody who had a motor car, or a bicycle and the energy, hared off to Roade, where in a small field Grahame-White had made a perfect landing at 7.55 pm. Paulhan won.

Both flights had been seen by thousands locally, and the phenomenon, like comets in the skies, was discussed for months afterwards in the pubs and clubs. Even in remote Buckinghamshire it was realised that the time might come when Britain might be invaded from the air, and unwelcome visitors from the

Continent might shoot at one with revolvers or shot guns from their planes. But the staggering event soon paled into insignificance with the achievements of the next few years. In April 1911 Mr Grahame-White flew over the area again, this time in a direct flight from Hendon to Birmingham, but very few turned out to see him.

Rather more excitement was aroused when, a few weeks later, a dashing young aviator made a forced landing in a field at Mount Farm, Simpson, which lay between the canal and the Watling Street (now the site of Mount Farm Industrial Estate). The machine collapsed, but the intrepid airman was unhurt. It was a Sunday, and small crowds in their Sunday best came to look and marvel. Among them were the daughters of Mr Janes, the farmer, and Miss Mary Sinfield, who for sixty years treasured the photograph we produce elsewhere. [5]

Even now it gives me a shiver of horror to think of anybody going up in the air in such a fantastic contraption.

---

[5] Miss Sinfield died in 1973, but the farmer's daughters, Mrs Clements and Mrs Pearson now live in Wordsworth Drive, Bletchley. I am grateful to Harold Hepworth for this information, and to Dr Peter Jarvis for the loan of the photograph.

15   Military Matters to 1919

ONE of the trade advantages that our local innkeepers lost with the advent of the railways was the quartering, victualling and transport of troops on the march. Before 1838 often a full battalion would rest and recuperate for a night or two at Fenny Stratford or Stony Stratford, and it can be imagined that the demand for ale from hundreds of thirsty soldiers was something that publicans delighted in meeting, even if they were not so pleased to billet them.

There were, as is related in chapter 1, a few experiments in 1822 in moving troops by canal, but this was slow motion transport at 2mph whereas the marching rate was about 3½mph.

From 1838 on troops with very few exceptions were moved by rail at over 30mph. The saving to the exchequer was great: the loss to our local public houses was greater in proportion and felt much more keenly.

There were, however, one or two exceptions; possibly the most important was that heavy artillery still had to go by road. In 1852 Stony Stratford rejoiced to have several batteries of heavy guns parked on the market square, even though it was quickly found that a few underground water pipes had been broken and drainage systems damaged. On such occasions as these, Stony Stratford assumed once again the mantle of a market town of great attractions, and the adjacent villages provided hundreds of sight-seers and beer quaffers.

Apart from such rare instances the only contacts with the army were through the militia. In the county, the Bucks militia was headed by the Lord Lieutenant whose main duty was to command the levies in times of disturbance and it may well be imagined that during the Napoleonic wars, when Bonaparte threatened to invade England, the militia in all parts had to be ready, just in case. In Buckinghamshire the first Marquess of Buckingham was Lord Lieutenant from 1782 to 1813, and it was his son, later the first Duke of Buckingham, who held the office from 1813 to 1839

– a period which covered not only the end of the Napoleonic war but also the 'Captain Swing' outrages and the Chartist riots.[1] His successor was Lord Carrington, a great Buckinghamshire landowner, who in 1860 took over the lease of Gayhurst House.

The recruiting and training of the militia had not altered much since Tudor days, but an attempt was made by the Militia Act of 1852 to raise the numbers for the country to 50,000 and each county was given a quota. The militia was actually embodied or called up during the Crimean War (1854), and the Indian Mutiny (1857), by which time it had been increased to well over 100,000 men.

In 1859 there was a scare that the Emperor of France, Napoleon III, intended to invade England. Certainly he had massed quite a large army facing the English Channel. The outcome of this was that volunteer companies of riflemen were formed in every town in Bucks. Anyone up to 80 years of age could join provided they could march with the rest. In 1861 the superintendent of Wolverton Works, J. E. McConnell, noting that there were 300 youths under 21 working in Wolverton Works who 'found the seductive amusements of the ale house too often irresistible' suggested to the Marquess of Chandos, the company chairman that a volunteer rifle company should be organised as a leisure time activity.[2] Approval was given, but the Wolverton Company (No 6) of the 1st Royal Bucks Volunteer Corps does not appear to have been formed until 1877. Four years later the Stony Stratford Company was created, and all went on annual camps which were greatly enjoyed.

In 1900 the Bletchley Company (No 9) was formed with Capt J. Chadwick in command. We have come across Mr Chadwick before as the surveyor to the Fenny Stratford UDC. He was to combine both roles for many years. It took a few years for the company to become as smart as other units, and even the *Wolverton Express* had its jokes at their expense, for it reported: 'The Bletchley Volunteers were greatly chagrined at their repeated failure to win the Battalion cup for smartness, and say their disappointment was brought about by one of their comrades

1 See chapter 3.
2 Information from Miss Moira Courtman, who, however, quotes the date as 1867, which it might be, but the Marquess of Chandos had resigned in 1861, and McConnell in 1862.

wearing his socks over the bottom of his leggings. The rest of the Battalion is now teaching him to pull up his socks.' Bletchley naturally replied with energy, and Colour Sergeant Brace said 'He didn't have his socks over his leggings. He wore shoes instead of boots, and his socks showed between.'[3]

Whatever the sartorial details Bletchley Volunteers did win the Smartness Cup at least twice.

In 1880 a Bearer Company (later RAMC) was also formed at Stony Stratford headed by the young, able and ambitious Dr W. H. Bull. This was part of the Home Counties Volunteer Brigade.

The Boer War (1899–1902) raised a fever of local patriotism which was reflected not only in the many appeals to 'drop a little shilling in my little tambourine for a gentleman in khaki ordered south' but the recruitment of hundreds of local lads from the volunteers into the local regiments and their actual service overseas.

In January 1900 a meeting was held at the Science and Art Institute at Wolverton when eighty-six men of the Wolverton Company of Rifle Volunteers signed on for service in South Africa. Their names are given in Ratcliff's *History of the Newport Hundreds*, pages 291–92. Five weeks later a dinner was given to those selected to serve. The following morning they paraded on the Square and marched off under the command of Major Williams and Lieutenant L. C. Hawkins to the railway station. Similar meetings, enlistments, farewell dinners and parades took

Of all the processions none could equal those arranged by a curious Stantonbury organisation called 'The Darktown Charity Organisation'. It was a most remarkable combination of a Organisation'. It was a most remarkable combination of a nigger minstrel troupe, decorated carts, clowns, a tin kettle band, giants and regal equestrians. In the summer of 1900 this organisation arranged four distinct carnivals – at Wolverton, Stony Stratford, Newport Pagnell and Stantonbury, the purpose of which was to collect money for the benefit of 'those called to South Africa and their dependents within six miles of Wolverton'. At each town the procession would start from some central point and process all around with dancing, singing, clowning and general bustling

3 *Bletchley Gazette* 3 May 1952.

all helping to increase the general merriment, and they collected quite a lot of money.

It was a frustrating war – but when the small town of Mafeking was relieved on 17 May 1900 everybody went mad. The long succession of defeats and frustrations was, as everyone thought, at an end. At Wolverton the news was received so joyously that the great railway works were full of singing cheering groups: work stopped for the day, bonfires were lit at night, oxen were roasted whole, and the public houses did a roaring trade. The celebrations went on for days. Children were given teas and medals, and almost everybody who had a horse dressed himself up and rode around looking like a popular general.

But in spite of all sorts of victories the war went on. It produced at least one man whose title to heroism was unquestioned – the 18 year old Trumpeter Frank Downing who won the DCM (a very rare decoration in those days) for great gallantry. He was in the Royal Bucks Hussars, and when in June 1901, they returned to England seventy-five of them were entertained royally at Buckingham. When Trumpeter Downing got away with his father (who was the Quarter-master of the Royal Bucks Yeomanry) they headed for their home town, Stony Stratford. At the bridge at Stony Stratford a huge crowd had gathered with a band, with clergy, and with the Church Lads Brigade. The confusion was understandable, but eventually Dr Bull (RAMC Lieut-Colonel) was understood to have made a speech of welcome and young Frank was escorted with all honours and much noise to his home at the corner of London Road.[4]

SIR JOHN FRENCH

But Frank Downing was not the only one to get a hero's reception. Everybody who came back, and nearly everyone did, was given a rousing welcome, and a gold watch. The Wolverton men of the Volunteers returned in May 1901. Amongst others they were welcomed by Mr C. A. Park, the superintendent of the railway works, who remarked that 'the only thing we regret is that you had not the opportunity of doing a little more fighting'.

This could not possibly have been said about another local hero, Lieutenant-General Sir John French who had been a brilliant

4 A fuller account of this appears in *The Nineteen Hundreds*. Frank Downing died in 1960.

cavalry leader during the whole war and had added lustre to British arms in battle after battle and campaign after campaign. Although he was an Irishman born in Kent he was more local than one would think. He had started life as a midshipman, but got into the army by the 'back door', ie, the Volunteers, and joined the 19th Hussars in 1874, and acquired a zest for polo.

A little later he met Eleanora Anna, second daughter of Richard Selby-Lowndes of 'Elmers', Church Green Road, Bletchley. She was one of eight sisters, known to the locals as the 'Eight Belles'. Only a few hundred yards from their home was the *Eight Bells* public house, and many were delighted with the allusion.[5]

But Lieutenant J. D. P. French was no catch in the matrimonial market, for although he was becoming a fine cavalryman he had only his subaltern's pay to live on, whilst Eleanora Anna, as one of eight daughters of a cadet branch of the Selby-Lowndes could hardly look forward to a substantial dowry. At last, in 1880 when Lt French learnt that he was to become captain and adjutant of his regiment (an adjutant got 2s a day extra) they decided to get married. Eleanora Anna was now 36. John French was 28.

Their earliest home seems to have been at Bracknell House, Bletchley, at the junction of Aylesbury Street and Vicarage Road, and doubtless there were many reunions here with Selby-Lowndes relatives from 'Elmers', Whaddon, Hanslope, Winslow and indeed all over the place.

In 1883 John French was promoted major and almost immediately got the chance of active service with his regiment in the Sudan under Lord Wolseley for the relief of General Gordon. His fine soldierly qualities were quickly appreciated and in 1885 he was mentioned in despatches and promoted lieutenant-colonel. Quick promotion![6]

Ten miles due north of Bletchley is the village of Hanslope with its soaring spire and attractive stone built cottages. At this time the lord of the manor was Edward Hanslope Watts, JP (1845–1912) whose ancestors had made a fortune or two in Bengal and had lived at the manor for generations, and were

---

5 The *Eight Bells* is first mentioned in 1779, but there had been a public house on the site since 1712. It was possibly named after the eight bells in the neighbouring Bletchley church. It was rebuilt about 1890 by Robert Holdom, and renamed the *Eight Belles* sometime after 1908. I am indebted to the Selby-Lowndes family of Bow Brickhill for family details.
6 *Life of Field Marshal Sir John French*, First Earl of Ypres, KT etc, by Gerald French, 1931.

related to the Earls of Liverpool (1846–1930). The manor was a commodious country house built in 1690 with nearly 200 acres of park land: just the sort of gentleman's house that Disraeli loved and probably visited.[7]

In 1868 Watts married Sophia Edith, another of the 'Eight Belles' and third daughter of Richard Selby-Lowndes. A few years later was a time of great agricultural depression, and it is small wonder that one of their farms, Yew Tree Farm, was untenanted. It was let to Lieut-Colonel John French around 1882.

In 1886 he was back in England, still finding it difficult to make both ends meet, and in 1890 he bought a dog-cart from Salmons of Newport, but for some reason only paid a fraction towards it. Salmons brought him up before the County Court at Aylesbury which ordered payment of the £15 2s 6d outstanding.[8]

He was a dedicated soldier, willing and eager to go anywhere on receipt of a telegram from the War Office. In 1891 he went off to India for a couple of years as OC of his regiment, and then a real catastrophe occurred. When he returned home in 1893 he was placed on half pay! This meant that there was no army job for him and that in a year or two he would be declared redundant. It will be gathered that our quick tempered and irritable Lieut-Colonel was now even more so. To say that he was 'not well off', was an understatement, and at 43 he was 'on the shelf'. Neither he nor his wife could get their standard of living down below what they were accustomed to. Local firms noticed this.

Suddenly in 1895, the whole picture changed. He was promoted colonel and given the post of Assistant-Adjutant at the Horse Guards. Here he did well. Four years later the Boer War broke out, and he went to South Africa in October 1899 as a local Major-General. Here his brilliant cavalry leadership brought him in 1900 promotion to Lieut-General and a KCB. Of all our generals in the Boer War, French was one of the few who enhanced his reputation.

Peace was signed in May 1902 and when Sir John returned from the war two months later, covered with laurels, he was given a tumultuous reception with Kitchener in London, and then took the train from Euston to Castlethorpe (for Hanslope) where he

7 It has housed government services since 1939.
8 *Bucks Standard* 13 April 1890.

was met at the station by a huge crowd. The horses were taken out of his carriage, and it was pulled through the gaily decorated streets of Castlethorpe and Hanslope to the Park, where his wife, family and all the squire's relations welcomed him. But Sir John was not a man to court popularity and was soon off on other military duties.

In 1902 he was given the most important post of the Aldershot Command and created a KCMG. He lived at Government House where he and Eleanora Anna received royalty, cabinet ministers and Selby-Lowndes' relatives in bewildering numbers.

The war had shown that whilst our soldiers could and would be heroes, neither the War Office nor most of the generals knew how to win a war. A relative handful of Boer farmers had defied the might of the British Empire for years, and the world had begun to wonder.

The Territorials

But the long needed shake-up in the army did not come for five years – when the new Liberal government put Lord Haldane into the War Office with a clear mandate to prepare for a possible continental war. But even he kept most of the old generals, for their popularity was enormous. It was not until Lord Haldane's Territorial and Reserve Forces Act of 1907 was passed that the old Volunteers disappeared and the new Territorial Army took its place.

In 1908 the Oxfordshire and Buckinghamshire Light Infantry, and the Royal Bucks Hussars with its depot at West Street, Buckingham, and a squadron commanded by Major Fenwick at Stony Stratford were our local units, and the 1st Bucks Royal Volunteer Corps now became the Bucks Territorial Battalion attached to the Oxfordshire and Buckinghamshire Light Infantry. In this battalion the old Nos 6 and 7 Companies at Wolverton became F and G Companies with Capt L. C. Hawkins in command, whilst the former Bletchley No 9 Company became I Company; still under Capt J. Chadwick.

The ambulance unit at Stony Stratford now became a Field Ambulance Unit of the 2nd South Midland Mounted Brigade (RAMC), and fifty-three men out of sixty-four volunteered for the new Territorial Ambulance Unit. Within a few weeks more enlistments had brought the strength up to six officers and 110 men, thus creating the first unit to be at full strength in the whole of the Southern Command, and it remained an example to all others.

In spite of all efforts to popularise the Territorials the Wolverton units were never up to strength and in 1912 lost many of those who signed on for four years in 1908. Every year there were, as in the Volunteer days, the annual camps. The location varied from Worthing or Shorncliffe to Swanage or Fort Widley.

Every year there were church parades and annual dinners of the various Territorial units. At one of these a very common complaint was ventilated. In these years men's clothing was certainly heavy and stiff, but even stiffer was the material from which uniforms were made. When the Territorials were served out with their new uniforms in 1908 the men could not help being smart on parade as they could scarcely bend. Colour-Sergeant W. L. Marsh, at the annual Territorial dinner of that year caused great hilarity when he expressed the hope that in future the uniforms 'might be a bit more pliable'.

THE MANOEUVRES OF 1913

At various times in our history north Bucks has been overrun by the military, and probably the most memorable time was during the Civil War when both sides manoeuvred and plundered, when Newport Pagnell was a defended military bastion and Great Brickhill the temporary encampment of thousands of Parliamentary troops. But now came a time when 40,000 men under arms and in full uniform, with all the trappings of war from guns to aircraft would encamp along our northern border for a couple of months in 1913.

The War Office or the Cabinet had decided that it was high time the modernised British army should be tested, and although we still had a few tribal wars going on in various parts of the empire, it was decided to organise grand scale manoeuvres on British soil to test out, if they could, everything from rifle marksmanship to the working of GHQ at war establishment. The idea was that the 'Brown' force of 40,000 men should advance from south of the river Ouse between Buckingham and Newport Pagnell and attack a 'White' army – token units amounting to 8,000 men – around Daventry. Aircraft were to take part – for reconnaissance purposes only – there were just thirty-four avail-

34   *Stony Stratford celebrates the coronation of 1902 by a procession which included the band and the great hand-painted banners of the Friendly Societies. The leading banner is that of the Duke of Buckingham Lodge of the Manchester Unity. The 'Cock' and the 'Bull' hotels are obscured by the banners. See p240.*

35   *Firing the anvils in celebration of the coronation of King George V, 1911. The setting is the Horse Fair Green at Stony Stratford. Three or four anvils were used. Photo: Buttrum, Stony Stratford. See pp237–38.*

36 *Staple Hall, Fenny Stratford when occupied by the Royal Engineers during the First World War. Courtesy of Mr A. O'Dell, Fenny Stratford. See p267*

37 *Bletchley Park arranged for cycle races and other athletic sports and the flower show in 1924. The building in the background is now the North Bucks Music Centre. Courtesy of Mr A. O'Dell, Bletchley.*

wan Corner, High Street, Bletchley.

38   The historic centre of Fenny Stratford. The old 'Swan' first mentioned in the 15th century is still standing, but the other houses on the corners have been demolished. Courtesy of Mrs Pacey, Woburn Sands.

39   Air crash at Simpson, 1911. See p254.

40 The declaration of the poll at Buckingham Town Hall, 1951 when Aidan
Crawley (right) was defeated by 54 votes. Next to him is Mrs Crawley. In the centre
is Guy Crouch the County Clerk, and then Major and Mrs Markham, with Major
Leslie Marler in between. Photo by Chapman, Buckingham.

able – and three airships were also available for the defending force.

The Territorials were not included in the scheme to any great degree. On 2 August they had started their annual fortnight's camp at Shorncliffe, and when they returned they had done their bit and were not invited to help either side. The week after their return the Wolverton cinema (Barber's) showed *The Battle of Paardeburg* and it drew packed houses.

Early in August regular troops were on the move from their barracks. The first to arrive were the 7th Field Company Royal Engineers whose job it was to prepare the camp sites at Stacey Hill and Warren Farm, Wolverton. These were also to include the headquarters of the 4th Division and a general hospital, whilst all around stretching to Stony Stratford the 10th and 11th Brigades would camp with various auxiliary forces. Wolverton Station was prepared for the reception of light artillery and thousands of troops.

On 23 August 156 men, 130 horses and 50 wagons of the Army Service Corps passed through Stony Stratford and made camp at Debbs Barn on the Wolverton Road. On 26 August the Royal Field Artillery were camped just opposite in Norman's Mill Meadows, and the Royal Irish Fusiliers were camped there too.

On Friday 29 August at 3 am the first troop train arrived at Wolverton as quietly as possible, but the fourth train three hours later with the Seaforth Highlanders aboard arrived to the skirl of pipes, which really awakened Wolverton. Following regiments played their way to the Stony Stratford camps. Whilst the infantry were detraining at Wolverton, the artillery were still coming by road, and on the same day 576 men, 590 horses, 38 wagons and 46 guns came through Stony Stratford.

On Saturday 30 August the 3rd Royal Dublin Fusiliers came by train, and as it was Saturday the girls at McCorquodale's printing works were free to welcome them. They did.

Within a few days 13,000 troops were quartered between Stony Stratford and the railway. The excitement of local boys and girls can be imagined. For the boys, the bands, the uniforms, the guns and even the tents were an excitement that was indescribable. For the girls, and particularly for the teenagers, the prospect of thousands of fine alert men in the pink of health coming into the vicinity created almost a mental delirium. Fathers might well have been advised to 'Lock up your daughters' – but not even the Particular Baptists went to that degree of austerity.

Training began at once, which meant plenty of fine marching to martial music, and other exercises like throwing a pontoon bridge across the river Ouse and manhandling guns through fords. And whilst there was an occasional night march, generally the troops were free in the evenings, and so were some of the girls.

Everybody made efforts to entertain them. Dances were held nightly: church choirs provided concerts, smoking concerts were held in all the best pubs. As for the military, they put on a Grand Military Tournament at Wolverton Park when about 6,000 people saw the Army at its best.

During the weeks that the soldiers were encamped around Wolverton and Stony Stratford they made friends galore. Almost every door was open to them, and whether they were Royal Dublin Fusiliers or Seaforth Highlanders they behaved with a gentlemanliness that was an infinite credit to their upbringing in Cork or Glasgow. Pipe Major Haywood and Drum Major Lockie of the Seaforth Highlanders came to our home at 58 Wolverton Road many times, and so did privates of the Royal Irish Fusiliers. I was 16 at the time – and I listened intently to their army experiences. I made up my mind to be a soldier. I had only two years to wait before I was eighteen – but then it seemed like eternity.

As for the officers, every stately home in north Bucks was open to them. The mansions were still as attractive as Disraeli had found them in 1857 with the possible exception of Stowe, and the hostesses felt themselves fortunate if they could capture a couple of captains for coffee.

The commander-in-chief, Field Marshal Sir John French (1852–1925) commanding the Brown army knew the area exceptionally well. He had just been promoted field marshal, and it was generally understood that if England were to be involved in a continental war he would command either the British Expeditionary Force or at any rate be in command of our fine little army whatever its job. His interest in the neighbourhood had been heightened by a most tragic event only twelve months earlier.

Murder most foul

Throughout this story of our section of north Bucks one may be
surprised by the relative absence of serious crime, and in fact the
last reference we made to a deliberate murder was as long ago
as 1805 when a Simpson shoemaker was murdered and robbed
at Denbigh Hall.

On 21 July 1912, the whole area was shocked by the shooting
of the lord of the manor, Edward Watts, at the main entrance to
Hanslope Park by his head gamekeeper on a Sunday morning
just after he and his wife were returning from church. Mrs Watts
whom we have met several times before, was Sophia Edith
(Selby-Lowndes) whose sister was the wife of Sir John French.
The gamekeeper, who was under sentence of dismissal, had got
drunk on an empty stomach with 'a jug of primrose wine' –
powerful stuff as many of these local home-made wines can be,
and it was a blazing hot day with temperatures in the 80s. The
gamekeeper was William Farrow, and after shooting Edward
Watts fatally twice, just missing Mrs Watts, he ran back into the
woods and shot himself. There was of course a probing inquest
and an immense funeral. There was much sympathy with Mrs
Farrow until she erected a headstone to her husband with the
inscription 'Waiting till all shall be revealed'.[9]

During the manoeuvres Field Marshal Sir John French's headquarters was very near Hanslope Park.

Possibly the high spot from many points of view was when
King George V came to Old Stratford to see the troops. There
was no press announcement about it, but we all knew when he
was coming. He and his staff were accompanied by foreign
military attachés. Their uniforms were pure Ruritania. Never in
all its history dating back to Roman times had Old Stratford
seen such sartorial glory.

On 22 September, the four-day battle began – opened by the
cavalry supported by cyclists. The Brown forces deployed for
attack, attacked the enemy's entrenched position, launched a
pursuit, and then broke off the pursuit with a sudden change of
direction just to test everybody.

Lots of things went wrong; there were great traffic congestions

9 For a full description of the murder see Gerald French's *The Hanslope Park Tragedy*,
Hove Shirley Press, 1968. I am also indebted to Walter Beesly, OBE of Bullington End,
Hanslope for his recollections. His mother was a witness at the inquest.

at Buckingham, which were not to be wondered at. Some of the locally hired 'weedy light horses' were quite unfitted for draught work. The cavalry *would* halt in fenced roads and become sitting targets. Military cyclists showed a great reluctance to leave their bikes even when attacked. Co-operation with air service was unclose. Farmers were upset by 'troops going through seed clover and roots when there was little or no military necessity for it'. The nibbling of haystacks by horses was another cause of irritation to the farmer, 'not so much from the actual amount eaten but because the appearance and the market price of the stack suffered'.[10]

Looking back with the advantage of hindsight one realises how pathetically inept these manoeuvres were. There were only 105 motor cars, mostly for the conveyance of top personnel, and 170 motor cycles. For troop movements and supplies there were 180 lorries, but also there were 15,000 horses (of which 3,000 were hired locally), and 3,000 carts or wagons. Nevertheless at the time everybody thought the manoeuvres a great success.

THE FIRST WORLD WAR

Within a year the First World War had broken out and all these men we had seen on manoeuvres were part of the British Expeditionary Force, and in retreat from Mons.

The impact of the war on north Bucks was immediate. The first impact was the calling up of men and horses. All men on army or navy reserve or in the Territorials were immediately ordered to their depots or coastal stations. The new drill hall near the railway station at Wolverton became a busy centre for mobilisation. Some firms like McCorquodales of Wolverton saw their managing director, Major L. C. Hawkins, and a score of men go off, and a month later three more of their best clerks (including C. W. Green) volunteered. The denuded firm tried desperately to cope.

Local authorities which had given all the encouragement they could to the Territorials in time of peace suddenly found themselves with only a skeleton staff. At Bletchley, the UDC not only saw its surveyor, Capt John Chadwick, 'embodied' but the whole of his staff. They were left with an elderly clerk, Thomas Best,

---

10 *Report on Army Exercise*, 1913. War Office January 1915. See also Crismus Parsons' delightful article on 'The 1913 manoeuvres' in *The Milton Keynes Journal* No 2, 1973.

and his son Thomas Best, Jnr. It was then that the Bletchley UDC stepped out of character and made a blunder. Hitherto it had been most careful of the pennies and the shillings, but now (8 September 1914) it was decided unanimously that 'In view of the fact that Mr John Chadwick has been called upon to serve the country on active service, leave of absence be granted him during the time the Territorial Forces remained mobilised, and that his salary be continued by the Council'. The minutes of the UDC continue:

> 'The position created by the absence of the Surveyor and his staff all of whom had been called for duty in the army was considered. It was decided to place the Clerk to the Council (Thomas Best) in charge of the Surveyors Department.'

A year later Thomas Best, Jnr was made deputy surveyor.

The council had a shock when in September 1915 the auditors ruled that the salary payments to Captain (now Major) John Chadwick were illegal and that the members of the council ought to be surcharged. The Local Government Board asked the council to explain. All they could do was to say that his salary as surveyor was £220 and that as a major he was now receiving £292 per annum. Nevertheless he had greatly helped the council with active advice during his periods of leave. The council salary was discontinued as from 29 September 1915, and nothing more was heard of the matter.

By 1915 there were hundreds of troops training in Bletchley, mostly billeted out. These included quite a large contingent of Royal Engineers at Staple Hall, Fenny Stratford. Amongst these was a young, insignificant sapper Bill Corsham, formerly a Post Office telegraphist who recalls 'I had a good time at the Interception Hut at Fenny Stratford, for whilst the others were out dancing I was signalling'. Later he became 'Uncle Vic' to the radio world, and opened up short wave communication even across the Atlantic and to Australia. Like all the others he was billeted out. In June 1915 the council resolved that 'In view of the greatly enhanced cost of living the billeting allowance of 2s 6d per day for board and lodging be increased to 3s 4½d' (17 pence in today's currency). By any standards it was a fantastically small amount.

In March 1916 Thomas Best who had been clerk for twenty years died. His son expected his job but the council by a seven

to two vote later decided to appoint Mr Charter Wilson at
£250 per annum. Thomas Best, Jnr resigned in June, very upset
and offended. A month later John Chadwick's son, Lieut Douglas
Chadwick, was killed in action, and month by month the casualty
list grew.

RATIONING

Early in 1917 it was evident that Britain was becoming very short
of sugar supplies and the first rationing system was introduced by
allowing each retailer half of his normal (1915) supplies, and he
was left to distribute this to households as fairly as his conscience
would allow. It was obviously an imperfect scheme, for whereas
some towns were expanding, like Bletchley, others with little
war work were dwindling. Food controllers were set up in
each district, and in February 1918 individual ration cards were
introduced. They were a melodramatic success, since they almost
abolished queues. It is astonishing what the British people will put
up with provided they think everybody is suffering alike: but
they hate queuing. To the ration of 8oz of sugar per week there
was now added meat and bacon, fats and lard, and later tea and
cheese were added, but now the British allotmenteers were in
action.

Even before the war, the great majority of working men had
an allotment and were deservedly proud of the magnificent
vegetables they grew. But more than this almost every other
allotment had a pig sty, and the county production of pigs in
1918 was an all time record. These various sheds, from the piggeries to tool sheds and even summer houses were mostly built
from anything available, from galvanised iron to old railway
carriages. Tar was the universal preservative, so that the view
over the allotments of any town or village in the area was not
much better than that of an Algerian shanty town. 'Dig for
victory' was the slogan, and victory came, for the first items to
be taken 'off the ration' were bacon and ham in July 1918. The
allotmenteers had won a great victory, but nobody got a medal
for carrying pig buckets.[11]

Jam was put on the ration in November 1918. It was about

11 The effort declined after the war and in 1924 we were importing £58 million worth
of pig products. Today we are importing ten times that figure, allotments are untenanted, and people grumble at the price of pork.

two years before sugar, the most difficult import of all, was taken off the ration (November 1920). The rush of the children for sweets that month is something no grocer or sweet shop will ever forget.

War Losses

Meanwhile the heavy cost had been counted at last. The austere war memorials that went up in 1919 or 1920 on village greens or in the local church showed what a terrible price had been paid for victory. Everybody knows of the sacrifices of the Somme, or Ypres or elsewhere where our young manhood was cut down in swathes. Few realised that with so many of the youth of the country slain, so many of the girls would never find husbands. Everybody rightly remembered the war widows, and their orphans, but nobody seemed to be able to think about, or to do anything about, the spinsters whose banns were never called.

Postscript

Field Marshal Lord French became Viceroy of Ireland in May 1918. He had a very troubled three years there, and was rewarded with an earldom in 1922. Much of the remaining three years of his life was spent in Paris. His widow survived him by many years and when she died in 1941 she was buried in Bletchley churchyard where a simple cross carries the inscription:

To the loving memory of
Eleanora Anna
Widow of the 1st Earl of Ypres
Daughter of Richard Selby Lowndes
1844 – 1941

Nearby their son, John Richard Lowndes French, second Earl of Ypres (1881–1958) is buried. The only Selby-Lowndes in our area now are at Bow Brickhill, where Mrs Geoffrey Selby-Lowndes aged 96, who was born a Selby-Lowndes and married a cousin, has been of great help. Though there are few family papers, there is a fine collection of family and hunting pictures.

16 North Bucks Politics and Trade Unionism, 1895–1951

THE Buckingham division, or the north Bucks constituency, has always been one of the most marginal in England, for it included eleven towns, about ninety villages or hamlets, and such varied interests as to make it almost unpredictable. It was created as a separate county division in 1885 when the qualifications for voting were widened and Buckinghamshire representation was halved, owing to the abolition of the borough constituencies of Buckingham, Wycombe and Marlow. Buckingham became the political centre of the new division, but already its power points were more at Wolverton and Bletchley.

The Liberals and Conservatives were strongly entrenched; there was as yet no Labour party – not even in Bletchley.

Up to about 1890 the Liberal cause had found several of its champions and chairmen from among the Verneys, and the Conservatives found some of their candidates, and often their chairmen, from among the Cottesloe family. But in 1891, with no Verney available, the Liberals chose Herbert Samuel Leon, who lived at Bletchley Park and was possibly the second greatest land-owner in Bletchley, for he owned about a square mile.

Leon had possibly never heard of Bletchley, other than as a railway junction, before 1883, for he was a London financier, head of the Stock Exchange firm of Leon Brothers, a leading firm of dealers in the American Stock Market. He was also a director of the Anglo-American Telegraph Company and at one time part proprietor of the *Daily News*, a very popular Liberal newspaper. He had made a fortune, and like so many city men who have been fortunate, decided to acquire a country estate. In 1883 he heard that Bletchley Park and the adjoining Home Farm were for sale; he bought them, fell in love with the area and became one of Bletchley's most dominant, most lovable and most criticised citizens.

As can be seen from his photograph (plate 24) he was already balding, but so was the Prince of Wales, and Leon's carefully tended moustache and beard again enhanced the resemblance to His Royal Highness. He soon became a familiar figure in the area for he decided firstly to enlarge the mansion in the Park and to surround it with trees of every kind, secondly to breed short-horn pedigree cattle on Home Farm, and thirdly to support the Liberal cause in north Bucks in every way he could.

His enlarged mansion we can still see today – opinions vary as to its architectural quality, but it is undoubtedly joyous Victorian with its gables, quirks and tall chimneys.[1] His shorthorn herd at Home Farm became a success, and some of the best beasts were exported to the Argentine. As for the local Liberal movement, it welcomed him with open arms, for he was generous and reliable. Certainly he looked the picture of absolute benevolence. Rail-waymen loved him. But he had his critics – mostly Conservatives – and that criticism when he became the Liberal candidate for north Bucks in 1891 scarcely stopped at terms like 'Jewish usurer'. A month later the sitting member, Capt E. H. Verney retired, and in the by-election Leon won by 381. In the General Election in the following year he beat W. W. Carlile by 449. The electorate was then about 11,000 since only male freeholders or those with lodging qualifications were enrolled, and the Liberal rejoicing was justified. That parliament lasted three years, and when the next General Election came Leon was again opposed by the pleasantly gruff Walter Carlile of Gayhurst. Carlile won by 436 votes. Conservatives were delighted, but once again the lesson was brought out that north Bucks was a most marginal constituency and never a safe seat for anybody.

Herbert Leon never stood for Parliament again but he became a Bletchley Councillor and a County Alderman and continued to aid the Liberal cause in diverse ways, including an annual grant of £500 to the Buckingham Liberal Association. For all his help to the Liberal cause and for his other philanthropies he was rewarded with a baronetcy in 1908. In 1909 he became sheriff of the county and was on Asquith's list of potential peers in 1911. In 1918 he became chairman of the Bletchley UDC. Every year he would open his grounds for the annual Bletchley Show which had up to 15,000 visitors and many county cricket matches were held on the superb pitch. He enjoyed being a host.

1 For illustrations see *Building Conservation in Milton Keynes* p19, and plate 22.

When he died in 1926 Lady Fanny Leon continued what was now a Bletchley tradition, and when she died in 1936 Bletchley's wonderful link with the Leon family was broken, but not forgotten.

We have wandered a little from the strict political history of north Bucks and we must now go back to see how Sir Herbert Leon's successor as MP was getting on. In 1900 Walter Carlile of Gayhurst stood again and beat the Hon Hubert Beaumont by 417, but by 1906 he had had enough of Westminster, and who can blame him when one remembers what a lovely place his home at Gayhurst was and is. He was rewarded with the OBE in 1920, which he did not much appreciate, and by a baronetcy in 1928, which he did. In 1915 when he was helping Sir Fabian Ware with his British Red Cross unit in France he recruited me to that unit as a clerk, and when thirty years later I became a parliamentary candidate and MP he gave me every conceivable assistance in a quiet, retiring way.

One of the oddest things about parliamentary elections was that although both the telegraph and telephone were now installed locally, the first results up to 1906 usually came by cycle. The racing cyclists of the local cycling clubs were faster than any other method then known of spreading the news. In that year telephones were installed at Wolverton and Stony Stratford, but there were only fifteen subscribers, mostly of course hotels and business premises. At Bletchley there were twenty.

When Walter Carlile stood down in 1906 his Conservative successor was the Hon T. F. Fremantle, son of Lord Cottesloe, but a new Verney was in the field, and F. W. Verney, a younger son of Sir Harry, the third baronet, romped in with a record majority of 1,580. Many of the campaign meetings were distinctly disorderly, windows were broken, free fights took place and much argument went on in the locals over many pints of beer, and not infrequently Saturday night political discussions at the local ended up with fisticuffs. Drunken enthusiasts sought to settle the fate of empires by giving each other a bloody nose or a black eye. Even the Suffragettes were active. A few years later, in August 1909 when the Prime Minister, the Right Honourable Herbert Asquith, came to Bletchley Park to speak in support of Verney, tremendous preparations were made to ensure that these 'wild women' did not molest him with their umbrellas or parasols. But one determined lady managed to chain herself to a tree in the park whilst others with speaking trumpets shrilled out 'Votes for Women' in the middle of the Prime Minister's speech. There was a stiff skirmish, several ladies were locked up for a few hours and the Prime Minister made a peaceful exit from Bletchley.

In Bletchley there were some who sympathised with the new Labour movement but most of these held that it was part and parcel of Liberalism. The Amalgamated Society of Railway Servants (later to become the NUR) included some who were more forthright, but generally there was a determination for trade unionists not to get involved in party politics. They felt they were more like a friendly society, and the annual parades with the great banners were one of the colourful events in a fairly drab period.

There were two General Elections in 1910, and north Bucks (or the Buckingham Division as it is still officially called) as a marginal constituency was hotly contested. In January 1910 F. W. Verney (Liberal) was triumphant over T. F. Fremantle with an insubstantial majority of only 111. Verney soon decided to seek a safer seat at Bournemouth and was succeeded as the Liberal choice by his nephew, Sir Harry Verney, the fourth baronet. In the December election the Conservative choice was Col F. T. H. Bernard of Chearsley Hill, but once again a Verney was triumphant by 327 votes. There were over 100 police at the declaration of the poll at Buckingham, but even this force could not prevent some ugly rushes and some egg throwing.

Behaviour throughout the elections was little better than in the 1900 or 1906 elections, and there was 'too much hooliganism at Wolverton' when the Conservatives held a meeting there. It was, in fact, a scene of continuous rowdyism, even the doors were broken, and Lord Desborough with his loud booming voice was the only speaker who could be heard at all.

THE WELLS BROTHERS OF BLETCHLEY

And now a new family comes into our north Bucks politics – the Wells family of Bletchley with two outstanding brothers, Oliver and Allen Wells. Oliver Wells was an outspoken socialist cobbler. He had not always been a cobbler, for he began his work-a-day career as a railwayman, actually as an engine cleaner. Then in 1899 he got involved in a railway accident and lost both legs below the knees. He was a formidable and charming person, and so was his younger brother, Allen, who was even more forthright, if that be possible. And there was a third brother, Costa.

In their youth these Wells brothers had heard of the abortive attempt of Bletchley railwaymen to form a branch of the Amalgamated Society of Railway Servants in 1872 and 1887, and the more successful attempt to form a local Co-operative Society in 1883 whose first president was Thomas Simmonds, a shunter, but he was killed whilst shunting nine days after becoming president.

But the Co-op grew, with railwaymen, including the Wells brothers, dominating its counsels and their wives doing the shopping at the new centre in Park Street. Co-op membership and sales were increased from 1886 on by the transfer to Bletchley Station of the personnel of the carpentry and other shops at Leighton Buzzard.

It is worth while recalling a story about Co-op premises that must be unique. In 1911 the Co-op bought 35 Bletchley Road. In 1925 their grocery manager, Mr W. J. Hing, began to live there. In 1941 it was decided to put a new water supply pipe in, and this meant taking up tiles in the pantry. To the astonishment of 'plain Charles Dickens' who was doing some of the work, he unearthed a rusty tin box under the tiles. It was found to contain £310 in gold coins, about £40 in silver, a 15-carat gold chain, and a silver watch inscribed 'G. F. Payne, Bedford, 1862'. Strenuous efforts were made to find the legal owners of this treasure trove, and it was revealed that a family by the name of Payne had lived there from about 1882 to 1900, but had no relatives. Finally a Coroner's Court (Mr E. T. Ray) formally seized the treasure on behalf of the Crown, and Charles Dickens, the finder, was rewarded by receiving about 75 per cent of the value of the find.

The staff at Bletchley Station was now about 300, of whom about eighty were engine drivers. In addition there were sixty men out at sub-depots whose actual homes were in the Bletchley area. There were forty-six engines at Bletchley and fourteen in the sub-depots.

In 1891 a local trade union was formed successfully at last. Its membership settled down to around sixty. From the first members paid 5d a week. In return for this there were death benefits up to £100, substantial help was organised for orphans, and help was given to members who were stood off or on short time. How valuable this help was was demonstrated early in 1893 when the railway company announced that all men over 70 in Wolverton Works would be discharged. There was neither pension nor gratuity from the company. It is perhaps not surprising that by 1897 union membership had risen to a peak of 219.

Amongst these new members was Allen Wells, and later on a younger brother, Costa. Costa however was soon in trouble. He began his career as a cleaner in the locomotive department at Bletchley, where engines were kept in tip-top readiness for shunting or any emergency. The temptation to drive an engine even a few yards was too much for him, and he opened the regulator just a bit to get the giant locomotive moving. It was one thing getting it moving, quite another stopping it, and the ponderous engine just crashed through the closed doors of the shed to the astonishment of all. Costa was dismissed, but he did manage to get a job in Wolverton Works for a time. This did not satisfy his ardent spirit, and he then decided to emigrate to Canada in 1912. The branch gave him a grant of 30s for his twelve years' membership, and he and his young wife sailed off to Canada.

The two remaining brothers now led a double campaign, firstly to get social justice for railwaymen, and secondly to get a local Labour party branch going. On the other hand many railwaymen were Liberal and saw no need for a socialist party.

Meanwhile railway discipline was rigid. Men were suspended for apparently trivial offences. For example, a goods carman was suspended because he refused to start another journey after 7 pm and after $13\frac{1}{2}$ hours on duty without overtime pay for the extra $3\frac{1}{2}$ hours he had already worked. The union helped by small grants and did infinitely more for widows, orphans and hospitals. It was a great-hearted movement, but industrially it had its limitations. There were annual church parades at Bletchley or Wolverton when the great banner and the Bletchley Station Brass Band were very much in evidence.

By August 1911 the discontent among many railwaymen reached a boiling point, and so did the weather. During the preceding three months there had been a drought, and in mid-August local temperatures were over 95°F in the shade, and the heat continued. Tempers were brittle. The four national unions, the Amalgamated Society of Railways Servants, the Associated Society of Locomotive Engineers and Firemen, the General

Railway Workers Union, and the United Pointsmen and Signalmen's Society, decided to call their men out on strike. Hurried meetings of railwaymen were called at Bletchley and Wolverton. At Bletchley Oliver Wells (the secretary) read out a telegram from the joint union headquarters, 'Your liberty at stake, all railwaymen must strike at once, loyalty to each other means victory'. At Wolverton about a third of the men, well over a thousand, came out, but at Bletchley railwaymen were not all keen on striking. Oliver Wells was reluctant to give advice, not being a railwayman himself, and Allen Wells was at work. The next day, Friday 18 August, an open meeting was called, and Allen Wells took the chair. The majority said they did not believe in strikes, they would lose their jobs, and in any case they thought more could be done by negotiation. Allen Wells replied with a fighting speech, urging the men to strike, and saying that whether they did or not, he would.

The meeting decided to defer a decision until Sunday. Allen Wells went on strike. He was the only Bletchley man that did, though at Wolverton many came out. By Sunday 20 August, the strike was over. Fortunately part of the settlement terms were that there should be no victimisation – so Allen kept his job. All those who stayed at work got an extra shining golden sovereign (almost an extra week's wage) from the company to take home. The unions for their part produced a medal with the inscription 'Railway Strike 1911. Loyalty to one another.' Local recrimination and bitterness were intense.

But Allen was unrepentant, and the next April (1912) he decided to stand for the Bletchley Ward of the UDC. He was opposed by that formidable Liberal, Sir Herbert Leon. The result was:

Sir Herbert Leon   142
Allen Wells   2

Rarely in the history of local elections can there have been such a crushing result. Obviously the railwaymen did not vote for Wells. The Wells brothers had reached the lowest point of their influence, for Oliver had been bottom of the poll for the Fenny Ward a year earlier and his uncertain attitude in the strike had earnt him no medals anywhere.

Bletchley did not like socialism or strikes, and in 1912 it did not like some of the views of the Wells brothers, but Wolverton did. On 29 March 1912 the Amalgamated Society of Railway

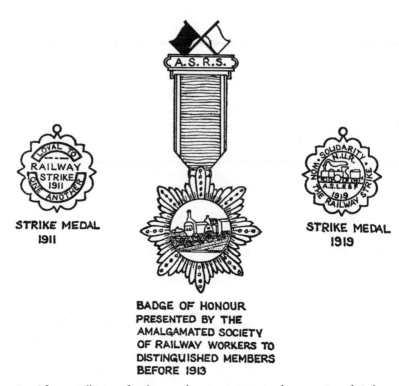

STRIKE MEDAL
1911

STRIKE MEDAL
1919

BADGE OF HONOUR
PRESENTED BY THE
AMALGAMATED SOCIETY
OF RAILWAY WORKERS TO
DISTINGUISHED MEMBERS
BEFORE 1913

Items from a collection of railway trade union insignia in the possession of Arthur Grigg of Bletchley.

Servants ceased to exist, and the National Union of Railwaymen was born. It included practically all existing railway unions except ASLEF (Associated Society of Locomotive Engineers and Firemen), which to this day preserves its separate identity. The new combination soon had a countrywide membership of nearly 18,000. Oliver Wells became the Bletchley branch secretary.

The local result of this was formidable. Almost every railwayman in Wolverton, Bletchley and all the other stations around belonged to a force that soon attained great unity and negotiating power. It built up a new loyalty. It developed new ambitions amongst which was the determination to control local councils in areas like Wolverton and Bletchley. Hitherto their candidates had been humiliatingly beaten with the exception of quiet George Sear, but from now on there was steady progress. In 1914 H. P.

Dimmock was elected to the Bletchley UDC, the first Labour and NUR councillor, and for thirty-nine years (during five of which he was chairman) he was a popular and devoted member of the Council.

When Oliver Wells was made a JP in 1917 it was proof that he was now well regarded by the Liberal establishment and by his own colleagues.

In that same year plans were laid for the creation of a constituency Labour party. At a packed meeting of the Wolverton Trades Council Oliver Wells moved a resolution to set it up. It was passed with determination, and Allen Wells was made its organising secretary, and everyone felt happy. For the next seven years he worked indefatigably at the job. And soon they had a Labour candidate, John Scurr.

For well over a century there had been only two parties in north Bucks. They were both strongly entrenched and well financed. The coming of the Labour party weakened the Liberals much more than the Tories, and Sir Harry Verney, the Liberal MP, was well aware that the Liberal party was already split right down the centre. He was an Asquithian Liberal – most others followed Lloyd George. Consequently Sir Harry did not get the 'coalition ticket' in 1918, and was defeated by the coalition Conservative, Capt George Bowyer. Much more humiliating was that he was soundly defeated for second place by John Scurr, the Labour candidate. Bowyer got over 12,000 votes, Scurr over 7,000 and Verney only just over 3,000.

So ended a great tradition. The first Verney of Claydon and Salden was returned as an MP for Bucks in 1483. For nearly five centuries there had rarely been a parliament without a Verney in it. It is a great record.

THE BOWYERS

The new Conservative member, Capt George Bowyer, had a good war record, and was an extremely hard worker who won the affection and support of the ex-service men of the 1914–18 war, and from his home at Weston Underwood he kept in touch with every corner of a large constituency. In all this, young George Bowyer was helped immeasurably by his wife, the Hon Daphne (Mitford), a daughter of the first Baron Redesdale. She was a strikingly beautiful woman of great charm.

M

After the First World War Labour was a vital political force in Bletchley, Wolverton and New Bradwell, but its combined strength was never enough to defeat the Conservatives entrenched in the villages and market towns, and so Captain George Bowyer continued to represent north Bucks.

Meanwhile the dissensions within the country were not restricted to purely party politics and in both 1919 and 1926 the whole of our area was afflicted by the railway strikes. In 1919 the unions won, and a medal was struck with the inscription 'Solidarity won the railway strike'. It was a different story in 1926.

THE GENERAL STRIKE, 1926

By any reckoning May 1926 was one of the saddest months in the history of Wolverton, New Bradwell, Bletchley and the adjacent villages. For nearly half a century the trade unions had been growing in membership, financial power and ambition. Every man in the great mining and transport industries was practically compelled to join an appropriate union, and union strength was such that scores of parliamentary seats were dominated and controlled in a way comparable to that of the old dukes and peers who owned rotten boroughs a century earlier. The unions provided much of the cash and the leadership for the Labour party, and some of their leaders saw no reason why they should not dominate any government. Their ultimate weapon was the General Strike. If all workers stopped working at their behest, the nation would be brought to a standstill, the government would be brought to its knees, and would have to concede the demands of the massed unions.

In Bletchley, New Bradwell and Wolverton, union influences were strong. At Bletchley Junction about 500 men were employed: in Wolverton Works nearly 4,500. All but a few were trade unionists.

The immediate cause of the General Strike of 1926 was discontent with pay and conditions in the mining industry, but on 1 May the Trades Union Congress took over and called a general strike of the vital services, including transport. It ceased to be a dispute about wages: it became a direct challenge as to who was to rule the country – parliament or the massed unions. The men were ordered to strike. Industries were paralysed, transport services came to a halt, and the press ceased to function.

Nearly every railwayman in Wolverton Works and at Bletchley, Leighton Buzzard and the smaller stations came out on strike. Station masters and many foremen did not. In addition to the railwaymen, the car workers at Salmons, Newport Pagnell and the girls at McCorquodales, Wolverton, came out too.

But on the other hand the farmers were determined their milk and eggs and meat should get to London or the smaller towns, and every conceivable vehicle from horse drawn carts to tractors did double and treble duty. A few trains run by enthusiastic volunteers, such as the exuberant students at Lathbury Park, got through to London. One student, Mr Cook, became an engine driver on the Dunstable line. The local UDCs and RDCs appointed special committees to ensure that coal got to the bakehouses and gas works and that milk and food was distributed. Dozens of special constables were sworn in, and regular police drafted to Wolverton and New Bradwell where trouble was expected.

The flaw in the strikers' arrangements was that the haulage and the garage industries were unaffected. Every haulage contractor in the area cheerfully did his bit with the distribution of food and milk. Even fish from Grimsby got through to Wolverton and Fenny Stratford by road. Other lorries picked up milk churns at local railway stations and conveyed them to the Hyde Park distributing depot. And the mails got through too.

Meanwhile the local strike committees, consisting of representatives of the NUR, ASLEF, and the NUVB were paying out strike pay at 24s a week, and seemed to be pleased with the call out and solidarity. At Bletchley the strikers' headquarters was at the Co-op Hall, Bletchley Road: at Wolverton the Empire cinema was the strike centre: and at Newport, 'The Poplars'.

The Bletchley committee organised the daily marches of strikers headed by the Station Band, carrying along with them the great banner of the Bletchley branch of the NUR, but there are few sadder sights than a striking trade union on the march. There were concerts and dances every evening in St Martin's Hall which were more cheerful.

But the zest diminished. Within a few days men were trickling back to Wolverton Works. The radio, now almost in every home, reported the Government's point of view. Within the week it was evident that the strike had lost much of its belligerent

heart, and on the ninth day the TUC caved in. It was unconditional surrender.

As in the strikes of 1911 and 1919, there was an aftermath of
bitterness and questioning in the railway towns, which was not
helped by the railway company's reprisals. On Thursday 10 May
1926 the Railway Managers Association posted the following
notice at Wolverton Works, and issued it to the local press:

'The injury to trade is believed to be so serious that for some
time full pre-strike services will not be required . . . Men will
be accepted for duty provided –

1) Every man who left his work without notice has broken
his contract of service, and the companies feel they must
reserve their right to dismiss him.

2) Those men in positions of trust who have gone on strike
will have their cases examined individually.

The companies feel compelled to make these reservations to
safeguard future peace and discipline on the railways. There
will be no wage reductions.'

These conditions, as the *Bucks Standard* reported on 12 May,
came as a bombshell to the railwaymen at Wolverton, New Bradwell, Bletchley, Newport Pagnell and the adjacent villages. There
was bitter dissatisfaction that the company should adopt such
drastic measures. In spite of this the men wanted to get back to
work, but now the union advised them that they must not
return on these terms. In consequence many men continued to
live in a condition of undesired idleness. The Newport line remained closed, and the LMS main line was far from normal.

Perhaps the greatest understatement of the time was made by
Mr Richardson at a meeting of the Wolverton UDC when he
said, 'I do not believe that any trade unionist in this area is enjoying the strike'.

Meanwhile another notice was posted, that only those who had
worked during the strike would be admitted to the works. On the
Thursday morning 3,000 men gathered outside the work gates
but only those 'for whom there was work' were allowed in.
When the works closed that evening the same 3,000 met the
'scabs' or 'black legs', and booed and sang at them all the way to
their various homes. It took great courage to be a non-striker in
1926. It says much for everybody that there was no untoward
incident.

The LMS meant to enforce 'peace with discipline' and to victimise the strike leaders, but fortunately Stanley Baldwin, the Prime Minister, made it clear that he wanted 'Peace in our time, O Lord', a far different phrase. The railway directors were checked, full work was soon resumed with no victimisation, and the dreadful month of May 1926 passed into history. The NUR did not issue a special strike medal, and their membership dropped by a third.

From now on the demand for the nationalisation of the railways was something that was not just a socialist dream, but practical politics.

SIR GEORGE BOWYER

We must now see how our local MP, Captain George Bowyer, was faring.

For almost a century an art of patronage had grown up by which cabinet ministers became hereditary peers in due course, and junior ministers became baronets even whilst in office, since this, though an hereditary title, did not mean translation to the House of Lords. This patronage was approved by everybody except a small band of republicans and zealous reformers who wanted to abolish the House of Lords or the Monarchy itself. When therefore Captain George Bowyer, who had won the Buckingham seat in 1918, became a Whip in 1926 (which was equal to a junior ministerial appointment) and vice-chairman of the Conservative party in 1930, no one was surprised, but many were delighted, when he became a baronet in 1933. He continued in his various appointments, including that of vice-chairman of the Conservative party, which meant a great deal of hard work, so that once again few were surprised and many delighted when in 1937 he was offered a peerage, and happily accepted – taking the name of Lord Denham of Weston Underwood.

JOHN WHITELEY

This meant a by-election, and the National-Conservative choice was a popular Bletchley man, Major John Whiteley who lived at the Grange, along the Buckingham Road. In the by-election of 1937 he had the smashing majority of 5,099.

Whiteley had little time to make his mark in Parliament. In 1939 as Lieutenant-Colonel commanding the Royal Bucks

Yeomanry RA he volunteered for war service and for the next few years was actively engaged. Then came a blow that really shook Bletchley and the constituency. On 4 July 1943 he was killed in an air crash at Gibraltar, along with General Sikorski the Polish Prime Minister and Commander in Chief, and Colonel Victor Cazalet, MP. It was a sad and sudden ending to several brilliant careers.

In *Who's Who* Brigadier Whiteley gave his hobbies as 'hunting, shooting, fishing and cricket'. He was an all-round sportsman, a fine soldier and would undoubtedly have made ministerial rank had he lived. I served in Parliament with him for six years and knew something of his sterling worth.

Whilst the war was on there was a political truce – and very few by-elections were contested. This time the Conservative choice fell on the eldest son of the great and autocratic Lord Kemsley, one of the great press barons of the epoch. The Hon G. Lionel Berry, was the man who was nominated and chosen for the Buckingham division in no time at all. His wife was the eldest daughter of the eleventh Marquess of Tweeddale.

There was some criticism of Berry. He can hardly be said to have wooed the constituency (anyway a war was on) and his duties as deputy chairman of Kemsley Newspapers did not give him a markedly high attendance in the House of Commons. People remembered that Sir George Bowyer had a record 100 per cent for years running, and the comparison was not favourable to his successor.

So in spite of the fact that Buckingham had been held by the Conservatives for nearly thirty years, it was still a marginal seat.

AIDAN CRAWLEY

When the General Election came suddenly in 1945 Berry had to face the young Aidan Crawley, who was an absolute find for the Labour party. Instead of offering the candidature to a horny-handed son of toil, or a stalwart of the NUR, they had chosen in 1938 this public school cricketer, son of a Canon of Windsor, educated at Harrow and Oxford, and a skilful journalist. During the war he served with the RAF, was shot down in 1941, and remained a prisoner until May 1945. He won the election in grand style, with a majority of 3,845.

Soon after his election in 1945 he bought a farm in Steeple

Claydon which almost entitled him to claim that he was a horny-handed son of toil. Anyway he was now a local resident, which Berry had never been. More than this, he soon became a fine parliamentarian and in 1946 was appointed Under-Secretary of State for Air. Handsome and blue-eyed, and a fine county cricketer, he won the affection of women and men alike. Bletchley particularly liked him, and when in July 1947 he scored a century in a county trial match and was then clean bowled by the young Ted James of Bletchley Town, nobody thought it diminished his cricket or political stature.

Meanwhile the north Bucks Tories were sadly surveying their bewildered ranks and determined to get a candidate of equal glamour to beat Crawley. They had a wide choice. The Conservative Central Office submitted a list of scores of would-be candidates, and then in November 1945 there was a local nomination, that of Major Frank Markham.

Major Markham, who had been born in Stony Stratford and had enjoyed being educated as an evening student at the Science and Art Institute in Wolverton and later worked his own way through Oxford University, had stood for Wolverton as a Labour candidate in the 1928 County Council Elections. He won the seat, but proved a poor County Councillor since in 1929 he was elected to Parliament as the Labour member for the Rochester division. In the next County Council elections at Wolverton in 1931 the Hon Daphne Bowyer stood as the Conservative candidate, and Mrs Boyce, wife of the dynamic headmaster of Wolverton Secondary School, stood as the Liberal candidate with unofficial Labour support. Mrs Boyce was elected; it was the first and only defeat that the Bowyers suffered.

In that same year, 1931, Major Markham remained loyal to Ramsey MacDonald (whose Parliamentary Secretary he then was), but did not fight in the ensuing General Election. From 1935 to 1945 he represented South Nottingham as a National MP (in alliance with the Conservatives) and now that this seat was recommended for abolition by redistribution, sought to represent his own home area.

Quite naturally the idea of his nomination did not appeal to many of the senior Conservatives in the Buckingham division who wanted a Tory gentleman in the great tradition. In the event, early in 1946, the candidature was won by young Peter Woodard, son of a canon, whose great-grandfather had founded the Woodard schools. He was good looking, a snappy dresser delighting in yellow waistcosts, and a light and amusing speaker.

Meanwhile Major Markham started *The History of Stony Stratford* in collaboration with Dr F. E. Hyde. It kept him busy.

But something went wrong, very wrong, with the Buckingham division, and within a year (November 1946) Peter Woodard had resigned, or had been compelled to resign, to the satisfaction of the Conservative caucus, and the Buckingham Conservative Association was again in the throes of selecting a candidate. Again a formidable list of Central Office nominees was considered, again the insuppressible Major Markham's name was put forward, this time by those areas where the Labour vote was strongest and the Conservatives most aggressive.

Finally four names were selected for the final ballot:

> Lt-Col R. L. Agnew
> S. F. Markham
> J. C. Rodgers
> G. R. Stevens

Although Markham topped the poll, Col Agnew of Turweston was a good second, so the caucus decided that this was not decisive and they asked the two top candidates if they would agree to tour the constituency having a series of meetings at which they both should speak and answer questions, and then have a great constituency meeting at which the final choice should be made. Both candidates agreed with pleasure – but no sooner were the meetings organised than the severest winter for a decade occurred. Coal was rationed and of poor quality. The word Shinwellite came into scientific vocabularies as a mineral that was sold as coal but would not burn.

Agnew and Markham ploughed through snow drifts in the unreliable cars of the period and held their meetings. The two candidates formed a warm friendship – they needed to – for helping one another out of snow drifts on the uncleared rolling roads of north Bucks was not a job to be undertaken without incredible good humour and push.

Eventually the worst of the winter passed, and at a great meeting held at the Science and Art Institute at Wolverton on

8 February 1947, and after the expected speeches, the ballot was taken. The result was astonishing:

Markham   371
Agnew   81

There was no doubt about the result. Colonel Agnew became vice-chairman of the party organisation and unity was secured. Perhaps the seal on unity was when Lord and Lady Denham asked Major and Mrs Markham to dine with them at Weston Underwood. It was a magnificent gesture and pleased many.

The Wolverton decision made a little bit of history: indeed it showed a break from 200 years of history. In the past every Tory or Conservative member of Parliament and indeed most Liberal ones had been connected with the peerage. Now for the first time the son of an insurance agent, who had left school at 14 and become a messenger boy at 5s a week at McCorquodales in Wolverton had become the Conservative standard bearer.

Buckingham with its memories of dukes and marquesses was somewhat appalled: Wolverton and Stony Stratford were almost delighted. One thing was certain: the old desire to have an aristocratic connection had faded away: without knowing quite why, the Buckingham Conservative division had chosen the son of a working man to be their spokesman. Henceforward they still loved dukes, but liked to see them as curators of stately homes.

The next General Election was held in February 1950, and Crawley triumphed by 1,500. It was a good win, but everybody read between the lines. Crawley's majority had been halved, even though the Prime Minister, Clement Attlee had personally visited Wolverton and Bletchley to speak for him. What couldn't happen next time?

As an indication of the relations between the candidates at this time, we quote a letter written by Aidan Crawley to Frank Markham immediately after the election:

'I hope you will not think it an impertinence if I write to say how much I admired the bearing of your wife and yourself at the Count – and indeed throughout the election. If we go into battle again it will be with added relish on my part because of the way you fought. And if the luck turns the other way I hope we can lose as well as you both did.'

They went 'into battle again' within a year. Every indication showed that Crawley would win. The poll of course was counted at Buckingham. And as the votes were counted and stacked it seemed that Crawley might be leading by 1,000. But there still remained the last odd bundles of votes on the tables. It turned out these were nearly all Markham's. In the result Crawley was passed on the post by fifty-four votes out of 45,000. The result after a recount was breathtaking:

Markham   22,688
Crawley   22,634

It was a skin of the teeth victory. Every village in the area claimed that it had produced Markham's victory. Crawley was naturally disappointed – and many felt that the Labour party owed him a less marginal seat. Possibly he would have got a safe seat and continued a brilliant career in politics, if he had not displeased the Bevanites.

In 1957 he resigned from the Labour party, sold his farm at Steeple Claydon, and became a television celebrity. He was a great loss to the Labour party, and the constituency. Later he was returned as Conservative MP for Derbyshire West (1962) and retained the seat in 1966.

It was to Bletchley that another Prime Minister came in 1955, the Rt Hon Antony Eden (later Lord Avon) to give Markham a hand. He had a far better reception than Asquith in 1909 and the Conservatives won the seat by a pleasant majority of 1,000 or so. Eden was pleased that they had won at all.

Just to round off the record, Frank Markham was knighted in 1953 on Winston Churchill's recommendation, and fought the seat again in 1959 defeating an unusual Labour candidate of great self confidence. When Sir Frank stood down in 1964 the seat went Labour – proving once again that north Bucks is one of the most marginal areas in England.

17 Brickmaking in north Bucks

CONSIDERING the enormous expanse of Oxford clay around Bletchley and Winslow it is perhaps surprising that it took so long for brick and tile making to develop into a local major industry. Anybody could make bricks if they could dig the right clay, mould it under the right conditions, and burn it with the required high heat. But these three variables were difficult to co-ordinate. Before the coming of the canal coal was scarce and dear, but from then on it was abundant and reasonably priced to anyone near a canal wharf. And no one bothered like the Israelites in Egypt that they had no straw.[1]

Brickmaking is probably the oldest plastic industry in the world. In its earliest simplicity, as practised in ancient Babylon and Egypt, clay was dug, worked with moisture into a state of plasticity, shaped in crude moulds, and left to dry out in the fierce tropical sun. Some of these 6,000 year old brick arches, walls, etc, have lasted until today. The Romans brought the arts and skills to Buckinghamshire, the Tudors gloried in bricks and tiles, and by 1800 some of our most attractive buildings in brick were already centuries old. Crawley Grange, Chicheley Hall and Willen church show what could be done locally.

In 1810 more bricks were made around Newport and Buckingham than in the Bletchley area. At Newport flat tiles then cost £2 per 1,000, and pantiles £1 per 1,000, whilst at Buckingham the hand-made bricks were about £2 per 1,000. Newport had three principal brick yards, in Clay Lane, in the Brick Field along the Broughton Road, and at Shipley Wharf in Green End until 1859 when the clay 'gave out'.[2] Both Great Linford and Simpson had brick yards next to the canal.

The coming of the railway in 1838 produced a great demand for bricks. Wolverton was a brick-made town, and railway tunnels, platforms, factory walls, etc, were all of brick. In fact it was the

1 *Exodus*, chapter 5.
2 Cole, *Echoes of the Past* p45.

age of brick, and bricks were made locally wherever suitable clay was available, and if a canal was nearby so much the better.

A mile south-east of Stony Stratford was a thriving kiln which flourished around 1850, and even Little Woolstone had a brick and tile manufactory for years.

Some of these brickmakers were builders too. In 1851 James Rose of Clay Lane, Newport Pagnell, built Great Woolstone rectory from designs by William Butterfield, at a cost of £611. This became the home of the Rev Edward Hill who comes so prominently into our chapter on schools.

A few brickmaking establishments included lime kilns, but there were quite separate ones at places like Wavendon and Little Brickhill. Somehow Brickhill could produce lime for 2s 4d the quarter of eight bushels, whilst at Wavendon it was 3s 6d the quarter, the greater cost possibly being due to the greater distance from the chalk supplies around Dunstable.

In Fenny Stratford the most prominent brickmaker around 1820–70 was a man of many activities, Gregory Odell Clarke, who set up business as a coal, timber, slate and iron merchant, and brick and tile maker, at Tan Yard Wharf, London Road. He was of course a wharfinger too. Clarke's brickworks were originally confined to the rear of Watling Terrace between the river Ouzel and the canal, but they were extended at some time prior to 1869 to include the land behind the canal wharf. Following his death, the works were run by his son, William Edward Clarke. Another brickyard was then opened at Simpson and by 1877 Clarke had brickworks, coal wharves and offices at Water Eaton, Woburn Sands and Ridgmont, whilst at Fenny Stratford he had built the large house, now Metalin's offices, and had installed outside his yard the largest lump of coal the town had ever seen.[3]

Others competed in the trade. Samuel Bragg had a small brickyard east of the canal down by the *White Hart*, Fenny Stratford, which changed hands in the late 1860s. Robert Holdom opened his own brickyard in the 1870s in Duncombe Street beside the Bletchley railway line. In 1876 yet another brickworks came into existence at Foxhole, Bletchley, where John Munday, a timber merchant, purchased the land, made bricks, and built houses with them in Albert Street and around. Up to this time

3. Information from Mr E. Legg.

less than a hundred men all told were engaged in brickmaking in north Bucks. Brickmakers came and went, and none appeared to have made a fortune unless they were builders too.

By 1907 *Kelly's Directory* records only half a dozen brick and tile makers in north Bucks, including Arthur W. Itter at Calvert Brickworks, and Read and Andrews, Newton Longville. The last named are of great interest to us.

READ AND ANDREWS

John Thornton Read was born in 1869. Just after 1890 he and his father (Thomas) opened a small traditional plastic brickworks on a 5-acre site half a mile north of Newton Longville near the Bletchley-Oxford railway branch line, and employed about a dozen men. Later Richard Andrews joined them and the firm of Read and Andrews made steady progress. Indeed they were the only brickmakers mentioned in *Kelly's Directory* for 1907 in the entire Bletchley area. Read was a generous local benefactor, a Baptist deacon for twenty-five years, and keenly interested in a number of hospitals. Mrs Hallowell of Newton Longville, his daughter, has a photograph of him, showing him as a bearded patriarch with the Bible on his knee. He was a man of great energy and greatly respected.

Read was also interested in the housing of his workmen and in 1910 Read and Andrews built a dozen houses facing their works and proudly put up the inscription:

MODEL
WORKMEN'S COTTAGES
1910
R & A

The village has enjoyed the unconscious joke for over half a century. They stand today, trim and pleasant, but as we shall see their outlook has changed, and the present Bletchley works are to the east of them.

Around 1919 Read and Andrews were joined by W. T. Lamb and Sons, builders' merchants, and the Bletchley Brick Company was formed in 1923 with a capital of £60,000.

'KNOTTS' AND 'FLETTONS'

Meanwhile two interesting words had come into local use from

Peterborough – 'knotts' and 'flettons'. The word fletton is of peculiar significance in the brickmaking industry, for it was at Fletton, near Peterborough, that around 1881 new and profitable methods of making bricks from Oxford clay were tried out and successfully developed.

It is difficult to describe the improvements, but briefly all bricks made prior to this were 'plastic' bricks. But beneath the over-burden and the top layers of clay (sometimes yellowish) are knotts, or clots of grey-green to dark brown shale, which have the peculiar property of providing some of the combustible material for burning the bricks. Once the bricks have been 'fired' they burn of their own accord, and fuel consumption can be as low as 1 cwt per 1,000 bricks, much less than the quantity required by other clays. The beds of knotts can vary in thickness from 20ft to 70ft.

The Fletton or 'knott' clay brick firms could therefore outsell anybody locally using the older methods, and it was only when they had to meet long transport charges that other firms could compete. So it was important that (prior to about 1920) brick-works should be next to railways both for the import of coal and the transport of bricks.

In 1924 Read and Andrews, or the Bletchley Brick Company as they were now known, changed over to the new methods, and two years later (September 1926) the *British Clay Worker* pub-lished a report on 'Knotts Clay in Buckinghamshire (Bletchley)', when the works, pits, etc, covered nearly 300 acres. The report ran:

'We have recently, on the invitation of Mr T. G. Read, joint managing director, paid a visit to the Bletchley works and seen one of the most recent and up-to-date equipments for the manufacture of pressed bricks. The works are an example of small beginnings worked up by the indefatigable zeal of the owner, to a large well-organised installation.

'Prior to this great extension, the clay beds overlying the "Knotts" were used to make wirecut bricks by the plastic process. Investigation, however, showed that the "Knotts" were of great depth and excellent quality.

'The present type of manufacture has been in operation only about $1\frac{1}{2}$ years, so that the quarry is not yet sufficiently developed to permit the installation of mechanical excavators. The clay is therefore still being "got" by manual labour. The upper yellow clay, about 10 ft. in thickness, is still being used in the old wirecut plant to make red wirecuts of common and facing quality, and an old continuous kiln, built nearly 30 years ago, is used for burning them. A rope railway, built by the Artex Company, takes this yellow clay across the main quarry to the wirecut plant . . . The four 9 ft. grinding pans are fed by means of special crushing rolls of unusual and novel type. From the pans, elevators raise the ground clay to piano wire screens, from which the screened material falls on to a steel band conveyor, on which it is mixed at several points prior to being swept off to the individual presses . . .

'The 14 presses are in one long line, turning out upwards of 80,000 bricks per day of 10 hours. In spite of the coal strike, means have been found to keep this plant in full operation without interruption.

'The bricks are burned in two transverse arch kilns. Each consists of 16 chambers, with a capacity of 35,000 bricks per chamber. From six to seven chambers per week are burned in each kiln, thus accounting for the whole production of the presses.

'The bricks, in process of being drawn from the kilns, were exceedingly well and uniformly burned, and, notwithstanding the large production, there was no stock whatever; bricks from the kilns were being loaded direct into trucks on the siding alongside.

'A third kiln of similar dimensions is in course of construction, and a fourth is projected, thus showing the intention of the company to increase, and shortly double, the present production.'[4]

Three years later (1929) the London Brick Company and Forders, whose previous activities had been mainly at Fletton near Peterborough, and around what is now Stewartby in Bedfordshire, acquired the Bletchley Brick Company from Read and his colleagues. At the same time their capital was raised to £2m – so that it was now about the largest brickmaking company in England.

In 1933 Read suffered the death of his wife and not only retired but moved to Grantham. During his lifetime he had seen Newton Longville, which had been a declining village up to 1891, rise from

---

4 I am indebted to J. P. Bristow of the London Brick Company for showing me this article, and for much other information.

a population of 415 in that year to nearly 1,000 in 1939. Shortly before his retirement new works were erected on the opposite side of the Newton Road. The old site is now allotment gardens and a lake of an acre or more in extent, and some land has been used for road widening. Close by can be seen the remains of the great kilns that were the pride and joy of John Thornton Read. His place was taken by his debonair and energetic son, Thomas George Read and the firm continued to prosper.

The Bletchley brickworks were now employing 400 men, and had a capacity for 700,000 pressed bricks a week. Apart from the railway they were the largest employer of labour in the whole of the Bletchley area. And now other firms and people were interested in Bletchley's clay deposits, and soon two other large brickworks were built and new brick chimneys challenged the sky line. Both the new works were close to the railway junction at Bletchley.

WATER EATON WORKS, FLETTONS LIMITED

The second large brickworks was created in 1929 for Flettons Limited whose main works were at Whittlesea, Peterborough. This works was built on Home Farm, Water Eaton and was capable of producing 60 million bricks per annum and about 200 men were employed up to the war years.

Capt W. G. Mells was for many years associated with the company, and was for a time on the Bletchley UDC.

SKEW BRIDGE WORKS, BLETCHLEY FLETTONS LIMITED

It was in 1933 that Read's old colleague, A. E. Lamb, commenced the building of a new works at Skew Bridge on a part of Slad Farm – the third largest works in the area. But whilst building was in progress a new company, Bletchley Flettons was formed and purchased the property, modified the design, and completed the building of the outstanding three-quarters. The new installation was bought by the London Brick Company and later christened 'Jubilee Works'. Somebody once described it as a white elephant; certainly it had its difficulties.

In 1934, shortly after they were opened, Bletchley Flettons Limited started to transport their bricks by road. In 1939 they boasted that a telephone order for bricks before 10 am could be completed before 4 pm, when bricks could be on the building site ready for use. By road transport there was less risk of damage to the bricks: shunting was more liable to cause damage to the bricks when they were transported by rail. An additional reason for the change was the poor service by the railway to the works – too few wagons when needed, and so on. The railway siding of Bletchley Flettons Limited eventually fell into disuse.

War Years and Post War Years

With the outbreak of the Second World War building, except for urgent military purposes practically stopped. Bletchley brickworks were closed down, so were the Skew Bridge works soon after, whilst Flettons Limited were on only a quarter of their possible production. With the peace of 1945 there came a tremendous demand for housing, consequently for bricks, and Bletchley brickworks and Flettons Limited were soon in full production, and indeed in 1946–47 were working day and night to satisfy the clamour of builders and young couples. Skew Bridge (Jubilee Works) was however in difficulties. The overburden was over 40ft deep and the lower clays less suitable, making working uneconomic. A new pit was then opened at Cold Harbour Farm, Loughton, and the knotts transported to the works by road. It found all the work it needed for a time.

Calvert Brickworks

In 1936 the title of the London Brick Company and Forders was shortened to London Brick Company, their capital was increased to £2.4m and they acquired Itters Brick Company at Calvert near the Claydons, 12 miles west of Bletchley. These works had started in a humble way in 1890, and for nearly fifty years had been run by the Itter family of Winslow, who also controlled Kings Dyke brickworks near Peterborough. They had been changed over to Fletton methods around 1900.

Under the new owners Calvert brickworks went ahead until the Second World War resulted in a limited production mainly due to great labour difficulties as at Bletchley. For a time German prisoners of war filled part of the gap, and when these were repatriated it became necessary to import labour from other areas, and considerable numbers of mid-European workers (EVW) and Polish ex-service men, entered the industry. Of recent years Italian, West Indian and Pakistani men have been employed in increasing numbers.

The situation in 1946 therefore was that the three brickworks in Bletchley were working to the limit, and still the demand for housing and for bricks was unabated. In December 1946 Flettons Limited asked the UDC and the Government to permit extended workings at Water Eaton (106 acres), Loughton Manor (175 acres), Skew Bridge (317 acres) and Cold Harbour (191 acres); and East-woods Limited asked for another site at Woburn Sands.[5] The companies argued that these applications were essential under time limiting requirements of the Town and Country Planning Act, and their purpose was to protect the rights of the companies to continue the extraction of clay. There was no desire or intention to build new works or increase the production of those then in operation, indeed in the consents there were rigid safeguards on the subject. Both Bletchley UDC and Newport RDC opposed these proposals, the chairman of the Bletchley UDC (Councillor Maycock) saying that these would 'create a string of brickworks which would strangle Bletchley like an octopus'. In January 1947 the Ministry said there could be no decision on the above until the Greater London plan had been decided, but in November 1947 the Government approved the new clay workings, and Flettons acquired 800 acres.[6]

But only a few months later in March 1948 the chairman of the London Brick Company, Sir Malcolm Stewart, Bt, announced that as the Government were slowing down house building, bricks were being stacked instead of being sold, the night shifts would have to be stopped.

In 1948 the London Brick Company increased its capital to £3m and in 1953 to £6m whilst in 1964 it was increased still further to £12m with a steady dividend record of about 17½ per cent. The firm now produces the astronomical figure of 3,500,000,000 bricks a year, of which 1,000 million come from Bedfordshire, and 700 million from north Bucks. Of these the greater production is from Calvert. Nowadays the Bletchley brickworks make 4¼ million bricks per week and employ 375 men, whilst the Jubilee Works (Skew Bridge) pro-

5 For map see Figure 9 in the *Interim Report*, Milton Keynes.
6 Local protests continued and in 1968 the *Interim Report* for Milton Keynes (pp19 and 57) said bluntly, 'These areas with permission for clay working are an unreasonable constraint on the planning of the new city. These permissions must be extinguished by whatever processes are appropriate'. These mostly were, but Water Eaton and Cold Harbour areas were retained.

duce 1,300,000 bricks per week and employ ninety men, but while these figures make brickworking a major industry in the Bletchley area, there was and still is more brickmaking activity at Calvert near Steeple Claydon where they have a capacity of 9,000,000 bricks a week.[7]

But all this combined was overshadowed by the tremendous production from the Stewartby region of Bedfordshire. Nevertheless in the post war years Bletchley's three outstanding brickworks – London Brick Company's Bletchley Works (the former Bletchley Brick Company on the Newton Longville-Bletchley border), Flettons Limited at Water Eaton and the London Brick Company's Jubilee Works near Slad Farm on the borders of Stoke Hammond were adding much to local prosperity. Then, around 1970 Milton Keynes Development Corporation bought up Flettons Limited partly for housing development and partly for park space.

Considering the numbers employed in brickmaking in north Bucks, it is perhaps surprising how little influence they exercised compared with the other two great industries, agriculture and railways. Very few brickmen ever stood for local councils, they had no great banners and held no great parades, and where the NFU, the NUR and ASLEF were always vocal and persistent, the brickmen were as quiet as chemists.

Possibly the reason is that whilst both agriculture and railways represented secure employment and steady careers (at any rate up till recently) brickmaking in the 1940s was a stop-and-go industry. It depended on housing, and housing depended on the Government's or the local council's opinion as to how many buildings should be produced. But other important reasons were that the percentage of workers of overseas origin was always greater than that on the railways, the farms or in commerce. And then the negotiation possibilities through the National Conciliation Board for the Fletton brick industry were always used to the full.

As Captain Mells says, 'The brickworker is generally a quiet and orderly person, and more interested in the pursuit of private interests than in setting the world to rights'. This of course did not prevent them from becoming very good boxers.

---

7 Information from J. P. Bristow of the London Brick Company, to whom I am indebted for much other material.

18　A Bigger, Better, Brighter Bletchley

IT is difficult to say when Bletchley first got an irrepressible desire to expand, but it could be that it was around 1930, when Lady Leon, the active widow of Sir Herbert Leon, and at that time a member of the UDC, persuaded the Council that as Bletchley was both the railway, postal and shopping centre for quite a large district it should extend to include the entire parishes of Bow, Great and Little Brickhill, Stoke Hammond, Newton Longville, Walton, Woughton and Water Eaton. The Council agreed to ask the astonished County Council to approve.

As can be imagined, there was dismay, opposition and resentment in most of these villages. Whatever happened they did not want to lose their identities or come under the Bletchley UDC. The fight went on in village schoolrooms and the committee rooms at Aylesbury and gradually the stubborn opposition from all around, with one exception, forced the County to turn down the entire proposal except for Water Eaton. And so in 1934 the administrative area of the Bletchley UDC was increased by 1,000 acres and an extra 300 population.

It was at once a valuable and expensive acquisition, for although the Duncombes had sold most of their land here in 1923 it was still a farming area though a few more houses had been built. It was lacking in adequate sewage, water and other services. The Council tackled these problems with zeal, and indeed Water Eaton was the first part of the UDC to have electric light.

But this mouthful by no means appeased the appetite of Bletchley, and now three other factors began to influence events. In July 1932, R. L. Sherwood was appointed the clerk (at a salary of £450 per annum). He enjoyed Bletchley, and Bletchley appreciated his services, for thirty years. Secondly in November 1933 there appeared the first issue of the *Bletchley Gazette*, which under its youthful editor, Ron Staniford, was soon campaigning for 'A Bigger, Better, Brighter Bletchley'. There was certainly need for a brighter Bletchley, for though it now had a second cinema and the usual variety of public houses, it was a dull place and no one could then accuse Bletchley people of undue effervescence. The third factor was the moving of the historic cattle market from Aylesbury Street in Fenny Stratford to Oliver Road, much nearer to Bletchley station. Fenny Stratford began to decay as a shopping centre, and Bletchley Road (later Queensway) became the new hub.

Another change that affected Bletchley was the resignation of John Chadwick in 1934 after or during a sad dispute in which legal proceedings were threatened. As surveyor for nearly forty years he had done a great deal for Bletchley whilst retaining his private practice as an architect. Among his creations were the Bletchley UDC offices, the schools on the opposite side of the road and the Fenny War Memorial there, which are all tributes to his skill, as well as other much praised buildings in Aylesbury Street. He was a unique figure, and it was a pity that his farewell was a mixed one.

There was no shortage of building land in and around Bletchley. As early as 1911, Sir Herbert Leon had offered ninety-three building plots for sale adjoining the Recreation Ground, but only ten were sold. The rest were turned into allotments during the First World War, and it was not until 1935 that the last of the plots were sold. The Duncombes too were anxious to sell land for building both in Bletchley and Water Eaton, but builders were unspeculative.

Whilst the Council were firming up their plans for Water Eaton yet another event happened which materially affected the development of Bletchley. In 1936 Lady Leon died, and soon after the entire estate of Bletchley Park was put up to auction. So long as this estate of about a square mile in the heart of Bletchley was firmly held in private hands the co-ordinated expansion of Bletchley was impossible. The estate stretched from the Watling Street to Shenley Road and from the old Rickley Lane to the Buckingham Road, though within it there were important pockets of church property, and other areas occupied by the railways.

At the auction in 1937 lot 1, which was the kernel of the estate including the house itself, with many beautiful trees and an avenue nearly a mile long running north and south, was bought by Hubert Faulkner, a local developer, who soon created Wilton

Avenue. Two years later the rest of lot 1 was bought by the Ministry of Works for the Foreign Office.

Lot 3, which was the cricket ground and its pavilion, were acquired by the Bucks Education Department. Most of the residential property (lots 4–8) was sold to the occupiers. Lots 9, 10 and 11 which were Home Farm and Denbigh Hall Farm, three-quarters of the entire area, remained in agricultural hands, as did lots 12–15, the fields along the Shenley Road.

Meanwhile, the industry of Bletchley had been almost entirely, in addition to the railway, 'bricks and brushes'. Imagine the excitement, therefore, when it was announced around 1936 that W. O. Peake Limited, the famous Rodex coat firm from St Albans, was to open a stylised modern branch in Bletchley. Initially it was to be close to the town centre, but fortunately planning was now beginning to show its hand, and the development was sited alongside the Watling Street – on a field on which the boys of Bletchley used to play cricket in summer – and skate in winter! This was the beginning of the Watling Street factory complex which flourishes today.[1]

Came the war, and the American Wico Company was licensed by the Government to manufacture sparking plugs and accessories in this country. What better place, thought the Ministry of Supply, than this lovely new factory of Peakes, in Bletchley. Ladies' coats were not really essential to the war effort, so out they had to go, finding other premises here and there to continue their work, while the Wico-Pacy group came in.

The focal area of all, Bletchley Park, was now firmly taken over by the Foreign Office, which had general control of the crypto-analytic sections of each defence service, which was later geared to produce about 300 cipher solutions a week.[2] The most ingenious and complicated mechanical devices were installed either in the mansion or in newly erected buildings of the severest wartime type of architecture. In fact 'architecture' was scarcely the word to apply to these grim buildings built in a hurry. Among these was Wilton Hall, a very plain red brick structure.[3]

Bletchley Park swiftly found accommodation for hundreds of

1 Information from Ron Staniford.
2 *Spy & Counter Spy*, Bernard Newman, p222.
3 It was only after it was sold to the Bletchley UDC in 1948 that it was given an internal face-lift of some artistic value, and until 1973 it was the largest hall in the entire district.

experts, and within a year the numbers had risen to thousands. The Park had become a conglomeration of different offices and training establishments which all brought into Bletchley a welter of new ideas, some of them very critical indeed. In addition there were the evacuees, and the RAF group signals camp over the Shenley Road–Rickley Lane area. Amongst those who served in Bletchley Park during the war years was Roy Jenkins, who soon after the war was to become a Labour MP, Home Secretary in 1965 and again in 1974, and a powerful leader in the Labour party. There were also hundreds of the sharpest minds in the Foreign Office and Defence Ministries, (including A. J. Allen the author, and Helen Rubenstein of Moral Rearmament), and it can be imagined that the dullness of the place accentuated sharply by rationing, and by the war-time black-out and travelling restrictions, did not create a very good impression on many who had come from universities or Whitehall, even though there were many high quality musical and dramatic entertainments at the Wilton Hall. It was out of the mouths of some of these wits that there came phrases like 'I spent a month in Bletchley last Sunday' or 'The only way out of Bletchley is through a bottle of gin', or 'In the midst of life we are in Bletchley'. The same of course could have been said of many army, navy or air force camps.

There was hardly a spare room or bed in the district. Bletchley was expanding, but in a way no one could have predicted.

All this had its repercussions. The Bletchley tradesmen and innkeepers, now meeting the demands of thousands of temporary inhabitants had an expansive time only limited by rationing, and they did not want to sink back after the war into the struggle for existence with a static population. They were naturally eager that Bletchley should grow. They wanted to expand voluptuously with the Government or the LCC paying for it all.

THE 'ULTRA' NERVE CENTRE

During these war years what was happening at Bletchley Park was most 'hush-hush' and it is only recently that we have been able to pull back the curtain of secrecy and see what a valuable contribution towards the winning of the war was made in the temporary buildings or in the house itself. Originally in 1939 the Secret Service had a bolt-hole here, but in 1940 they returned to

London, and the Park was handed over to another Foreign Office set-up known as the 'Ultra' organisation. Its task was to gather German coded signals, to crack them, and then to distribute the information properly. The man in charge was Group Captain F. W. Winterbotham, who has waited many years for the clearance of his narrative.[4] Early successes of 'Ultra' were such that in 1942 they even intercepted Rommel's reports to Hitler and so gave Montgomery adequate time to prepare for El Alamein and to start a series of glorious victories. Churchill asked 'Ultra' that they should enable him to follow these battles from the German side. German coded signals were now picked up, uncoded and translated 'within minutes'. The original staff of about a hundred was expanded to about five thousand.

But this was only one of 'Ultra's' superb achievements. The great Duke of Wellington had said that the business of war was 'guessing what was at the other side of the hill'. Thanks to 'Ultra', our statesmen, military commanders and Eisenhower too, knew not only what was on the other side of the hill, but the other side of the ocean. 'Ultra' scanned the world, German messages in particular were picked up and the most intricate codes were cracked. The Germans never knew what was happening otherwise Bletchley might have become the most bombed-out small town in Britain.

During these war years Bletchley had many unobtrusive visitors, as of course befitted a cloak and dagger centre of considerable importance. But there was one who had no connection with cryptograms, codes or the secret service in any way: he was Professor Leslie Abercrombie (1879–1956) who amongst other activities was consultant to the London County Council for the rebuilding and planning of London and Professor of Town Planning at University College, London. In 1942(?) he was asked to produce a 'Greater London Plan' and his enquiries led him to many talks with R. L. Sherwood, Bletchley's clerk, and councillors such as the experienced C. D. Flack. In December 1944 J. F. Smithie was appointed surveyor and engineer to the Bletchley UDC.

When in 1944 Abercrombie produced his 'Greater London

---

4 See *Sunday Telegraph* for 28 July 1974 which has a preview of his book, *The Ultra Secret* was published in October 1974. Both King George VI and Churchill came to Bletchley to witness the marvels of the 'Oracle of Bletchley' as the author tells me.

Plan' most people in Bletchley were delighted, for amongst other things he recommended Bletchley for development as a 'new town' with an eventual population of 50,000.

One of the great lessons of the war was that London was too large and too vulnerable. Its population must be diminished, its industries induced to emigrate here, there and everywhere, and somehow the LCC would pay partly for this lightening of its own population density.

Actually less than one page of the report was devoted to Bletchley, Wolverton and Newport Pagnell. Bletchley was described as having some light industries, mainly concerned with clothing and electrical goods which made little use of the railway and relied on road transport. Abercrombie suggested that Bletchley might take a part of London's surplus population. He pointed out that the town had excellent rail, road and canal communications which made it eminently suitable for people and industry. The best site for industry was to the north-east of the town; this part of Bletchley was not residentially attractive and would need a large amount of improvement, such as the provision of shopping facilities, before people could live there.[5] The conclusion swiftly reached was that Wolverton and Newport should stay very much as they were, with a little easily controlled expansion, but that Bletchley should be developed particularly to the north-east and north-west. During the war years the Bletchley Council had decided to keep the rates up although few public works were carried out, and so built up a reserve fund that was used to buy up land.

The Second European War ended on 8 May, 1945 with the unconditional surrender of the German forces, and almost immediately afterwards the Abercrombie report was approved in principle by the Government. Two months later it was 'enthusiastically greeted' by the Bletchley UDC (14 August, 1945, the day when Japan surrendered), who not only asked the Government to designate Bletchley as a place 'suitable for large scale development' but ordered that a plan be prepared to indicate how it might be achieved.[6]

At last it looked as if Bletchley's ten year urge for 'A Bigger,

5 Abercrombie, *The Greater London Plan*, London, 1944, section 456.
6 J. F. Smithie's article on 'Post-war Bletchley' in the Bletchley Pageant Souvenir Booklet.

Better, Brighter Bletchley' – so persistently advocated by the *Bletchley Gazette*, was really likely to come into being. In October 1945 the Council bought the Manor Farm estate, Water Eaton (off Aylesbury Street), and this, with other land acquisitions, set the programme going. But there were lions in the way. First of all the Foreign Office and other Government departments were most reluctant to give up Bletchley Park, and it was difficult to get any labour. Some German and Italian prisoners of war were released from local farms, but the Italians were very slow, and could not understand why they were not immediately repatriated.

The Chestnut estate was ready for the builders in October 1945, closely followed by Brookdale (Larch Grove). The first house was completed and occupied on 20 June 1946.

Housing had been a dominant question during the General Election of 1945, and labour won a smashing victory. Lewis Silkin, MP, the new Minister of Town and Country Planning, was as eager as Bletchley Council to see hundreds of houses built in record time. Election pledges were at stake, and Bletchley was probably the most co-operative and go-ahead UDC in the country.

The Government perhaps hoped that Bletchley would be the first of the 'New Towns', and draft plans were now produced for one of 60,000 people centred on Bletchley Park. Naturally these plans were the subject of the closest but most secret consultations between Bletchley and the Ministry. On the Bletchley side the chairmen during the next few years were:

1945 and 1946:	Syd Maycock
1947 and 1948:	Spen Johnson
1949 to 1951:	Harold Price
1952 and 1953:	Ernest Fryer

but the Council, possibly to ensure greater secrecy, had appointed a Development Committee, whose chairman was usually one of the above. In addition to these there were of course the town clerk, R. L. Sherwood, and the surveyor, John Smithie.

On the Ministry side there was one of the most likeable and electric figures ever produced by the Civil Service, Dame Evelyn Sharp, who was created a DBE in 1948. No one who came in contact with her could doubt her extraordinary ability and her fascinating charm. [7]

7 She became Permanent Secretary to the Ministry of Housing and Local Government 1955–66, and was then created a baroness.

Meanwhile the Wico-Pacy group, now very attached to Bletchley, built themselves a handsome factory further north on the Watling Street. Other firms followed rapidly,[8] and soon Bletchley could boast a score of light industries.

And now the planners came more to the front, men with stars in their eyes and drawing boards in front of them. In echelon to these were the property owners who had displaced the old squires, and who knew that whilst agricultural land was only worth £100 an acre, such land with planning permission was worth many times more. Some became councillors.

Nor were the local press oblivious to the fact that more people meant greater circulations. More industries meant more advertisments, the life blood of any newspaper.

By any standards 1947 was a very trying year for Bletchley. At this time north Bucks needed 7,000 houses but only 300 had been completed since 1945 and only another 700 were under construction. There were shortages, nation-wide, of bricks, glass and timber, and of firm decisions.

In February 1947 the Ministry for Town and Country Planning let it be known that Bletchley was to be recommended not as a 'satellite' town but as an 'expanded' town, and in May 1947 it published its *Memorandum on the Greater London Plan*. According to this a million people were to be dispersed from Greater London to 'satellite' towns, and another 200,000 to 'expanded' towns such as Aylesbury, which was to increase from 14,500 to 44,500, and Bletchley from 7,500 to 40,000 (paragraph 28).[9]

In that month Lewis Silkin, the Minister, came to a tea party at the Council Chambers, but only the eight Labour councillors and a few officials were invited to meet him. It appears that Councillor Maycock made it clear that a firm decision on Bletchley's future would be welcomed both by the Council and by local industry, since all important plans were being deferred. But apparently Silkin could only reply that 'no decision had yet been reached . . . but that he was casting covetous eyes on Bletchley . . . and was eager to arrange for the import of Londoners . . .'.[10]

In June 1947 worried farmers urged that the Minister should be asked whether Newton Longville, the Brickhills, Woughton,

8 Information from Ron Staniford.
9 Also Appendix C, Table 4.
10 *Wolverton Express* 10 May 1947, etc.

Simpson, and the area up to Denbigh Hall would be urbanised, but there were no replies to these and many other questions. It was then, 14 June 1947 that Major Markham advised the Bletchley Council 'not to wait for the dithering Minister, but to go ahead with their own plans'.

In July 1947 selected councillors and officials of the UDC saw 'high officials' of the Ministry and from this time onwards there were almost monthly secret discussions either at the Ministry or on 'neutral' ground. It was rumoured that the estimate for building up Bletchley to 50,000 or 60,000 population was £30,000,000 to £40,000,000, and Bletchley representatives were naturally determined that the cost to Bletchley ratepayers should be minimised. Progress was difficult.

At the end of 1947 it looked as if 'A Bigger, Better, Brighter Bletchley' idea was either dead or at least dying. All the same in December the local papers published the outline plans for the Manor Farm estate of 342 houses and garages, but the cautionary words were added 'The site will be tackled when work on existing sites at Water Eaton, Newton Road, and Westfield Road is completed'.

There were still more lions in the path, and it was becoming evident early in 1948 that the Government were dragging their feet and that the Bucks County Council were not enthusiastic. Lewis Silkin told a Council deputation a little later that owing to water difficulties only another 10,000 additional people could be accommodated in the Ouse valley.[11]

Certainly there was some reason for this, for the new sewage works and increased demands for water for domestic and industrial use led possibly to overpumping, and in May 1948 the well at Sandhouse (see chapter 12) collapsed. New boreholes were created but the resultant 'brown water' due to iron 'pollution' gave Bletchley a bad name for years. The Sandhouse works in Heath and Reach were developed until they could produce a million gallons of water per day – a vast improvement on the 100,000 gallons of Chadwick's day.

In 1948 the Ministry announced that the 'new town' scheme must be abandoned because there seemed to be no way of coping with the sewage and general drainage problems that would

11 J. F. Smithie's 'Post-war Bletchley' in the Bletchley Pageant Souvenir Booklet.

result. The fact was that the Great Ouse River Authority had carefully and at great length considered the implications of a new town of 60,000 people on the already stretched water supplies drawn mainly from the river Ouse or its catchment area, and at length warned the Government that considering the increasing demands of Bedford and the area down to the sea they could not see how ever increasing demands could be met. There were probably other reasons for the Ministry's change of policy for by about 1948 the Labour Government had built over 200,000 houses and then there was a desperate balance of payments situation and difficulties with America. Money was tight. Bletchley went even a long way to borrow from Holland, but the idea was scotched 'from above'.[12]

After another period of indecision it was decided that the whole of the expansion allocated to north Bucks (10,000 people) should be in or around Bletchley. Bletchley, although disappointed at not becoming a town of 50,000 or 60,000 welcomed the new plans, and went steadily ahead with its limited building programme. The 500th house was opened by Aneurin Bevan in 1950. Housing allocation was becoming increasingly difficult. The Saints estate was begun in 1951.

Bletchley was still determined to expand, and in June proposed to the boundary commissioner that the urban area should be increased sevenfold. Their proposals were much wider than those put forward in 1930. Bletchley would take over ten villages from the Newport Rural District Council, five from Winslow and two from Wing, so that the new Bletchley would include:

Milton Keynes	Whaddon
Little Woolstone	Newton Longville
Great Woolstone	Drayton Parslow
Wavendon	Mursley
Woburn Sands	Woughton
Bow Brickhill	Loughton
Little Brickhill	Shenley Church End
Great Brickhill	Shenley Brook End
Stoke Hammond	

Once again, as in 1930, there was a shock of horror in most of these villages, and opposition was formidable.

12 Information from Harold Price.

Even as late as 1948 every village contained an ingredient of
seperateness, hard to define, which made it subtly different from
its neighbours and vastly different from Bletchley. It was as
though each were an island kingdom steeped in its own heritage
and traditions, and welcoming communion with the outside
world only when the needs of trade or entertainment demanded.

It was about this time that Mr Lewis Silkin came to Bletchley
again.[13] The Conservative candidate's views on his visit were
printed at length in the local press:

'A fortnight ago Mr. Lewis Silkin, Minister of Town and
Country Planning, came to Bletchley.

'Everyone expected Mr. Silkin, after two years of cogita-
tion, to tell us what decisions had been arrived at, but all he
could say was that he had not yet made up his mind. Mr.
Maycock who followed told the Minister that until the
Ministry had made up its mind, Bletchley was left in a state
of not knowing what its future was to be.

'But the question that was not put was, if the Minister
cannot make up his own mind about the future of Bletchley,
why should not Bletchley make up its own mind? Bletchley
wants to grow. From the scenic and amenities point of view
it has had a poor start, and if Bletchley is to grow, everybody
wants it to grow into a beautiful town. Why then shouldn't
Bletchley evolve its own plans for the future? Fifty years ago
two very interesting towns not so far away were planned –
Letchworth and Welwyn, in Hertfordshire. They were
planned as Garden Cities. Today we can see the result; they
are among the loveliest of all the modern towns in the
country, and are the admiration and envy of American and
continental visitors. Here are clean, well laid out towns, with
well designed homes, amenities and services.

'My suggestion is that Bletchley should not wait for the
Ministry to make up its mind; but should start now to plan
and mould its own future. The U.D.C. might start with the
question: "What is the ideal size of the town we want
Bletchley to be?", and then to secure the finest architect or
town planner available to plan such an ideal town, based
upon the best that the garden cities of Letchworth or

13 He was created a baron in 1950.

Welwyn have to offer. The whole of the U.D.C. might pack into a charabanc and spend a day or two in Welwyn or Letchworth, and see for themselves what local initiative can do. At the same time they might go on just a few miles to Stevenage, and see what a muddle the Ministry has created there.

'The vital question is, will Bletchley plan its own future, or shall this be done by a Ministry out of touch with local feelings or aspirations?'

It will be appreciated that a Labour Council with now a 9–3 majority, did not welcome the views of the Tory candidate, and proceeded along its own troubled path. Finally the pattern for 'A Bigger, Better, Brighter Bletchley' was set by the Bletchley Town Map and Development Plan of March 1951, authorised by the County Council. This envisaged a growth in population from 10,284 in December 1950 to 19,300 in 1971, of which 7,000 would be in Bletchley, 1,500 in Fenny Stratford, and the rest at Newton Longville. The proposals included an allocation of 730 acres for the brick industry, 140 acres for industrial development and 696 acres for residential development. All this would mean a reduction by 900 acres of agricultural land, but since this was Grade IV it was not expected many would grumble.

Nor was much opposition expected from archaeologists or historians, for page 3 states 'There are few, if any, buildings of archaeological or historic interest', and page 4 says 'There are no monuments scheduled under the Ancient Monuments Act of 1931. No list of buildings of special archaeological or historic interest under section 30 of the Town and Country Planning Act, 1947 has been supplied'.

In short this meant that neither the County nor Bletchley itself thought the district had a single building worthy of preservation. Small wonder that it took the Bletchley Rectory Cottages Museum Trust over ten years to persuade the UDC to take an active part in preserving them instead of destroying them.[14]

At that time 861 persons were employed by the railway, 778 by the brick companies, 408 in engineering and 337 in the brush works, so it looked as if Bletchley would become more than ever a brick town, but with a dozen more light industries, and that the majority of the new population would be Londoners.

14 See Vol I *History of Milton Keynes* p184.

Quite early on the question was raised as to the cost of this expansion and the burden on the rates. Harold Price was certain that the Council would only co-operate if they could be assured that there would be 'no undue burden on the rates'. But the Ministry said this was an indefinable phrase. However, all heads got to work to produce an Act of Parliament that would be fair.

The Council did well over its land acquisitions and leasehold factory development, and later the town's leisure centre and swimming pool were paid for out of the profits of land and factory sales. In spite of all the disappointments and setbacks, Bletchley continued to grow. In August 1952 the first Londoners moved into Bletchley under the new schemes,[15] and the new Town Development Act of that year included special retrospective financial provisions which helped Bletchley, but even then there were delays in settling more of London's overspill population in Bletchley.[16]

The Act was a most important one from Bletchley's point of view and it owed much to the solid creative work put in by Bletchley councillors. Harold Hepworth, writing in the *Bletchley Gazette Extra* on 29 March 1974 referred to Harold Price as 'the Councillor who led the deputations and some of whose phrases were incorporated word for word in the 1952 Town Development Act'.

Beneath the chaffering and the bargaining there was an unspoken idealism that never surfaced. Bletchley has no poets – otherwise someone might have spoken thus to London:

> Give us your tired, your poor
> Your huddled masses yearning to breathe free,
> The bombed-out sufferers of the nation's war,
> Send these, the tempest tossed, to me
> We light the lamp of welcome by their door.[17]

At that time the local MP was Frank Markham and the Bill came up for detailed scrutiny before the House and its Committees. Writing in the *Bucks Standard* on 8 March 1952 Frank Markham said:

'The Bill does not mention Bletchley, but the Minister of

---

15 Article by John Smithie in the Bletchley Pageant Souvenir Booklet, 1974.
16 Previous Acts were the Distribution of Industry Act, 1945; the New Towns Act, 1946, and Town and Country Planning Act, 1947.
17 With apologies to the Statue of Liberty, Ellis Island.

311

Housing did, and it is apparent that what is in view is the expansion of the residential area to the north-west, and the development of an industrial area to the north along the lines of the railway and the A.5 road. In a few years' time Bletchley will (if the Bill goes through) have an additional 1,500 houses, a dozen new factories, and 7,500 more people. . .

'Now comes the final question, how much will it all cost, and where is the money to come from? The houses will cost £2,500,000 or more, land purchase and site works possibly £600,000, and special services another £40,000. In all, over £3,000,000 will be required for the first five years of the programme. Obviously, even with the housing and other subsidies, that will be a big bill for bigger Bletchley, most of which will have to be found from the rates . . .

'I suspect that in the case of Bletchley the new state assistance might amount to between £40,000 and £70,000 over the first few years. Much, however, depends upon how the Bill fares in its final stages. There are already scores of amendments down on the paper, and many babies are a great disappointment to their parents when they grow up.'

In August 1953 Harold Macmillan, then Minister of Housing and Local Government opened Bletchley's 1,000th post-war council house. He of course met the leading councillors. Harold Price was still pressing the 'No undue burden' theme and Macmillan gently queried who would pay if not the Bletchley ratepayers? The answer was made that it was a *national* responsibility! A sweet smile closed the matter![18]

The Cockney sparrows soon found themselves at home, and indeed the birth rate jumped to 20.1 compared with 17.6 for the rest of the country. These incomers knew nothing and cared nothing for local pride or history. Indeed there was not a single popular book or pamphlet that could give them a historic consciousness. They came to Bletchley for more living room, for economic or professional advancement, they stayed because they liked Bletchley, and within a few years one of them, J. F. Cassidy, was a councillor and a chairman.[19]

18 Information from Harold Price. The Bletchley rate was then 28s 6d in the £.
19 It is pleasing to note that in 1953 Arthur Bates, former Bletchley Council surveyor, was awarded the OBE. In 1960 John Smithie was awarded the same honour and Harold Price in 1961. A few years later Spen Johnson received the OBE, too.

However many came, there was no unemployment save for the rheumaticky older generation and the usual trifling interval when changing jobs.

TROUBLE ON THE RAILWAYS

Meanwhile the railway situation was becoming chaotic. In January 1948 the railways were nationalised – the hopes of many railway workers were achieved at last – but with this decision there came the news that 200 dismissals were threatened locally in the traffic section. More and more people bought cars and more and more firms bought lorries. Railway receipts went down and down. Hugh Dalton, the Labour Chancellor of the Exchequer from 1945 to 1947 described the railway system as a collection of old iron.

During the war, railways had been stretched to the utmost, and there was neither money nor labour to bring back the old glorious standards of efficiency. Railway nationalisation did not provide swift remedies, and the exalted hopes of the old Bletchley and Wolverton Labour stalwarts soon began to look tattered and even drab as realities were faced. During 1950 20 per cent of the Bletchley staff left. There was never a shortage of complaints at the branch meeting of the NUR. Some of the Polish members who had remained over from the war compared their treatment to that meted out to Belsen camp victims.[20]

In 1953 the men of the NUR struck for better wages, (the minimum wage was then about £4 12s 6d per week). Three of their members promptly joined ASLEF who were not on strike. The NUR got their rises, but the men in ASLEF did not benefit, so now they went on strike, and the NUR went on working. The bitterness can be imagined. As Grigg says, 'The more loquacious strikers actively encouraged a vendetta of hate and ostracism when the strike was over'.[21]

The railway management were superbly tactful, and even paid the strikers their last week's pay off railway premises so as to minimise confrontations between them and the NUR, but the seventeen-day strike ended in more bitterness.

And yet the NUR was still the strongest trade union in

---

20 Grigg, *In Railway Service* p131.
21 Grigg, *In Railway Service* p137.

Bletchley and rarely had less than three members on the Council.

The flourishing brick industry, as we have seen, now employed as many men as the railway, but produced only a couple of councillors in a decade.

Another social change was the twilight or blight that descended over Fenny Stratford and is still there. When Manor Farm estate was built Aylesbury Street and the High Street were still reputable shopping areas, but as the new estates opened to the west the Fenny shops lost more of their trade to the new shops in Bletchley Road (now the Queensway). Gradually the name of Fenny Stratford was left off more and more signposts. A historic town dwindled to a scrubby suburb. It was as if the new vigorous town of Bletchley wanted to forget or ignore its links with the past, and the new Bletchley coat of arms might well have had as its motto 'Go west, young man, go west'. Everybody was very surprised when the UDC instead chose a line from Cicero: 'Progrediens Confirmatur Animus' which few councillors, not being old Etonians, could translate. They were told it meant 'Our spirit is strengthened by advancing' which sounds rather like the motto of a merchant bank.

By the end of the 1960s there had been a complete revolution throughout the whole of the Bletchley area. The old squire and landlord, often the benevolent autocrat of his village, had passed. The friendly and respected families of the Duncombes, etc, still had their descendants living locally, but they were no longer the landlords.

The state, with its agents, the County Council and the Bletchley UDC and the local RDCs, was the greatest landlord. The railways, the canals, the gas and the electricity undertakings, had been state property for a decade or more, as were mansions such as Hanslope Park, Whaddon Hall, and Bletchley Park. Nearly all the schools, with their increasing acreages, belonged to the state in addition to an ever-growing road system which often eliminated entire farms. Even the factories were mainly leased from the Council, and almost all the major recreational facilities were municipal.

The old landlords had been bought out, or taxed out of existence. The new landlords can never be bought out and they cannot be taxed out of existence. The old landlords played a tremendous part in local affairs. They were independent critics of the state and its agents. The new landlords are the state itself or its agents.

This is perhaps the greatest change that has taken place in Bletchley and district since the Enclosure Awards or the Norman Conquest. But even greater changes were to come and our 'Bigger, Better, Brighter Bletchley' was to be merged into the new city of Milton Keynes.

But that of course is another story.

Certain it is that old loyalties will diminish and new loyalties will arise, and that the new loyalties will be to Milton Keynes, the greatest new city in England. It is our hope to see that the new city, by remembering and preserving the best of its exciting past, helps everybody to make the best of the future.

We hope that future generations will be able to say, as St Paul said nearly 2,000 years ago, 'I am a citizen of no mean city'. *Acts* 21.39.

Appendix

The Medieval Building, Fenny Stratford, by Paul Woodfield, Conservation Officer, Milton Keynes Development Corporation

In Fenny Stratford, north of the canal bridge and behind the 1930 period office block of Valentin Ord and Nagle, glucose refiners, lies an extensive medieval timber-framed building. This building has, due to the numerous accretions which have accumulated on all sides in recent times, often been overlooked, and although noted in detail by the surveyor for the Royal Commission on Historic Monuments in 1912 when more complete, it has until recently escaped being statutory listed. Sir Frank Markham, who has been one of the few who have long realised the importance of this building, used his good offices with Messrs Valentin Ord and Nagle, who kindly allowed me free access over some months in early 1974 for this survey to be prepared.

The building, an isometric sketch of which is shown on page 173, is composed of a two- or three-bay building facing Watling Street, with a two-bay rear wing, a parallel range of at least four bays originally some 32m to the rear, and a block of five bays at right angles linking the two.

By its position alone, the northern or front block would appear to be the earliest structure. The western bay, or two bays which until demolished in 1939 formed an arched gateway across the entrance to Bull Yard, were fortunately described in the 1912 survey as having a central arched braced collar beam truss, the principals rising from quasi-hammer beams supported by brackets from raised wall posts with ogee terminals. Two trusses only defining the eastern bay now survive, with a narrow half bay enclosing a large stone stack with openings for hearths to the ground floor eastern bay and the western first floor bay. This stack now terminates in three curtailed diagonal brick stacks of 15th or 16th century type. The surviving roof structure is of queen post type with clasped purlins and wind-braces, and with the internal

truss collar and tie grossly cambered. Ceiling beams with chamfered and stopped ends occur in both the surviving and demolished
bays, thus there is little possibility of an original open hall. Both
front and rear elevations were jettied, the jetty beam facing
Watling Street being moulded and the now completely enclosed
rear elevation still retains large scantling tension braces of Kentish
type.

Of the rear wing to the front block little survives except the
three simple clasping purlin roof trusses, the lower floors having
been rebuilt in brickwork in the 18th century. The rear jetty
and elevational details of the front block, and the incompetence
of the roof junction point to this rear wing being secondary to the
first construction. In the end rear bay, the narrower of the two,
an existing stack is, by its position, assumed to be a successor to an
original hearth in this bay.

The building parallel to the street and at the rear of the site
survives in two bays only although four bays were present at the
time of the RCHM survey. The details of this building much
resemble the front block, and the jetties which occurred on at
least three sides, supported by dragon beams now removed,
together with the lack of alignment through to the front of the
site, point to this building being erected as an independent
structure in the first instance. The major difference is that it is
provided with two clasped purlins instead of one. Little detail
remains to be seen but truss 'L' appears to have originally been
open. The 1912 survey draws attention to a curiosity, the rear wall
being built up on 12in diameter stones, perhaps from a mill. These
can no longer be seen.

Between the 'L' shaped front buildings and the building last
described, a large block of five bays was subsequently inserted
linking the two. This structure is similar in construction to the
other buildings and is still entirely within the medieval tradition,
and similarly appears to have been originally floored throughout
at first floor level with one jetty at least on the western yard side.
Today there is no trace whatsoever of the group floor arrangements, though the earlier survey records a moulded doorframe
in the southern bay of the western elevation. The jetty is now
underbuilt in modern brick and the floor replaced in concrete. The
first floor elevation has apparently one large window to each bay,
and the vertical studding has suppressed straight tension bracing.

Internally, the two bays D-E-F represent the major room, with the centre truss 'E' retaining the quasi-hammer posts and arch bracing in the front block. This northern bay had moreover above the wall plate on the west side a wall painting of 16th century type illustrating a bipedal cat playing a fiddle amid loosely drawn foilage. This conceit is now preserved in Aylesbury Museum (illustration: *Record of Bucks* XII No 1). To the south of this two-bay room, beyond a close studded partition, the remaining three bays appear to have formed one large hall 71ft × 21ft (approximately) the upper, northern end emphasised in its importance by the moulding of the soffite of the tie beam and braces.

The date and purpose of this building complex is not easily determined from documentary sources or detailed investigation. The front and far rear building are demonstrably the earliest, with the rear wing to the former preceding the last and major development, the five-bay hall. From details, and the bay space allowed for the stack, the earliest phase cannot be much earlier than the mid-15th century, even if the brickwork is a later insertion, which is impossible. Thus the rear wing must interpolate between this date and the erection of the five-bay rear block, itself so similar in construction as to be not more than fifty years later. The front block has, in addition to its more domestic scale, obvious means of heating and can be assumed to be a residence, which was enlarged to fulfil a growing need. No stack survives, or is indicated throughout the rest of the complex, and thus a civic or community use must be sought. Apart from the obvious need for hospices on Watling Street throughout the medieval period and later, which more probably would occupy a ground floor position, as at the Merchant Venturers Hall, York (1447) the only major secular requirement is for a guildhall or woolhall for civic and guild functions where a large and dignified assembly space was required. Such structures are known elsewhere in the area, at Long Crendon, and King Sutton but nowhere outside major medieval towns are they of the scale approaching the Fenny Stratford building.

In Volume I of the *History of Milton Keynes and District*, pages 147–48, Sir Frank Markham sets out the terms of a licence obtained of Henry VII by the citizens of Fenny Stratford to found a guildhall and appoint a chaplain. It appears that they had sued for this licence for some time before, and when it was finally granted in 1497 they were doubtless in a position to build it immediately. It is possible, though unproven, that the five-bay block represents this enterprise, the upper assembly rooms being approached from a stair located in a wing or an external structure. The ground floor would then provide hospice accommodation with separate access from the courtyard through the door noted by the Royal Commission. The earlier building on Watling Street may therefore have served as accommodation for the chaplain to the stone chapel of St Margaret and St Katherine which is known to have stood on the site of the present church. Although, without more evidence, these attributions of use must remain speculative, reason should be sought for this building complex being disproportionately large in relation to the modest late medieval chapelry of Fenny Stratford. This situation is further aggravated if the lining of the property boundary of the garage, north of the *Bull*, with the rear medieval wing is taken to be evidence for a return of the medieval structure on the north-west side, enclosing a courtyard. Fenny Stratford lived by Watling Street, the greatest arterial highway of the land. When account is taken of the great ranges of medieval buildings erected in pilgrimage centres like Walsingham, this group of buildings may be better explained.

Whatever the final interpretation will be, there is no doubt that the buildings, the largest secular medieval structures in north Buckinghamshire, are of outstanding interest and importance.

INDEX

Compiled by Keith Tull

321

60–61, 63–64, 75–76, 79, 86, 93, 98,
158, 164–66, 194–96, 208, 229, 234,
242, 261–62, 266, 271, 288–89
Buckinghamshire railways, 93 *seq*
Bucks: County Council, 153–54, 206–07,
219, 221–22, 247–48, 285, 310, 314
Education committee, 153, 301
Light infantry, 261
Militia, 1, 255
Parliamentary representation, 41; see
also Politics
Royal Hussars, 36–37, 79, 258
Territorials, 167, 261–68
Volunteers, 237
Yeomanry, RA, 283–84
Bull:
family, Newport Pagnell, 136
T. P., 134n
William, of Newport Pagnell, 127–28
Dr W. H., 257–58
Bury, Edward, 78, 185
Bury engines, 74–75, 185
Busby, Dr Richard, 29
Butterfield, William, 147n, 290

Calvert, Frederick, 98, 102; see also
Verney
Brickworks, 295–96
Calverton, 17, 19–20, 44, 47, 51, 58, 146
Canals, 1–2, 4–5, 11, 60, 63, 65–66, 73,
117–19, 161–62, 166, 171–72, 183, 188,
214, 289–90
Canham family, 133, 136
Capell, Rev G. M., 245
Carlile, Sir Walter, 246, 272–73
Carrington, (family name Smith), Lord,
17–18, 21, 256
Carter, George, 26
Cassidy, J. F., 312
Castlethorpe, 35, 48, 65, 77, 138, 199,
260–61
Caunt, Ben, 85–87
Cave, George, 174–75
Cecil, James, Marquess of Salisbury, 17
Chadwick:
John, 213–14, 218, 256, 261, 266–67,
300, 307
Douglas, son of John, 268
Chandos:
Family papers, 195
Title of, 8, 13
Marquess of, 37, 79, 89, 109, 186, 256;
see also Buckingham, Dukes of
Chapman:
Mary, 199
Chartists, 38–39
Cheddington, 70–96
Chew, Thomas, 116

Chicheley, 289
Church of England, 136–39; see also
Clergy
Cinema; see Sports and Pastimes
Clarke:
Gregory, Odell, Fenny Stratford, 119,
172, 290
John, Deanshanger, 229
'Nobby', Pugilist, 87–88
William Edward, son of G. O., 290
Claydon, 18, 43
Station 100–04
Clements, family, of Dropshort, 114
Clergy, 25, 42, 48, 83–84, 88, 108, 125–39,
150, 155, 159–60, 191, 220, 222, 229,
245; see also Education, Noncon-
formists, Roman Catholics
Clifton Reynes, 193
Clovis, Louis, (Bonaparte), 202
Coaches (horse), 55, 60, 68–69, 75–76,
199, 230–31, 248–51, 266
Coales, Francis, 45
Cobb, Henry P., 221
Cobbett, William, 31
Cobham, Lord, 9; see also Temple
Cole:
James, of Newport, 37
Rev William, of Bletchley, 127, 171,
228–29, 239, 251
Condensed Peptonised Milk Company
(Buckingham), 166, 217
Congregationalists, 134
Church, Stony Stratford, 238; see also
Nonconformists
Congreve, J. F., 57
Constable, Philip, 171–72
Cook, Mary Ann, 180; see also Industries –
Brushmaking
Cooke, Rev Edward, 48
Co-operative Societies:
Bletchley, 275, 281
Leighton Buzzard, 275
Coronations, 240 *seq*
Corsham, Bill, (Uncle Vic), 267
Cosgrove, 4, 48, 58, 60, 71, 77, 175, 193
Cottesloe:
Family, 271
Lord, 21, 273; see also Fremantle
Courtman, Moira, vii, 90n, 91, 189
Cowley, Amos, 157
Cowley's Parchment Works, 231
Cowper, William, 3, 134–35
Crawley:
Grange, 289
North, 193
Crawley, Aidan, 284–85, 287–88
Creed, Richard, 63–64
Crudge, Rev James, 129–31
Culverhouse, Abraham, 200